Beginning Hibernate

Second Edition

Jeff Linwood and Dave Minter

Apress®

Beginning Hibernate, Second Edition

ISBN-13 (pbk): 978-1-4302-2850-9

ISBN-13 (electronic): 978-1-4302-2851-6

Printed and bound in the United States of America 9 8 7 6 5 4 3 2 1

President and Publisher: Paul Manning
Lead Editor: Jonathan Gennick
Technical Reviewer: Sumit Pal
Editorial Board: Clay Andres, Steve Anglin, Mark Beckner, Ewan Buckingham, Gary Cornell, Jonathan Gennick, Jonathan Hassell, Michelle Lowman, Matthew Moodie, Duncan Parkes, Jeffrey Pepper, Frank Pohlmann, Douglas Pundick, Ben Renow-Clarke, Dominic Shakeshaft, Matt Wade, Tom Welsh
Coordinating Editor: Debra Kelly
Copy Editor: Sharon Terdeman
Production Support: Patrick Cunningham
Indexer: BIM Indexing & Proofreading Services
Artist: April Milne
Cover Designer: Anna Ishchenko

Distributed to the book trade worldwide by Springer-Verlag New York, Inc., 233 Spring Street, 6th Floor, New York, NY 10013. Phone 1-800-SPRINGER, fax 201-348-4505, e-mail orders-ny@springer-sbm.com, or visit www.springeronline.com.

For information on translations, please e-mail rights@apress.com, or visit www.apress.com.

Apress and friends of ED books may be purchased in bulk for academic, corporate, or promotional use. eBook versions and licenses are also available for most titles. For more information, reference our Special Bulk Sales–eBook Licensing web page at www.apress.com/info/bulksales.

The source code for this book is available to readers at www.apress.com.

Contents at a Glance

Contents

About the Authors

Jeff Linwood has been involved in software programming since he had a 286 in high school. He got caught up with the Internet when he got access to a UNIX shell account, and it has been downhill ever since.

When he's not playing on the computer, his hobby is running ultramarathons. Jeff is based in Austin, Texas and helps large companies solve tough problems with content management, search engines, and web application development. Jeff also co-authored *Professional Struts Applications* (Apress), *Building Portals with the Java Portlet API* (Apress), and *Pro Hibernate 3* (Apress).

Dave Minter has adored computers since he was small enough to play in the boxes they came in. He built his first PC from discarded, faulty, and obsolete components; and he considers that to be the foundation of his career as an integration consultant. Dave is based in London, where he helps large and small companies build systems that "just work." He wrote *Beginning Spring 2: From Novice to Professional* (Apress) and co-authored *Building Portals with the Java Portlet API* (Apress) and *Pro Hibernate 3* (Apress).

About the Technical Reviewer

Sumit Pal has about 16 years of experience with Software Architecture, Design & Development on a variety of platforms, including Java, J2EE. Sumit has worked in SQLServer Replication group while with Microsoft for two years and with Oraclc's OLAP Server group while with Oracle for seven years.

Apart from Certifications like IEEE-CSDP and J2EE Architect, Sumit also has an MS in Computer Science from Asian Institute of Technology, Thailand.

Sumit has keen interest in database internals, algorithms, search engine technology, data mining, and machine learning.

Sumit has invented some basic generalized algorithms to find divisibility between numbers and also invented divisibility rules for prime numbers less than 100.

Sumit loves to play badminton and swim. He is also an amateur astrophysicist and is incorporating green habits into his daily life.

Acknowledgments

Jeff and Dave would like to thank the staff of Apress for their consistent good humor in the face of looming deadlines. Particular thanks are due to Debra Kelly, our ever-present project manager, for keeping this book on the rails; and to Patrick Meader, for correcting our dodgy spelling and grammar. Thanks to Fran Parnell, as well, for managing the project in its early stages. Special thanks to Jonathan Gennick for his contributions and particularly for his help directing the new edition. Thanks also to Steve Anglin for letting us write for Apress and to Sumit Pal for his contributions as technical reviewer. Finally, thanks are due to the Hibernate team for producing an awesome piece of software.

Jeff would like to thank Cheri for putting up with endless late nights to meet chapter deadlines; he would also like to thank Rocky for giving him a reason to put the laptop away on a sunny day. He would also like to thank his friends Roman and Jason for reviewing parts of the book.

Introduction

Hibernate is an amazing piece of software. With a little experience and the power of annotations, you can build a complex, database-backed system with disturbing ease. Once you have built a system using Hibernate, you will never want to go back to the traditional approaches.

While Hibernate is incredibly powerful, it presents a steep learning curve when you first encounter it—steep learning curves are actually a good thing because they impart profound insight once you have scaled them. Yet gaining that insight takes some perseverance and assistance.

Our aim in this book is to help you scale that learning curve by presenting you with the minimal requirements of a discrete Hibernate application, explaining the basis of those requirements, and walking you through an example application built using to them. We then provide additional material to be digested once the fundamentals are firmly understood. Throughout, we provide examples, rather than relying upon pure discourse. We hope that you will continue to find this book useful as a reference text long after you have become an expert on the subject.

Who This Book Is For

This book assumes a good understanding of Java fundamentals and some familiarity with database programming using the Java Database Connectivity (JDBC) API. We don't expect you to know anything about Hibernate—but if you buy this book, it will probably be because you have some exposure to the painful process of building a large database-based system.

All of our examples use open source software—primarily the Hibernate API itself—so you will not need to purchase any software to get started with Hibernate development. This book is not an academic text. Our focus is instead on providing extensive examples and taking a pragmatic approach to the technology that it covers.

To true newcomers to the Hibernate API, we recommend that you read at least the first three chapters in order before diving into the juicy subjects of later chapters. Very experienced developers or those with experience with tools similar to Hibernate will want to skim through the latter half of the book for interesting chapters. Readers familiar with Hibernate will want to turn to the appendixes for discussion of more arcane topics.

How This Book Is Structured

This book is informally divided into three parts. Chapters 1 through 8 describe the fundamentals of Hibernate, including configuration, the creation of mapping files, and the basic APIs. Chapters 9 through 11 describe the use of queries, criteria, and filters to access the persistent information in more sophisticated ways. Chapter 12 is a case study that starts with an existing database, and then shows you how to map that database to a Java application using Hibernate.

Finally, the appendixes discuss features that you will use less often, or that are peripheral to the core Hibernate functionality. The following list describes more fully the contents of each chapter:

Chapter 1 outlines the purpose of persistence tools and presents excerpts from a simple example application to show how Hibernate can be applied. It also introduces core terminology and concepts.

Chapter 2 discusses the fundamentals of configuring a Hibernate application. It presents the basic architecture of Hibernate and discusses how a Hibernate application is integrated into an application.

Chapter 3 presents the example application from Chapter 1 in its entirety, walking you through the complete process of creating and running the application. It then looks at a slightly more complex example and introduces the notion of generating the database schema directly from Hibernate annotations.

Chapter 4 covers the Hibernate life cycle in depth. It discusses the life cycle in the context of the methods available on the core interfaces. It also introduces key terminology and discusses the need for cascading and lazy loading.

Chapter 5 explains why mapping information must be retained by Hibernate and demonstrates the various types of associations that can be represented by a relational database. It briefly discusses the other information that can be maintained within a Hibernate mapping.

Chapter 6 explains how Hibernate lets you use the annotations to represent mapping information. It provides detailed examples for the most important annotations, and discusses the distinctions between the standard JPA 2 annotations and the proprietary Hibernate ones.

Chapter 7 explains how the XML-based mapping files can be used to represent mapping information in Hibernate. It provides examples for all of the most common mapping types and reference notes for the more obscure ones.

Chapter 8 revisits the Hibernate `Session` object in detail, explaining the various methods that it provides. The chapter also discusses the use of transactions, locking, and caching, as well as how to use Hibernate in a multithreaded environment.

Chapter 9 discusses how Hibernate can be used to make sophisticated queries against the underlying relational database using the built-in Hibernate Query Language (HQL).

Chapter 10 introduces the Criteria API, which is a programmatic analog of the query language discussed in Chapter 9.

Chapter 11 discusses how the Filter API can be used to restrict the results of the queries introduced in Chapters 9 and 10.

Chapter 12 is a case study chapter that illustrates how to use Hibernate with an existing database. This chapter draws on topics covered in the previous 11 chapters to demonstrate a common use case.

Appendix A presents a large number of peripheral features that do not warrant more extensive coverage in a beginner-level text. The chapter discusses the basics, with examples, of the support for versioning and optimistic locking, the provision for persisting and retrieving maps of information, and some of the obscure limitations of Hibernate and various ways that these can be worked around. It also discusses the use of events and interceptors. The chapter briefly touches on Hibernate Search, which bridges Lucene and Hibernate.

Appendix B discusses how the Hibernate Tools toolset can be used to enhance development with the Eclipse development environment and the Ant build tool. It also explains how the Ant code-generation tasks can be customized.

Appendix C discusses how Hibernate can be integrated into the Spring API. The integration of Hibernate as the persistence layer of a Spring application is complex, so we present a working example, including the entire bean definition file, with discussions of the appropriate way to manage the session in the Spring MVC environment. This chapter also discusses how Spring can enforce the proper transactional boundaries when using Hibernate.

Appendix D discusses some topics of interest to developers who are working with a preexisting base of code that was built using version 2 of Hibernate. We present the various approaches for coexisting with Hibernate 3 code, as well as for migrating a Hibernate 2 code base to the Hibernate 3 API.

Downloading the Code

The source code for this book is available to readers from www.apress.com, in the Source Code/Download section. Please feel free to visit the Apress web site and download all the code from there.

Contacting the Authors

We welcome feedback from our readers. If you have any queries or suggestions about this book, or technical questions about Hibernate, or if you just want to share a really good joke, you can e-mail Dave Minter at dave@paperstack.com and Jeff Linwood at jlinwood@gmail.com.

CHAPTER 1

■ ■ ■

An Introduction to Hibernate 3.5

Most significant development projects involve a relational database. The mainstay of most commercial applications is the large-scale storage of ordered information, such as catalogs, customer lists, contract details, published text, and architectural designs.

With the advent of the World Wide Web, the demand for databases has increased. Though they may not know it, the customers of online bookshops and newspapers are using databases. Somewhere in the guts of the application a database is being queried and a response is offered.

While the demand for such applications has grown, their creation has not become noticeably simpler. Some standardization has occurred around the Java Persistence API with the release of Enterprise Java Beans 3.0. Hibernate 3.5 is an implementation of the Java Persistence API standard, which replaced older Java persistence solutions such as the entity beans from Enterprise Java Beans 2.

There are solutions for which some sort of object-relational mapping (ORM) like Hibernate is appropriate, and some for which the traditional approach of direct access via the Java Database Connectivity (JDBC) API is appropriate. We think that Hibernate represents a good first choice, as it does not preclude the simultaneous use of these alternative approaches.

To illustrate some of Hibernate's strengths, in this chapter we will show you a brief example using Hibernate and contrast this with the traditional JDBC approach.

Plain Old Java Objects (POJOs)

In our ideal world, it would be trivial to take any Java object and persist it to the database. No special coding would be required to achieve this, no performance penalty would ensue, and the result would be totally portable.

In this ideal world, we would perhaps perform such an operation in a manner like that shown in Listing 1-1.

Listing 1-1. A Rose-Tinted View of Object Persistence

```
POJO pojo = new POJO();
ORMSolution magic = ORMSolution.getInstance();
magic.save(pojo);
```

There would be no nasty surprises, no additional work to correlate the class with tables in the database, and no performance problems.

Hibernate comes remarkably close to this, at least when compared with the alternatives—but alas, there are configuration files to create and subtle performance issues to consider. Hibernate does, however, achieve its fundamental aim—it allows you to store POJOs in the database. Figure 1-1 shows how Hibernate fits into your application between the client code and the database.

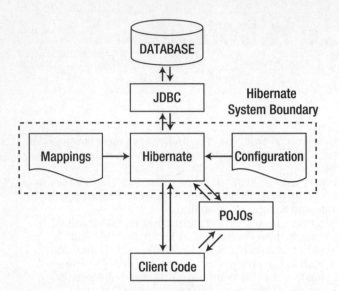

Figure 1-1. The role of Hibernate in a Java application

The common term for the direct persistence of traditional Java objects is object-relational mapping—that is, mapping the objects in Java to the relational entities in a database.

POJOs can be any Java object at all. Hibernate allows you to persist POJOs with very few constraints. Listing 1-2 is an example of a simple POJO to represent a message.

Listing 1-2. The POJO Used in this Chapter's Examples

```
public class Message {
   private Message() {
   }

   public Message(String messageText) {
      this.messageText = messageText;
   }

   public String getMessageText() {
      return messageText;
   }
}
```

```
    public void setMessageText(String messageText) {
        this.messageText = messageText;
    }

    private String messageText;
}
```

The sole condescension to Hibernate here is the provision of a private default constructor. Hibernate demands that all POJOs to be stored should provide a default constructor; but even that can be worked around when third-party classes fail to satisfy this limited requirement (we will demonstrate this in Appendix A).

Origins of Hibernate and Object-Relational Mapping

If Hibernate is the solution, what was the problem? One answer is that doing things the right way when using JDBC requires a considerable body of code, and careful observation of various rules (such as those governing connection management) to ensure that your application does not leak resources. The gargantuan body of code in Listing 1-3 is required to populate the example Motd object from the database even when you know the appropriate message identifier.

Listing 1-3. The JDBC Approach to Retrieving the POJO

```
public static List getMessages(int messageId) throws MessageException {
    Connection c = null;
    PreparedStatement p = null;
    List list = new ArrayList();

    try {

        Class.forName("org.postgresql.Driver");
        c = DriverManager.getConnection(
                "jdbc:hsqldb:testdb;shutdown=true",
                "hibernate",
                "hibernate");
        p = c.prepareStatement(
                "select message from motd");

        ResultSet rs = p.executeQuery();

        while(rs.next()) {
            String text = rs.getString(1);
            list.add(new Message(text));
        }
        return list;

    } catch (Exception e) {
        log.log(Level.SEVERE, "Could not acquire message", e);
        throw new MotdException(
                "Failed to retrieve message from the database.", e);
```

```
    } finally {
      if (p != null) {
        try {
          p.close();
        } catch (SQLException e) {
          log.log(Level.WARNING,
                "Could not close ostensibly open statement.", e);
        }
      }

      if (c != null) {
        try {
          c.close();
        } catch (SQLException e) {
          log.log(Level.WARNING,
                "Could not close ostensibly open connection.", e);
        }
      }
    }
  }
```

Some of this can be trimmed down; there are various techniques that allow you to reduce the boilerplate code for opening connections and logging problems, but the basic logic that pulls the object instance from the ResultSet becomes more complex as the object itself does. Once the object includes references to other objects—or worse yet, other collections of objects—these "manual" techniques start to look more and more flawed.

Hibernate As a Persistence Solution

Hibernate addresses a lot of these points, or alleviates some of the pain where it can't, so we'll address the points in turn.

Hibernate does not require you to map one POJO to one table. A POJO can be constructed out of a selection of table columns, or several POJOs can be persisted into a single table.

Hibernate directly supports inheritance relationships and the various other relationships between classes.

Though there is some performance overhead while Hibernate starts up and processes its configuration files, it is generally perceived as being a fast tool. This is very hard to quantify, and, to some extent, the poor reputation of entity beans may have been earned less from their own faults than from the mistakes of those designing and deploying such applications. As with all performance questions, you should carry out tests rather than relying on anecdotal evidence.

In Hibernate it is possible, but not necessary, to specify the mappings at deployment time.

Hibernate persistence has no requirement for a J2EE application server or any other special environment. It is, therefore, a much more suitable solution for stand-alone applications, command-line tools, client-side application storage, and other environments in which a J2EE server is not immediately available.

Hibernate uses POJOs that can very easily and naturally be generalized for use in other applications. There is no direct dependency upon the Hibernate libraries, so POJOs can be put to any use that does not require persistence; or they can be persisted using any other "POJO-friendly" mechanism.

Hibernate presents no problems when handling serializable POJOs.

Any Java object capable of being persisted to a database is a candidate for Hibernate persistence. Therefore, Hibernate is a natural replacement for ad hoc solutions, or as the persistence engine for an application that has not yet had database persistence incorporated into it. Furthermore, by choosing Hibernate persistence, you are not tying yourself to any particular design decisions for the business objects in your application.

A Hibernate Hello World Example

Listing 1-4 shows how much less boilerplate is required with Hibernate than with the JDBC approach from Listing 1-3.

Listing 1-4. The Hibernate Approach to Retrieving the POJO

```
public static List getMessages(int messageId)
   throws MessageException
{
   SessionFactory sessions =
      new AnnotationConfiguration().configure().buildSessionFactory();
   Session session = sessions.openSession();
   Transaction tx = null;
   try {
      tx = session.beginTransaction();

      List list = session.createQuery("from Message").list();

      tx.commit();
      tx = null;
      return list;

   } catch ( HibernateException e ) {
      if ( tx != null ) tx.rollback();
      log.log(Level.SEVERE, "Could not acquire message", e);
      throw new MotdException(
            "Failed to retrieve message from the database.",e);
   } finally {
      session.close();
   }
}
```

Even for this trivial example there would be a further reduction in the amount of code required in a real deployment—particularly in an application-server environment. For example, the `SessionFactory` would normally be created elsewhere and made available to the application as a Java Native Directory Interface (JNDI) resource.

Note that the manual coding to populate the message object has not been eradicated—rather, it has been moved into an external configuration file that isolates this implementation detail from the main logic.

Some of the additional code in the Hibernate 3 example given in Listing 1-4 actually provides functionality (particularly transactionality and caching) beyond that of the JDBC example.

5

Mappings

As we have intimated, Hibernate needs something to tell it which tables relate to which objects. In Hibernate parlance, this is called a mapping. Mappings can either be provided through Java annotations, or through an XML mapping file. In this book, we will focus on using annotations, as we can mark up the POJO Java classes directly. We find that using annotations gives us a clear picture of the code and what we are trying to accomplish. Hibernate also takes a configuration-by-exception approach for annotations – if we are satisfied with the default values that Hibernate provides for us, we do not need to explicitly provide them as annotations. For instance, Hibernate uses the name of the POJO class as the default value of the database table the object maps to. In our example, if we are satisfied with using a database table named message, we do not need to define it in the source code.

Listing 1-5 shows the Message POJO with annotations for mapping the Java object into the database.

Listing 1-5. The POJO with mapping annotations

```
import javax.persistence.Entity;
import javax.persistence.Id;

@Entity
public class Message {
    private Message() {
    }

    public Message(String messageText) {
        this.messageText = messageText;
    }

    public String getMessageText() {
        return messageText;
    }


    public void setMessageText(String messageText) {
        this.messageText = messageText;
    }

@Id
    public Integer getId() {
        return id;
    }


    public void setId(Integer id) {
        this.id = id;
    }
     private String messageText;
     private Integer id;


}
```

Summary

In this chapter, we have considered the problems and requirements that have driven the development of Hibernate. We have looked at some of the details of a trivial example application written with and without the aid of Hibernate. We have glossed over some of the implementation details, but we will discuss these in depth in Chapter 3.

In the next chapter, we will look at the architecture of Hibernate and how it is integrated into your applications.

CHAPTER 2

■■■

Integrating and Configuring Hibernate

Compared to other Java persistence solutions, integrating Hibernate into a Java application is easy. The designers of Hibernate avoided some of the more common pitfalls and problems with the existing Java persistence solutions, and created a clean but powerful architecture. In practice, this means that you do not have to run Hibernate inside any particular J2EE container or framework—Hibernate 3.5 only requires Java 2 Standard Edition (J2SE), version 5.0 (or later).

At first, adding Hibernate to your Java project looks intimidating—the distribution includes a large set of libraries. To get your first Hibernate application to work, you have to set up the database, the mapping files or annotations, the configuration, and your plain old Java objects (POJOs). After you have done all that, you need to write the logic in your application that uses the Hibernate session to actually do something! But once you learn how to integrate Hibernate with your application, the basics apply for any project that uses Hibernate.

If you already have an application that uses Hibernate 2, the migration path from Hibernate 2 to Hibernate 3.5 is easy. While Hibernate 3.5 is not completely backward-compatible, most of the changes are additional features that you can integrate into your existing application as you see fit. The Hibernate developers provided implementations of the core Hibernate 2 objects in Hibernate 3.5 with the Hibernate 2 methods for backward compatibility. We discuss the differences between Hibernate 2 and Hibernate 3.5 in more depth in Appendix D.

One of the key features of Hibernate's design is the principle of least intrusiveness—the Hibernate developers did not want Hibernate to intrude into your application more than was necessary. This led to several of the architectural decisions made for Hibernate. In Chapter 1 you saw how Hibernate can be applied to solve persistence problems using conventional Java objects. In this chapter, we explain some of the configuration details needed to support this behavior.

The Steps Needed to Integrate and Configure Hibernate

This chapter explains configuration and integration in detail, but for a quick overview, refer to the following bulleted list to determine what you need to do to get your first Hibernate application up and running. Chapter 3 leads you through the building of a pair of small example applications that use Hibernate. The first of these is as simple as we could make it, so it is an excellent introduction to the following necessary steps:

1. Identify the POJOs that have a database representation.

2. Identify which properties of those POJOs need to be persisted.

3. Annotate each of the POJOs to map your Java object's properties to columns in a database table (covered in more detail in Chapter 7).

4. Create the database schema using the schema export tool, use an existing database, or create your own database schema.

5. Add the Hibernate Java libraries to your application's classpath (covered in this chapter).

6. Create a Hibernate XML configuration file that points to your database and your mapped classes (covered in this chapter).

7. In your Java application, create a Hibernate `Configuration` object that references your XML configuration file (covered in this chapter).

8. Also in your Java application, build a Hibernate `SessionFactory` object from the `Configuration` object (covered in this chapter).

9. Finally, retrieve Hibernate Session objects from the `SessionFactory`, and write your data access logic for your application (create, retrieve, update, and delete).

Don't worry if you don't understand every term or concept in the preceding list. After reading this chapter, and then going through the example in the next chapter, you will know what these terms mean and how they fit together.

Understanding Where Hibernate Fits in Your Java Application

You can call Hibernate from your Java application directly, or you can access Hibernate through another framework. You can call Hibernate from a Swing application, a servlet, a portlet, a JSP page, or any other Java application that has access to a database. Typically, you would use Hibernate to either create a data access layer for an application or replace an existing data access layer.

Hibernate supports Java Management Extensions (JMX), J2EE Connector Architecture (JCA), and Java Naming and Directory Interface (JNDI) Java language standards. Using JMX, you can configure Hibernate while it is running. Hibernate may be deployed as a JCA connector, and you can use JNDI to obtain a Hibernate session factory in your application. In addition, Hibernate uses standard Java Database Connectivity (JDBC) database drivers to access the relational database. Hibernate does not replace JDBC as a database connectivity layer—Hibernate sits on a level above JDBC.

In addition to the standard Java APIs, many Java web and application frameworks now integrate with Hibernate. Hibernate's simple, clean API makes it easy for these frameworks to support Hibernate in one way or another. The Spring framework provides excellent Hibernate integration, including generic support for persistence objects, a generic set of persistence exceptions, and transaction management. Appendix C explains how Hibernate can be configured within a Spring application.

Regardless of the environment that you are integrating Hibernate into, certain requirements remain constant. You will need to define the configuration details that apply—these are then represented by a `Configuration` object. From the `Configuration` object, a single `SessionFactory` object is created; and from this, `Session` objects are instantiated, through which your application accesses Hibernate's representation of the database.

Deploying Hibernate

To integrate Hibernate with your Java application, you will need to use several Java libraries. The first library is the Java Archive (JAR) file for your JDBC driver, which you will need to find for your specific relational database. The Hibernate download does not include any JDBC drivers. You must obtain these yourself—typically, the database provider will offer them as a separate download, or they may be bundled with your database installation.

Because every relational database—and hence every JDBC driver—behaves slightly differently, the Hibernate team created *dialects* to abstract away the differences. These dialects define the SQL variant and the specific database features to use for each vendor's database. Every project that uses Hibernate must specify one dialect in the Hibernate configuration file. We discuss dialects in more detail further on in the chapter. The Hibernate web site also contains a platform-specific FAQ that offers some solutions to several vendor-specific questions.

If you encounter problems getting Hibernate to work with older JDBC versions, disable the following two JDBC 2–specific features: batch update and scrollable result sets. Use the following configuration values for Hibernate (we discuss the specifics of this configuration later in this chapter):

```
hibernate.jdbc.batch_size=0
hibernate.jdbc.use_scrollable_resultsets=false
```

Once you have configured the JDBC driver, your next step is to deploy `hibernate3.jar` with your application. This JAR file is provided with the Hibernate 3.5 binary distribution. The file contains the classes in the `org.hibernate` package, along with several DTD and XML Schema files. You will then need to deploy the other required libraries.

Required Libraries for Running Hibernate 3.5

Hibernate requires several libraries beyond `hibernate3.jar`. These libraries are included in the `lib/required` directory of your Hibernate 3.5 installation. Besides the libraries in `lib/required`, Hibernate also uses a JPA library, which is included in the `lib/jpa` directory.

Hibernate 3.5 also requires a bytecode library to function. There are two bytecode libraries shipped with the Hibernate distribution – javassist and CGLib. With Hibernate 3.5, you need to use one or the other. In this book, we will use javassist, as it is the default library.

■ **Note** If you are already using CGlib in your application, or if you would like to try it for performance or memory usage testing, you will need to set a JVM level property or a property in hibernate.properties (not the Hibernate configuration XML file). The property's name is `org.hibernate.bytecode.provider`, and the new value should be cglib. To change this in an application server environment, you will probably need to specify it as a system property for the application server's JVM. If everything is working well, use the default Hibernate bytecode library, javassist, as it is likely to be better supported in future versions of Hibernate.

There are several optional libraries included with the Hibernate 3.5 distribution. If you build Hibernate from source, a few of these are necessary for Hibernate to compile. Other libraries provide connection pools, additional caching functionality (the `Session` cache is mandatory), and the JCA API.

JMX and Hibernate

JMX is a standard API for managing Java applications and components—mostly accessed through MBeans, which represent wrappers for services and resources. Hibernate provides two MBeans for JMX: `HibernateServiceMBean` and `StatisticsServiceMBean`. Both of these are interfaces that reside in the `org.hibernate.jmx` package. The `HibernateService` and `StatisticsService` classes implement the interfaces and reside within the same package. The `HibernateServiceMBean` provides getter and setter methods for many of the Hibernate configuration properties, including the data source, transaction strategy, caching, dialect, and other database options. It also provides a mechanism for adding mapping files to the configuration. When the `HibernateServiceMBean` starts, it creates a `Configuration` object from its properties and mapping files, and then builds a `SessionFactory` object. The `SessionFactory` object binds to the JNDI location specified on the JMX MBean, and your Java application can then use standard JNDI calls to obtain the session factory.

The other MBean supplies statistics. Hibernate can log statistics about the performance of query execution, caching, and object entity operations. Using a JMX console, an administrator can enable statistics and then access up-to-date performance indicators through the console.

The advantage of JMX over programmatic access to these features is that administrators or other non-developers may change properties at run time through a standardized JMX console that is independent of Hibernate and applies to a range of other frameworks and components.

Hibernate Configuration

Before you create a session factory, you must tell Hibernate where to find the mapping information that defines how your Java classes relate to the database tables. Hibernate also requires a set of configuration settings, which are usually supplied as a standard Java properties file called `hibernate.properties`, or as an XML file named `hibernate.cfg.xml`.

We recommend using the XML format. This allows you to specify the location of the mapping information from the configuration files—the alternative (when using properties files) being to programmatically supply this information to Hibernate through the `Configuration` class.

Listing 2-1 is a reprint of Listing 1-4 from the previous chapter, which shows a complete usage of Hibernate from within an application. The parts of this listing that deal with configuration and integration are highlighted.

Listing 2-1. The Hibernate Approach to Retrieving the POJO

```
public static List getMessages(int messageId)
    throws MessageException
{
    SessionFactory sessions =
        new AnnotationConfiguration().configure().buildSessionFactory();
    Session session = sessions.openSession();
```

```
    try {
        session.beginTransaction();
        List list = session.createQuery("from Message").list();
        session.getTransaction().commit();
        return list;

    } catch ( HibernateException e ) {
        if ( session.getTransaction() != null )
            session.getTransaction().rollback();

        log.log(Level.SEVERE, "Could not acquire message", e);
        throw new MotdException(
                "Failed to retrieve message from the database.",e);
    } finally {
        session.close();
    }
}
```

As you can see, we called the `configure()` method on the `org.hibernate.cfg.AnnotationConfiguration` class without any arguments. This tells Hibernate to look in the classpath for the configuration file. The default name for the configuration file is `hibernate.cfg.xml`—if you change it, you will need to pass that name explicitly as an argument to the `configure()` method. We discuss the `configure()` method and XML configuration in more detail later in this chapter.

The `configure()` method returns an instance of `AnnotationConfiguration`, which can be used to obtain a Hibernate `SessionFactory` instance by calling the `buildSessionFactory()` method, as follows:
`public SessionFactory buildSessionFactory() throws HibernateException`

The `SessionFactory` is a heavyweight object, and your application should use one Hibernate `SessionFactory` object for each discrete database instance that it interacts with. The `SessionFactory` relies on the Hibernate configuration properties, which we detail in the next section of this chapter The `SessionFactory` object is thread-safe, so you can reuse the session factory in applications with multiple threads – such as most web applications.

After you have obtained the `SessionFactory`, you can retrieve Hibernate `org.hibernate.Session` objects. While the `SessionFactory` is a heavyweight object, the `Session` objects are lightweight. You perform your persistence operations using `Session` objects. Each thread in your application should get a separate `Session` object from the session factory.

To sum up, there are three classes that you need to use: `AnnotationConfiguration`, `SessionFactory`, and `Session`.

- Use the `AnnotationConfiguration` class to read (and to set) configuration details.

- Use the `AnnotationConfiguration` object to create a `SessionFactory` object.

- Use the `SessionFactory` object to create `Session` objects as needed.

A typical application will have one `AnnotationConfiguration` object, which will only be used in initialization. There will be one `SessionFactory` object that will exist throughout the life cycle of the application. Your application will ask this `SessionFactory` object for a `Session` any time it needs to work with the database. The application could retrieve an object, make some property changes, and then persist it, all within one session, and then close down the `Session` object.

Hibernate Properties

Typically, you will specify your Hibernate configuration in a properties file called `hibernate.properties` in the root directory of your application's classpath, or as identified values in a `hibernate.cfg.xml` file. Hibernate has an extensive list of properties for configuration (see Table 2-1).

While the list of properties you can use for configuration is extensive, the number of properties you will probably use in your Hibernate applications is a lot smaller. At its simplest, you just need to tell Hibernate where to find a database to connect to and tell Hibernate what type of database it is (MySQL, SQL Server, Oracle, etc.). Following is a simple example of a Hibernate properties file that configures a database connection to an HSQL database and also turns on SQL logging statements for debugging:

```
hibernate.connection.driver_class = org.hsqldb.jdbcDriver
hibernate.connection.url = jdbc:hsqldb:file:exampledb;shutdown=true
hibernate.connection.username = admin
hibernate.connection.password = password
hibernate.dialect = org.hibernate.dialect.HSQLDialect
hibernate.show_sql = true
```

Unless you provide a JDBC connection programmatically in your application, you must either configure a JDBC connection here or specify the JNDI name of a container-provided JDBC connection. You must also configure the SQL dialect appropriate to the database that you are using. All the other properties take sensible default values, so they do not need to be explicitly stated.

Table 2-1. Hibernate Configuration Property Names and Descriptions

Property Name	Description
hibernate.c3p0.acquire_increment	The C3P0 database connection pool improves performance of Hibernate applications by managing database connections. Instead of connecting to the database every time a connection is asked for, the connection pool keeps a collection of open database connections for the application to use. There are several C3P0 configuration properties for Hibernate. After the connection pool is completely utilized, determines how many new connections are added to the pool.
hibernate.c3p0.idle_test_period	Determines how long to wait before a connection is validated.
hibernate.c3p0.max_size	The maximum size of the connection pool for C3PO.
hibernate.c3p0.max_statements	The upper limit for the SQL statement cache for C3PO.
hibernate.c3p0.min_size	The minimum size of the connection pool for C3PO.
hibernate.c3p0.timeout	The timeout for C3PO (in seconds).

Property Name	Description
hibernate.cache.provider_class	Specifies a class that implements the org.hibernate.cache.CacheProvider interface.
hibernate.cache.query_cache_factory	Specifies a class that implements the org.hibernate.cache.QueryCacheFactory interface for getting QueryCache objects.
hibernate.cache.region_prefix	The prefix to use for the name of the cache.
hibernate.cache.use_minimal_puts	Configures the cache to favor minimal puts over minimal gets.
hibernate.cache.use_query_cache	Specifies whether to use the query cache.
hibernate.cache.use_second_level_cache	Determines whether to use the Hibernate second-level cache.
hibernate.cglib.use_reflection_optimizer	Instead of using slower standard Java reflection, uses the CGLib code generation library to optimize access to business object properties. The application may be slower at startup if this is enabled, but with faster runtime performance.
hibernate.connection.autocommit	Allows autocommit mode to be used for the JDBC connection (not usually a good idea).
hibernate.connection.datasource	The DataSource name for a container-managed data source.
hibernate.connection.driver_class	The JDBC driver class.
hibernate.connection.isolation	The transaction isolation level for the JDBC connection.
hibernate.connection...............	Passes any JDBC property you like to the JDBC connection—for instance, hibernate.connection.debuglevel=info would pass a JDBC property called debuglevel.
hibernate.connection.password	The database password.
hibernate.connection.pool_size	Limits the number of connections waiting in the Hibernate database connection pool.
hibernate.connection.provider_class	The class that implements Hibernate's ConnectionProvider interface.

Continued

Property Name	Description
hibernate.connection.url	The JDBC URL to the database instance.
hibernate.connection.username	The database username.
hibernate.default_catalog	The default database catalog name that Hibernate uses to generate SQL for unqualified table names.
hibernate.default_schema	The default database owner name that Hibernate uses to generate SQL for unqualified table names.
hibernate.dialect	The SQL dialect to use for Hibernate; varies by database. See this chapter's "SQL Dialects" section.
hibernate.generate_statistics	Determines whether statistics are collected.
hibernate.hbm2ddl.auto	Automatically creates, updates, or drops the database schema on startup and shut down. There are three possible values: create, create-drop, and update. Be careful with create-drop!
hibernate.jdbc.batch_size	The maximum batch size for updates.
hibernate.jdbc.batch_versioned_data	Determines whether Hibernate batches versioned data, which depends on your JDBC driver properly implementing row counts for batch updates. Hibernate uses the row count to determine whether the update is successful.
hibernate.jdbc.factory_class	The class name of a custom implementation of the org.hibernate.jdbc.Batcher interface for controlling JDBC prepared statements.
hibernate.jdbc.fetch_size	Determines how many rows the JDBC connection will try to buffer with every fetch. This is a balance between memory and minimizing database network traffic.
hibernate.jdbc.use_get_generated_keys	Determines Hibernate's behavior with respect to generated keys. If this property is set to true, and if the database driver supports the JDBC 3.0 generated keys API, Hibernate will retrieve generated keys from the statement after it executes an SQL query.

Property Name	Description
hibernate.jdbc.use_scrollable_resultset	Determines whether Hibernate will use JDBC scrollable result sets for a user-provided JDBC connection.
hibernate.jdbc.use_streams_for_binary	Determines whether binary data is read or written over JDBC as streams.
hibernate.jndi.class	The InitialContext class for JNDI.
hibernate.jndi.<JNDIpropertyname>	Passes any JNDI property you like to the JNDI InitialContext.
hibernate.jndi.url	Provides the URL for JNDI.
hibernate.max_fetch_depth	Determines how deep Hibernate will go to fetch the results of an outer join. Used by Hibernate's outer join loader.
hibernate.order_updates	Orders SQL update statements by each primary key.
hibernate.proxool	Prefix for the Proxool database connection pool.
hibernate.proxool.existing_pool	Configures Proxool with an existing pool.
hibernate.proxool.pool_alias	The alias to use for any of the configured Proxool pools previously mentioned.
hibernate.proxool.properties	Path to a Proxool properties file.
hibernate.proxool.xml	Path to a Proxool XML configuration file.
hibernate.query.factory_class	Specifies an HQL query factory class name.
hibernate.query.substitutions	Any possible SQL token substitutions that Hibernate should use.
hibernate.session_factory_name	If set, causes the Hibernate session factory to bind to this JNDI name.
hibernate.show_sql	Logs the generated SQL commands.
hibernate.sql_exception_converter	Specifies which SQLExceptionConverter to use to convert SQLExceptions into JDBCExceptions.

Continued

Property Name	Description
`hibernate.transaction.auto_close_session`	Automatically closes the session after a transaction.
`hibernate.transaction.factory_class`	Specifies a class that implements the `org.hibernate.transaction.TransactionFactory` interface.
`hibernate.transaction.flush_before_completion`	Automatically flushes before completion.
`hibernate.transaction.manager_lookup_class`	Specifies a class that implements the `org.hibernate.transaction.TransactionManagerLookup` interface.
`hibernate.use_identifier_rollback`	Determines whether Hibernate uses identifier rollback.
`hibernate.use_sql_comments`	Generates SQL with comments.
`hibernate.wrap_result_sets`	Turns on JDBC result set wrapping with column names.
`hibernate.xml.output_stylesheet`	Specifies an XSLT stylesheet for Hibernate's XML data binder. Requires `xalan.jar`.
`jta.UserTransaction`	The JNDI name for the `UserTransaction` object.

XML Configuration

As we have already mentioned, Hibernate offers XML configuration capabilities. To use them, you must create an XML configuration file, normally called `hibernate.cfg.xml`, and place it in the root of your application's classpath. The XML configuration file must conform to the Hibernate 3 Configuration DTD, which is available from `http://hibernate.sourceforge.net/hibernate-configuration-3.0.dtd`.
    Listing 2-2 shows an example XML configuration for Hibernate.

Listing 2-2. An XML Configuration for Hibernate

```
<?xml version="1.0" encoding="utf-8"?>
<!DOCTYPE hibernate-configuration SYSTEM ➡
"http://hibernate.sourceforge.net/hibernate-configuration-3.0.dtd">
<hibernate-configuration>
    <session-factory>
 <property name="hibernate.connection.driver_class">org.hsqldb.jdbcDriver</property>
        <property
```

```
name="hibernate.connection.url">jdbc:hsqldb:file:exampledb;shutdown=true</property>
        <property name="hibernate.connection.username">admin</property>
        <property name="hibernate.dialect">org.hibernate.dialect.HSQLDialect</property>
        <property name="connection.password">password</property>
        <property name="show_sql">true</property>

        <mapping jar="hibernate-mappings.jar"/>
        <mapping class="com.apress.hibernate.User"/>
    </session-factory>
</hibernate-configuration>
```

When you use the XML configuration file, you do not need to use the `hibernate.` prefix for properties. As you can see in Listing 2-2, the `dialect` property is simply `dialect`, not `hibernate.dialect`. However, we usually elect to include the prefix for the sake of consistency. If you are already using `hibernate.properties`, `hibernate.cfg.xml` will override any settings in `hibernate.properties`. Both of these files should be located in the root of your application's classpath.

In addition to specifying the properties listed in Table 2-1 to configure a session factory, with the `<property>` tag you can also configure mapping files, caching, listeners, and the JNDI name for the session factory in the XML configuration. Listing 2-2 includes two `<mapping>` elements that identify a JAR file containing mapping files and a specific class with Hibernate annotations that is available on the classpath, respectively. We discuss mapping file configuration in the next section and caching in Chapter 9.

After placing your XML configuration file in the root directory of the classpath, you will need to call one of the `configure()` methods on your application's `AnnotationConfiguration` object. With the default file name (`hibernate.cfg.xml`), you can call `configure()` with no arguments. If you used a different file name (for instance, because you have production, staging, user acceptance test, and development environments, with different databases), use one of the following methods on a `AnnotationConfiguration` object:

- `public AnnotationConfiguration configure(String) throws HibernateException`: Loads the XML configuration from a resource accessible by the current thread's context class loader

- `public AnnotationConfiguration configure(URL) throws HibernateException`: Retrieves the XML configuration from a valid URL

- `public AnnotationConfiguration configure(File) throws HibernateException`: Uses an XML configuration file on the file system

Annotated Classes

Once you have created your annotated classes for Hibernate, it needs to know where to find them. Before you create the session factory, add them to your `AnnotationConfiguration` object, or specify them in the `hibernate.cfg.xml` XML configuration file. If you choose to add the annotated classes directly to an instance of `AnnotationConfiguration`, use one of the following methods:

- `addClass(Class)`: Takes a Java class name (such as `com.hibernatebook.config.Example`), which is then inspected for Hibernate annotations and added as a mapped class

- `addJar(File)`: Adds any annotated classes in the specified JAR file to the `AnnotationConfiguration` object

The `addJar()`method is the most convenient because it allows you to load all of your Hibernate annotated classes at one time. This method simplifies code configuration, layout, and refactoring.

As an alternative to specifying the locations of the mapping information in the code, you can instead use the `<mapping>` element in the `hibernate.cfg.xml` XML configuration file. For annotated classes, the `<mapping>` element has two possible attributes—`jar` and `class`—which map to the `addJar()`and `addClass()` methods on the `AnnotationConfiguration` object.

```
<?xml version="1.0" encoding="utf-8"?>
<!DOCTYPE hibernate-configuration SYSTEM ➡
"http://hibernate.sourceforge.net/hibernate-configuration-3.0.dtd">
<hibernate-configuration>
    <session-factory>
        <mapping jar="hibernate-mappings.jar"/>
        <mapping class="com.apress.hibernate.User"/>
    </session-factory>
</hibernate-configuration>
```

We suggest using the XML configuration file to specify the mappings, as that way you can easily use application frameworks such as Spring that will configure your Hibernate session factory for you.

Naming Strategy

If your project has an existing standard for naming database tables or columns, or you would like to specify exactly how Hibernate maps Java class names to database table names, you can use Hibernate's *naming strategy* functionality. Custom naming strategies specify how Hibernate maps Java class names to database table names, properties to column names, and the name of a table used to hold a collection of properties for a Java class. A naming strategy may also override the table names and column names specified in the Hibernate mapping documents—for instance, you might use this to enforce a consistent application-wide prefix to table names.

Although you can explicitly specify the names of all of the tables and columns in the mapping document, if you have clear and consistent rules for naming already, implementing a custom naming strategy can save a lot of time and frustration. Equally, if you decide to add a prefix to all database table names after the fact, it is easy to do so with a naming strategy, while it would be a pain to correct these in every Hibernate mapping document.

■ **Note** Using Hibernate with an existing well-specified database often means creating a custom naming strategy for Hibernate. If the database tables have a prefix, it may be cleaner to implement a naming strategy that adds that prefix than to specify the full table name with a prefix in every Hibernate mapping document.

A custom naming strategy must implement the `org.hibernate.cfg.NamingStrategy` interface or extend one of the two provided naming strategy classes, `org.hibernate.cfg.DefaultNamingStrategy` or `org.hibernate.cfg.ImprovedNamingStrategy`. The default naming strategy simply returns the unqualified Java class name as the database table name. For instance, the table name for the Java class `com.hibernatebook.AccessGroups` would be `AccessGroups`. The column name would be the same as the property name, and the collection table would have the same name as the property.

The improved naming strategy adds underscores in place of uppercase letters in mixed-case table and column names, and then lowercases the name. For instance, the same `com.hibernatebook.AccessGroups` Java class would correspond to a database table named `access_groups`.

Neither of these naming strategies takes into account the case in which you have two classes with the same name in different packages in your application. For instance, if you had two classes, `com.hibernatebook.webcast.Group` and `com.hibernatebook.security.Group`, both would default to a table named `Group`, which is not what you want. You would have to explicitly set the table name in the mapping of at least one class.

Once you have created a naming strategy, pass an instance of it to the `AnnotationConfiguration` object's `setNamingStrategy()` method, as follows:

```
public AnnotationConfiguration setNamingStrategy(NamingStrategy namingStrategy)
```

You must call this method *before* building the session factory from the `AnnotationConfiguration`. For example, here's the code for using the `ImprovedNamingStrategy` naming strategy:

```
AnnotationConfiguration conf = new AnnotationConfiguration()
conf.setNamingStrategy(ImprovedNamingStrategy.INSTANCE);
```

Using a Container-Managed Data Source

When running in an environment with a JNDI server, Hibernate can obtain a data source through a JNDI lookup. You must use the `hibernate.connection.datasource` property to specify the JNDI name, and then you may set the optional `hibernate.jndi.url` and `hibernate.jndi.class` properties to specify the location of the container's JNDI provider and the class name of the container's implementation of the JNDI `InitialContextFactory` interface. You may also use the `hibernate.connection.username` and `hibernate.connection.password` properties to specify the database user your application uses. For example, your `hibernate.properties` file might have these lines for a WebLogic 7.0 managed data source:

```
hibernate.connection.datasource=java:/comp/env/jdbc/TestDB
hibernate.connection.username=dbuser
hibernate.connection.password=dbpassword
hibernate.jndi.url=t3://localhost:7001
hibernate.jndi.class=weblogic.jndi.WLInitialContextFactory
```

Typically only the mandatory `datasource` property is needed.

The Session Factory

You use the Hibernate session factory to create `Session` objects that manage connection data, caching, and mappings. Your application is responsible for managing the session factory. You should only have one session factory unless you are using Hibernate to connect to two or more database instances with different settings, in which case you should still have one session factory for each database instance.

In order to maintain backward compatibility with Hibernate 2, the Hibernate 3 session factory can also create `org.hibernate.classic.Session` session objects. These "classic" session objects implement all of the Hibernate 3 session functionality in addition to the deprecated Hibernate 2 session methods. We briefly discuss the changes in core functionality between Hibernate 2 and 3 in Appendix D.

You obtain a session from the `SessionFactory` object using one of the four `openSession()` methods. The no-argument `openSession()` method opens a session, with the database connection and interceptor specified in the `SessionFactory`'s original configuration. You can explicitly pass a JDBC connection to use, a Hibernate interceptor, or both as arguments to the remaining `openSession()` methods.

```
public org.hibernate.classic.Session openSession()
    throws HibernateException

public org.hibernate.classic.Session openSession(Interceptor interceptor)
    throws HibernateException

public org.hibernate.classic.Session openSession(
                Connection connection,
                Interceptor interceptor)

public org.hibernate.classic.Session openSession()
    throws HibernateException
```

We discuss Hibernate interceptors in Appendix A. You can also retrieve metadata and statistics from the `SessionFactory`.

The other important method on the session factory is `close()`. The `close()` method releases all the resource information used by the session factory and made available to the `Session` objects. It is therefore important that any related `Session` objects have been closed before invoking this to close the session factory.

When the session factory closes, it destroys the cache for the entity persisters and collection persisters, and also destroys the query cache and the timestamps cache. Then the session factory closes the JDBC connection provider and removes the current instance from its JNDI object factory binding.

```
public void close() throws HibernateException
```

The Hibernate developers designed their implementation of the `SessionFactory` interface to be scalable in a multithreaded application.

SQL Dialects

JDBC abstracts away many of the underlying connection details for each relational database, yet every relational database supports a different set of features and uses a slightly different version of SQL. Among the features that differ between relational databases are the syntax for marking identity columns, column data types, available SQL functions, foreign key constraint syntax, limits, GUID support, and support for cascade deletes.

Hibernate abstracts away all of these changes into *dialect* classes. Each supported database has its own dialect. When Hibernate constructs an SQL query, it obtains appropriate syntax information for the current database from the dialect. Hibernate 3 comes with over 20 different dialects. All of these standard dialects are supplied within the `org.hibernate.dialect` package. Table 2-2 shows the supported databases in Hibernate 3 and their corresponding dialect classes.

Table 2-2. Supported Databases and Dialect Class Names for Hibernate 3.5

Database Name	Dialect Class Name
DB2/390	DB2390Dialect
DB2/400	DB2400Dialect
DB2	DB2Dialect
Derby	DerbyDialect
Firebird	FirebirdDialect
FrontBase	FrontBaseDialect
H2	H2Dialect
HSQLDB	HSQLDialect
Informix	InformixDialect
Ingres	IngresDialect
InterBase	InterbaseDialect
JDataStore	JDataStoreDialect
Mimer SQL	MimerSQLDialect
Mckoi	MckoiDialect
MySQL 5	MySQL5Dialect
MySQL (< 5.x)	MySQLDialect
MySQL with InnoDB tables	MySQLInnoDBDialect
MySQL with MyISAM tables	MySQLMyISAMDialect

Continued

Database Name	Dialect Class Name
Oracle9*i*	Oracle9Dialect
Oracle9*i* (DataDirect drivers)	DataDirectOracle9Dialect
Oracle (< 9.x)	OracleDialect
PointBase	PointbaseDialect
PostgreSQL	PostgreSQLDialect
Progress	ProgressDialect
RDMS for Unisys OS2200	RDMSOS2200Dialect
SAP DB	SAPDBDialect
SQL Server	SQLServerDialect
Sybase	SybaseDialect
Sybase 11	Sybase11Dialect
Sybase Anywhere	SybaseAnywhereDialect
Times Ten 5.1	TimesTenDialect

Configure your chosen dialect by supplying the fully qualified dialect class name as the value for the `hibernate.dialect` configuration property.

Through Hibernate Query Language (HQL), Hibernate provides object-querying functionality that is database-independent. Hibernate translates the HQL queries into database-specific SQL using hints provided by the SQL dialect classes. We discuss HQL in more detail in Chapter 9.

Hibernate also provides a native SQL facility, which is especially useful for porting existing JDBC applications to Hibernate or for improving the performance of complicated queries.

Summary

In this chapter, we explained how to integrate Hibernate into your Java applications. We also detailed the configuration options for Hibernate, including the available Hibernate property settings. We discussed how naming strategies aid in the creation of consistent company- or application-wide database table-naming conventions, and how they help you to map your Hibernate classes to databases with existing naming conventions. Finally, we discussed how Hibernate uses dialects to manage the different behaviors of different database platforms.

In the next chapter, we build and configure a pair of simple Hibernate applications that illustrate the core Hibernate concepts discussed in the first two chapters.

CHAPTER 3

■ ■ ■

Building a Simple Application

In this chapter, you'll take another look at some of the steps necessary to get the example from Chapter 1 up and running. You'll also build a somewhat larger application from scratch. All of the code in this book is available for download from the Apress site (www.apress.com).

Installing the Tools

To run the examples in this chapter, you will need to install a number of tools. You will require a JDK (Java 6 or higher), the Hibernate and Hibernate Tools distributions, the Ant build tool, the Simple Logging Facade for Java distribution, and the HSQLDB database. Table 3-1 lists the specific tools you will need and where you can find them.

Table 3-1. The Tools Used in This Book

Tool	Version	Download Location
Hibernate	3.5.1	http://hibernate.org
Hibernate Tools	3.2.4	http://hibernate.org
Java JDK	6.0	http://java.sun.com
Ant	1.8.0	http://ant.apache.org
Simple Logging Facade for Java	1.5.11	http://www.slf4j.org
HSQLDB	2.0.0	http://hsqldb.org

Hibernate and Hibernate Tools

The latest version of Hibernate is always available from http://hibernate.org, under the menu link named "Download." Various older versions and additional libraries are available from the resulting page, but you should select Hibernate Core 3.5.1 or a later version. Download the archive and unpack it to a local directory. The unpacked archive contains all the source code for Hibernate itself, a JAR library built from this source, and most of the library files that are necessary to run the sample.

You should then download Hibernate Tools from the same site. Hibernate Tools provides various plug-ins for the Ant build tool and the free Eclipse IDE. In this chapter, we make use of the Ant plug-ins only, but we discuss the Eclipse features in Appendix B. Again, the archive should be downloaded and unpacked to a local directory. This archive does not include the source code (which is available elsewhere on the `www.hibernate.org` site, if you decide to take a look at it). We use the Commons Logging framework library and the Freemarker library (packaged with the distribution) for our schema export task. They are added to the tools classpath in the Ant build file.

Simple Logging Facade for Java (SLF4J) 1.5.11

Hibernate relies on the Simple Logging Facade for Java (SLF4J) to allow you to pick your favorite logging system and use it for your application and for Hibernate, rather than forcing you to use one just for Hibernate. Typically, you might use the JDK logging, the open source Logback project, or the open source Log4J project. In this case, we are keeping things simple, so we will use the SLF4J simple logging. SLF4J works by figuring out which implementation of the SLF4J API is available on the classpath, and then uses that. So we will need to unpack the SLF4J distribution and add the path of logging implementation we plan to use to the build.properties file for our application.

Because we are using the simple logger, we do not need to include a logging properties file in our classpath. You can use other loggers for your projects, however, by specifying the corresponding SLF4J implementation to use.

HSQLDB 2.0.0

The database we will be using in our examples is the HSQL database. This is written in Java and is freely available open source software. While we used version 2.0.0 for our examples, we expect that any later version will be suitable. HSQL is derived from code originally released as "Hypersonic." You may encounter the term in some of the HSQL documentation and should treat it as synonymous with "HSQL." We may also refer to the product as HSQLDB when it might otherwise be mistaken for Hibernate Query Language (HQL), whose acronym is distressingly similar!

Our examples are tailored to HSQL because HSQL will run on any of the platforms that Hibernate will run on, and because HSQL is freely available with minimal installation requirements. However, if you want to run the examples with your own database, then the differences should boil down to the following:

- The Hibernate dialect class

- The JDBC driver

- The connection URL for the database

- The username for the database

- The password for the database

You will see where these can be specified later in this chapter. You will notice that where we specify the URL for connection to the database, we often append a `shutdown=true` attribute. This fixes a minor problem in which HSQLDB does not write its changes to disk until a `Connection` object is closed (something that may never happen when a connection is being managed by Hibernate's own connection pooling logic). This is not necessary on non-embedded databases.

Ant 1.8.0

You will want to install the Ant build tool. We will not attempt to explain the `build.xml` format in detail; if you are familiar with Ant, then the example build script provided in this chapter will be enough to get you started—if not, then Ant is a topic in its own right. We would recommend *Enterprise Java Development on a Budget*, by Christopher M. Judd and Brian Sam-Bodden (Apress, 2004), for good coverage of open source tools such as Ant.

While Ant in general lies outside the scope of this book, we will discuss the use of the Hibernate tasks used by our scripts.

Listing 3-1 provides the Ant script to build the example for this chapter.

Listing 3-1. *An Ant Script to Build the Chapter 3 Examples*

```
<project name="sample">

    <property file="build.properties"/>

    <property name="src" location="src"/>
    <property name="bin" location="bin"/>
    <property name="sql" location="sql"/>
    <property name="hibernate.tools"
        value="${hibernate.tools.home}${hibernate.tools.path}"/>

    <path id="classpath.base">
        <pathelement location="${src}"/>
        <pathelement location="${bin}"/>
        <pathelement location="${hibernate.home}/hibernate3.jar"/>
        <pathelement location="${slf4j.implementation.jar}"/>
        <fileset dir="${hibernate.home}/lib" includes="**/*.jar"/>
        <pathelement location="${hsql.home}/lib/hsqldb.jar"/>
    </path>

    <path id="classpath.tools">
        <path refid="classpath.base"/>
        <pathelement
            location="${hibernate.tools.lib}/commons-logging-1.0.4.jar"/>
        <pathelement
            location="${hibernate.tools}/freemarker.jar"/>
        <pathelement
            location="${hibernate.tools}/hibernate-tools.jar"/>
    </path>

    <taskdef name="htools"
        classname="org.hibernate.tool.ant.HibernateToolTask"
        classpathref="classpath.tools"/>
```

```
<target name="exportDDL" depends="compile">
 <mkdir dir="${sql}"/>
    <htools destdir="${sql}">
       <classpath refid="classpath.tools"/>
       <annotationconfiguration
          configurationfile="${src}/hibernate.cfg.xml"/>
       <hbm2ddl drop="true" outputfilename="sample.sql"/>
    </htools>
</target>

<target name="compile">
    <javac srcdir="${src}" destdir="${bin}" classpathref="classpath.base"/>
</target>

<target name="populateMessages" depends="compile">
    <java classname="sample.PopulateMessages" classpathref="classpath.base"/>
</target>

<target name="listMessages" depends="compile">
    <java classname="sample.ListMessages" classpathref="classpath.base"/>
</target>

<target name="createUsers" depends="compile">
    <java classname="sample.CreateUser" classpathref="classpath.base">
       <arg value="dave"/>
       <arg value="dodgy"/>
    </java>
    <java classname="sample.CreateUser" classpathref="classpath.base">
       <arg value="jeff"/>
       <arg value="jammy"/>
    </java>
</target>

<target name="createCategories" depends="compile">
    <java classname="sample.CreateCategory" classpathref="classpath.base">
       <arg value="retro"/>
    </java>
    <java classname="sample.CreateCategory" classpathref="classpath.base">
       <arg value="kitsch"/>
    </java>
</target>

<target name="postAdverts" depends="compile">
    <java classname="sample.PostAdvert" classpathref="classpath.base">
       <arg value="dave"/>
       <arg value="retro"/>
       <arg value="Sinclair Spectrum for sale"/>
       <arg value="48k original box and packaging"/>
    </java>
```

```
        <java classname="sample.PostAdvert" classpathref="classpath.base">
            <arg value="dave"/>
            <arg value="kitsch"/>
            <arg value="Commemorative Plates"/>
            <arg value="Kitten and puppies design"/>
        </java>
        <java classname="sample.PostAdvert" classpathref="classpath.base">
            <arg value="jeff"/>
            <arg value="retro"/>
            <arg value="Atari 2600 wanted"/>
            <arg value="Must have original joysticks."/>
        </java>
        <java classname="sample.PostAdvert" classpathref="classpath.base">
            <arg value="jeff"/>
            <arg value="kitsch"/>
            <arg value="Inflatable Sofa"/>
            <arg value="Leopard skin pattern. Nice."/>
        </java>
    </target>

    <target name="listAdverts" depends="compile">
        <java classname="sample.ListAdverts" classpathref="classpath.base"/>
    </target>

</project>
```

The properties file imported in the first line provides the paths to your installed libraries, and you should adjust it as appropriate (as shown in Listing 3-2). If you unpack Hibernate 3.5.1, it will create a directory called `hibernate-distribution-3.5.1`, which we have renamed to `hibernate-3.5.1` and placed in a directory called `hibernate`; we have done something similar with the HSQL database directory.

The Hibernate Tools archive currently unpacks to two directories (`plugins` and `features`). We have created a parent directory to contain these called `hibernate-tools-3.2.4`. The path to the appropriate JAR file (`hibernate-tools.jar`) within the unpacked directory is dependent upon the specific Hibernate Tools version, so we have added the `hibernate.tools.path` property to point our build script at this. We also added a path to the Hibernate libraries contained in the Hibernate Tools distribution so that we can load the Commons Logging library for our Hibernate Tools to use.

Listing 3-2. The `build.properties` *File to Configure the Ant Script*

```
# Path to the hibernate install directory
hibernate.home=/hibernate/hibernate-3.5.1

# Path to the hibernate-tools install directory
hibernate.tools.home=/hibernate/hibernate-tools-3.2.4

# Path to hibernate-tools.jar relative to hibernate.tools.home
hibernate.tools.path=/plugins/org.hibernate.eclipse_3.2.4.GA-R200905070146-H18/lib/tools

# Path to hibernate-tools hibernate libraries relative to hibernate.tools.home
hibernate.tools.lib.path=/plugins/org.hibernate.eclipse_3.2.4.GA-R200905070146-
H18/lib/hibernate
```

```
# Path to the SLF4J implementation JAR for the logging framework to use
slf4j.implementation.jar=/slf4j/slf4j-1.5.11/slf4j-simple-1.5.11.jar

# Path to the HSQL DB install directory
hsql.home=/hsqldb/hsqldb_2.0.0
```

Aside from the configuration settings, the only oddity in the `build.xml` file is the configuration and use of a Hibernate-specific Ant task. The `taskdef` (shown in Listing 3-3) makes this task available for use, using the appropriate classes from the `tools.jar` file.

Listing 3-3. Defining the Hibernate Tools Ant Tasks

```
<taskdef name="htools"
    classname="org.hibernate.tool.ant.HibernateToolTask"
    classpathref="classpath.tools"/>
```

This task provides several subtasks, but in this chapter we will only make use of the `hbm2ddl` subtask. This reads in the mapped classes and configuration files and generates Data Definition Language (DDL) scripts to create an appropriate schema in the database to represent our entities. This way we do not need to maintain the database schema creation scripts ourselves, changing it every time we add, change, or remove something from our Hibernate mappings. This is very useful when designing new applications that use Hibernate.

Table 3-2 shows the basic directories that our build script assumes, relative to the example project's root.

Table 3-2. The Project Directories

Directory	Contents
src	Source code and configuration files (excluding those directly related to the build)
bin	Compiled class files
sql	Generated DDL scripts

The root of the project contains the build script and build configuration file; it will also contain the database files generated by HSQL when the `exportDDL` task is run.

The Ant Tasks

Table 3-3 shows the tasks contained in the Ant build script.

Table 3-3. *The Tasks Available in the Example Ant Script*

Task	Action
exportDDL	Creates the appropriate database objects. It also generates a script that can be run against an HSQL database to re-create these objects if necessary.
compile	Builds the class files. This task is a dependency of all the tasks except exportDDL (which does not require the class files), so it is not necessary to invoke it directly.
populateMessages	Populates the database with a sample message.
listMessages	Lists all messages stored in the database by populateMessages.
createUsers	Creates a pair of users in the database for the Advert example.
createCategories	Creates a pair of categories in the database for the Advert example.
postAdverts	Creates several adverts in the database for the Advert example.
listAdverts	Lists the adverts in the database for the Advert example.

Creating a Hibernate Configuration File

There are several ways that Hibernate can be given all of the information that it needs to connect to the database and determine its mappings. For our Message example, we used the configuration file hibernate.cfg.xml placed in our project's **src** directory and given in Listing 3-4.

Listing 3-4. *The Message Application's Configuration File*

```
<<!DOCTYPE hibernate-configuration PUBLIC
"-//Hibernate/Hibernate Configuration DTD 3.0//EN"
    "http://hibernate.sourceforge.net/hibernate-configuration-3.0.dtd">

 <hibernate-configuration>
  <session-factory>
    <property name="hibernate.connection.url">
        jdbc:hsqldb:file:testdb;shutdown=true
    </property>
    <property name="hibernate.connection.driver_class">
        org.hsqldb.jdbcDriver
    </property>
    <property name="hibernate.connection.username">sa</property>
    <property name="hibernate.connection.password"></property>
    <property name="hibernate.connection.pool_size">0</property>
```

```
    <property name="hibernate.dialect">
        org.hibernate.dialect.HSQLDialect
    </property>
    <property name="hibernate.show_sql">false</property>

    <!-- "Import" the mapping resources here -->
    <mapping class="sample.entity.Message"/>

  </session-factory>
</hibernate-configuration>
```

The various database-related fields (`hibernate.connection.*`) should look pretty familiar from setting up JDBC connections, with the exception of the `hibernate.connection.pool` property, which is used to disable a feature (connection pooling) that causes problems when using the HSQL database. The `show_sql` value, set to `false` in our example, is extremely useful when debugging problems with your programs—when set to `true`, all of the SQL prepared by Hibernate is logged to the standard output stream (i.e., the console).

The SQL dialects, discussed in Chapter 2, allow you to select the database type that Hibernate will be talking to. You must select a dialect, even if it is `GenericDialect`—most database platforms accept a common subset of SQL, but there are inconsistencies and extensions specific to each. Hibernate uses the dialect class to determine the appropriate SQL to use when creating and querying the database. If you elect to use `GenericDialect`, then Hibernate will only be able to use a common subset of SQL to perform its operations, and will be unable to take advantage of various database-specific features to improve performance.

■ **Caution** Hibernate looks in the classpath for the configuration file. If you place it anywhere else, Hibernate will complain that you haven't provided necessary configuration details.

Hibernate does not require you to use an XML configuration file. You have two other options. First, you can provide a normal Java properties file. The equivalent properties file to Listing 3-4 would be as follows:

```
hibernate.connection.driver_class=org.hsqldb.jdbcDriver
hibernate.connection.url=jdbc:hsqldb:file:testdb;shutdown=true
hibernate.connection.username=sa
hibernate.connection.password=
hibernate.connection.pool_size=0
hibernate.show_sql=false
hibernate.dialect=org.hibernate.dialect.HSQLDialect
```

As you'll notice, this does not contain the resource mapping from the XML file—and in fact, you cannot include this information in a properties file; if you want to configure Hibernate this way, you'll need to directly map your classes into the Hibernate `Configuration` at run time. Here's how this can be done:

```
Configuration config = new Configuration();
config.addClass( sample.entity.Message.class );
config.setProperties( System.getProperties() );
SessionFactory sessions = config.buildSessionFactory();
```

Here, `Message.class` is the compiled output from the `Message.java` code given in Listing 3-5 (and briefly discussed in Chapter 1). If you don't want to provide the configuration properties in a file, you can apply them directly using the -D flag. Here's an example:

```
java -classpath ...
   -Dhibernate.connection.driver_class=org.hsqldb.jdbcDriver
   -Dhibernate.connection.url= jdbc:hsqldb:file:testdb;shutdown=true
   -Dhibernate.connection.username=sa
   -Dhibernate.connection.password=
   -Dhibernate.connection.pool_size=0
   -Dhibernate.show_sql=false
   -Dhibernate.dialect=org.hibernate.dialect.HSQLDialect
   ...
```

Given its verbosity, this is probably the least convenient of the three methods, but it is occasionally useful when running tools and utilities on an ad hoc basis. For most other purposes, we think that the XML configuration file is the best choice.

Running the Message Example

With Hibernate and a database installed, and our configuration file created, all we need to do now is create the classes in full, and then build and run everything. Chapter 1 omitted the trivial parts of the required classes, so we provide them in full in Listings 3-5 through 3-7, after which we'll look at some of the details of what's being invoked.

Listing 3-5. The Message POJO Class

```
package sample.entity;

import javax.persistence.Entity;
import javax.persistence.Id;
import javax.persistence.GeneratedValue;

@Entity
public class Message {

   private Message() {

   }

   public Message(String messageText) {
      this.messageText = messageText;
   }
```

```
    public String getMessageText() {
        return messageText;
    }

    public void setMessageText(String messageText) {
        this.messageText = messageText;
    }

@Id
@GeneratedValue
    public Integer getId() {
        return id;
    }

    public void setId(Integer id) {
        this.id = id;
    }
    private String messageText;
    private Integer id;

}
```

Listing 3-6 shows a simple application to populate the messages table with examples.

Listing 3-6. The Code to Create a Sample Message

```
package sample;

import java.util.Date;

import org.hibernate.Session;
import org.hibernate.SessionFactory;
import org.hibernate.cfg.AnnotationConfiguration;

import sample.entity.Message;

public class PopulateMessages {
    public static void main(String[] args) {
            SessionFactory factory =
                new AnnotationConfiguration().configure().buildSessionFactory();
            Session session = factory.openSession();
            session.beginTransaction();

            Message m1 = new Message(
                "Hibernated a message on " + new Date());

            session.save(m1);
            session.getTransaction().commit();
            session.close();
    }
}
```

Finally, Listing 3-7 shows the full text of the application to list all the messages in the database.

Listing 3-7. The Message Application

```
package sample;

import java.util.Iterator;
import java.util.List;

import org.hibernate.Session;
import org.hibernate.SessionFactory;
import org.hibernate.cfg.AnnotationConfiguration;

import sample.entity.Message;

public class ListMessages {
   public static void main(String[] args)
   {
      SessionFactory factory =
         new AnnotationConfiguration().configure().buildSessionFactory();
      Session session = factory.openSession();

      List messages = session.createQuery("from Message").list();
      System.out.println("Found " + messages.size() + " message(s):");

      Iterator i = messages.iterator();
      while(i.hasNext()) {
         Message msg = (Message)i.next();
         System.out.println(msg.getMessageText());
      }

      session.close();
   }
}
```

The Ant target exportDDL will create an appropriate schema in the HSQLDB database files. Running the populateMessages task will create a message entry (this can be invoked multiple times). Running the listMessages task will list the messages that have been entered into the database so far.

■ **Caution** Because we have selected the drop="true" option for the hbm2ddl subtask of our exportDDL target, running this script will effectively delete any data in the named tables. It is rarely a good idea to run such a script from a machine that has database access to the production environment because of the risk of accidentally deleting your production data!

The appropriate classpath entries have been set up in the Ant build script. To run a Hibernate application, you need the hibernate.jar file from the root of the Hibernate distribution, and a subset of the libraries provided in the `lib` subdirectory. You will need all of the libraries in the `lib/required` subdirectory and the Javassist library in the `lib/bytecode/javassist` subdirectory. You will also need the JPA 2 library in the `lib/jpa` subdirectory. The optional libraries aren't needed for this example. The ant build file for this example includes all of the libraries in the Hibernate distribution, both optional and required.

Most of the work required to get this example running is the sort of basic configuration trivia that any application requires (writing Ant scripts, setting classpaths, and so on). The real work consists of these steps:

1. Creating the Hibernate configuration file

2. Writing the POJOs (introduced in Chapter 1)

3. Adding Hibernate mapping annotations to the POJOs

Persisting Multiple Objects

Our example in Chapter 1 was as simple a persistence scenario as you can imagine. In the next few sections of this chapter, we will look at a slightly more complicated scenario.

Our example application will provide the persistence technology for an online billboard application, as shown in Figure 3-1.

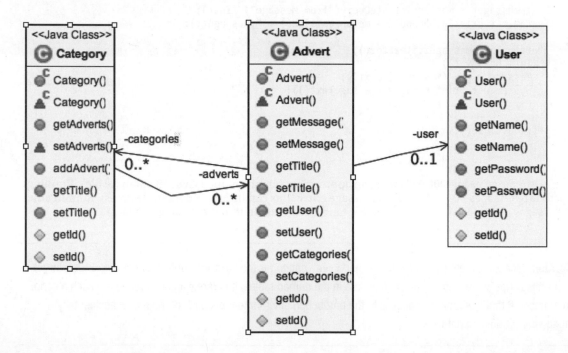

Figure 3-1. The online billboard classes

This is a gross simplification of the sort of classes that would be required in a production application. For example, we make no distinction between the roles of users of the application, but it should suffice to show some of the simpler relationships between classes.

Particularly interesting is the many-to-many relationship between categories and advertisements. We would like to be able to have multiple categories and adverts, and place any given advert in more than one category. For example, an electric piano should be listed in the "Instruments" category as well as the "Electronics" category.

Creating Persistence Classes

We will begin by creating the POJOs for the application. From the class diagram, we know that three classes will be persisted into the database (see Listings 3-8, 3-9, and 3-10). Each class that will be persisted by Hibernate is required to have a default constructor with at least package scope. They should have get and set methods for all of the attributes that are to be persisted. We will provide each with an id field, allowing this to be the primary key in our database (we prefer the use of surrogate keys, as changes to business rules can make the use of direct keys risky).

■ **Note** A surrogate key is an arbitrary value (usually numeric), with the data type depending on the number of objects expected (e.g., 32-bit, 64-bit, etc.). The surrogate key has no meaning outside the database—it is not a customer number, a phone number, or anything else. As such, if a business decision causes previously unique business data to be duplicated, this will not cause problems since the business data does not form the primary key.

As well as the default constructor for each class, we provide a constructor that allows the fields other than the primary key to be assigned directly. This allows us to create and populate an object in one step instead of several, but we let Hibernate take care of the allocation of our primary keys.

The classes shown in Figure 3-1 are our POJOs. Their implementation is shown in Listings 3-8, 3-9, and 3-10.

Listing 3-8. The Class Representing Users

```
package sample.entity;

public class User {
    private long id;
    private String name;
    private String password;

    public User(String name, String password) {
        this.name = name;
        this.password = password;
    }
}
```

```
    User() {
    }

    public String getName() {
        return name;
    }

    public void setName(String name) {
        this.name = name;
    }

    public String getPassword() {
        return password;
    }

    public void setPassword(String password) {
        this.password = password;
    }

    protected long getId() {
        return id;
    }

    protected void setId(long id) {
        this.id = id;
    }
}
```

*Listing 3-9. The Class Representing Categories (Each Having an Associated Set of **Advert** Objects)*

```
package sample.entity;

import java.util.HashSet;
import java.util.Set;

public class Category {
    private long id;
    private String title;
    private Set<Advert> adverts = new HashSet<Advert>();

    public Category(String title) {
        this.title = title;
        this.adverts = new HashSet<Advert>();
    }

    Category() {
    }

    public Set<Advert> getAdverts() {
        return adverts;
    }
```

```
    void setAdverts(Set<Advert> adverts) {
        this.adverts = adverts;
    }

    public void addAdvert(Advert advert) {
        getAdverts().add(advert);
    }

    public String getTitle() {
        return title;
    }

    public void setTitle(String title) {
        this.title = title;
    }

    protected long getId() {
        return id;
    }

    protected void setId(long id) {
        this.id = id;
    }
}
```

Listing 3-10. The Class Representing Adverts (Each Instance Has an Associated User Who Placed the Advert)

```
package sample.entity;

public class Advert {
    private long id;
    private String title;
    private String message;
    private User user;

    public Advert(String title, String message, User user) {
        this.title = title;
        this.message = message;
        this.user = user;
    }

    Advert() {
    }

    public String getMessage() {
        return message;
    }
```

```java
    public void setMessage(String message) {
        this.message = message;
    }

    public String getTitle() {
        return title;
    }

    public void setTitle(String title) {
        this.title = title;
    }

    public User getUser() {
        return user;
    }

    public void setUser(User user) {
        this.user = user;
    }

    protected long getId() {
        return id;
    }

    protected void setId(long id) {
        this.id = id;
    }
}
```

We will have to add annotations to these POJOs to support Hibernate, as we will show in the next section. We have also chosen to provide package-scoped default constructors to support use of the (optional) lazy-loading feature of Hibernate. Most existing applications will contain POJOs "out of the box" that are compatible with Hibernate.

Creating the Object Mappings

Now that we have our POJOs, we need to map them to the database, representing the fields of each directly or indirectly as values in the columns of the associated tables. We take each in turn, starting with the User class.

The first step is to tell Hibernate to map the class with the @Entity annotation. We also need to tell Hibernate that we would like the database table that stores the User class to be named AdUser because user is a reserved keyword in many databases. We do this with the @Table annotation, which we supply with the name of the database table we would like to use instead of the default.

The next step is to map the fields on the class. The User class has three fields, as follows:

> *The* id *field*: Corresponds to the surrogate key to be used in, and generated by, the database. This special field is handled by the @Id annotation. We specify that it should be generated by the database, rather than by the application, by using the @GeneratedValue annotation. We can use the default, which is to use the database's native generator.

The name *field*: Represents the name of the user. It should be stored in a column called name. It has type String. We do not permit duplicate names to be stored in the table. To model this unique constraint, we use the @Column annotation and set the unique attribute on the @Column annotation to true. When we create the database schema from the annotated POJOs, the name column for the aduser table will have a unique constraint that the database will enforce for us.

The password *field*: Represents a given user's password. It should be stored in a column called password. It has type String.

Bearing these features in mind, the updated Java class in Listing 3-11 should be extremely easy to follow.

Listing 3-11. The Mapping of the User *Class into the Database*

```
package sample.entity;


import javax.persistence.Column;
import javax.persistence.Entity;
import javax.persistence.GeneratedValue;
import javax.persistence.Id;
import javax.persistence.Table;

@Entity
@Table(name="AdUser")
public class User {
    private long id;
    private String name;
    private String password;

    public User(String name, String password) {
        this.name = name;
        this.password = password;
    }

    User() {
    }

    @Column(unique=true)
    public String getName() {
        return name;
    }

    public void setName(String name) {
        this.name = name;
    }

    public String getPassword() {
        return password;
    }
}
```

```
    public void setPassword(String password) {
        this.password = password;
    }

    @Id
    @GeneratedValue
    protected long getId() {
        return id;
    }

    protected void setId(long id) {
        this.id = id;
    }
}
```

The **Category** mapping presents another type of relationship: many-to-many. Each **Category** object is associated with a set of adverts, while any given advert can be associated with multiple categories. In addition to the annotations we discussed in the previous example, we will need to use the **@ManyToMany** and **@JoinTable** annotations. We used generics for the collections, so Hibernate will know which classes are mapped on either end of the many-to-many relationship.

The **@ManyToMany** annotation indicates that the **Category** class has a many-to-many relationship with the **Advert** class. This many-to-many relationship is bidirectional, which means that the **Advert** class has a collection of **Category** objects, and the **Category** class has a collection of **Advert** objects. For many-to-many relationships, we need to tell Hibernate which class is the owner of the relationship. For bidirectional many-to-many relationships, either side can be designated as the owner. For this example, the **Category** class will be the owner.

The details of the join table that contains the links between the two classes in a many-to-many relationship go on the owner class. The **Category** class owns the relationship, so we add a **@JoinTable** annotation. The **@JoinTable** annotation indicates that the relationship requires the creation of an additional link table, so we specify the name of the table containing that information.

When we map the **Advert** class, we will also need to add a **@ManyToMany** annotation, but we will need to point back to the **Category** class as the owner with the **mappedBy** attribute on the **@ManyToMany** annotation. We do not need to specify the join table on the **Advert** class.

Again, this is complicated when described, but if you look at the example table from Listing 3-14, the need for each field in the mapping becomes clear (see Listing 3-12).

Listing 3-12. The Mapping of the Category Class into the Database

```
package sample.entity;


import java.util.HashSet;
import java.util.Set;
import javax.persistence.Column;
import javax.persistence.Entity;
import javax.persistence.GeneratedValue;
import javax.persistence.Id;
import javax.persistence.JoinColumn;
import javax.persistence.JoinTable;
import javax.persistence.ManyToMany;
```

```java
@Entity
public class Category {
    private long id;
    private String title;
    private Set<Advert> adverts = new HashSet<Advert>();

    public Category(String title) {
        this.title = title;
        this.adverts = new HashSet<Advert>();
    }

    Category() {
    }

    @ManyToMany
    @JoinTable(name="link_category_advert")
    public Set<Advert> getAdverts() {
        return adverts;
    }

    void setAdverts(Set<Advert> adverts) {
        this.adverts = adverts;
    }

    public void addAdvert(Advert advert) {
        getAdverts().add(advert);
    }

    @Column(unique=true)
    public String getTitle() {
        return title;
    }
     public void setTitle(String title) {
        this.title = title;
    }

    @Id
    @GeneratedValue
    protected long getId() {
        return id;
    }

    protected void setId(long id) {
        this.id = id;
    }
}
```

Finally, we represent the **Advert** class (see Listing 3-13). We add the **@ManyToMany** annotation to the class to represent the bidirectional relationship with the **Category** class. As discussed, we will need to point back to the **Category** class as the owner with the **mappedBy** attribute. The **mappedBy** attribute points to the field on the **Category** class that contains the **Advert** classes (in this case, **adverts**).

This class also introduces the many-to-one association, in this case with the User class. Any given advertisement must belong to a single user, but any given user can place many different advertisements.

Listing 3-13. The Mapping of the Advert Class into the Database

```java
package sample.entity;

import java.util.HashSet;
import java.util.Set;
import javax.persistence.Entity;
import javax.persistence.GeneratedValue;
import javax.persistence.Id;
import javax.persistence.JoinColumn;
import javax.persistence.ManyToMany;
import javax.persistence.ManyToOne;

@Entity
public class Advert {
    private long id;
    private String title;
    private String message;
    private User user;
    private Set<Category> categories;

    public Advert(String title, String message, User user) {
        this.title = title;
        this.message = message;
        this.user = user;
        this.categories = new HashSet<Category>();
    }

    Advert() {
    }

    public String getMessage() {
        return message;
    }

    public void setMessage(String message) {
        this.message = message;
    }

    public String getTitle() {
        return title;
    }

    public void setTitle(String title) {
        this.title = title;
    }
```

```
@ManyToOne
@JoinColumn(name="aduser")
public User getUser() {
        return user;
}

public void setUser(User user) {
    this.user = user;
}

@ManyToMany(mappedBy="adverts")
public Set<Category> getCategories() {
    return categories;
}

public void setCategories(Set<Category> categories) {
    this.categories = categories;
}

@Id
@GeneratedValue
protected long getId() {
    return id;
}

protected void setId(long id) {
    this.id = id;
}
}
```

Once you have mapped the classes, you need to tell Hibernate where to find them. The simplest way to do this is to add them to a Hibernate configuration file, as we did in Listing 3-4. Because we haven't changed the way we connect to the database, we can reuse that configuration file and add mappings for our classes.

For our example, take the configuration file described in Listing 3-4 and add the following three mapping resource entries:

```
<mapping class="sample.entity.Advert"/>
<mapping class="sample.entity.Category"/>
<mapping class="sample.entity.User"/>
```

after the following line:

```
<mapping class="sample.entity.Message"/>
```

This section may seem confusing, as it is something of a flying visit to the subject of mappings and some of their whys and wherefores. We provide a more in-depth discussion of mapping in later chapters—specifically, general mapping concepts in Chapter 5, and mapping your Java objects with annotations in Chapter 6. We also discuss how to use the older XML mapping documents in Chapter 7.

Creating the Tables

With the object mapping in place and our Hibernate configuration file set up correctly, we have everything we need to generate a script to create the database for our application by invoking the exportDDL task. This builds the entities shown in Figure 3-2.

Even though we can generate the database directly, we also recommend taking some time to work out what schema you would expect your mappings to generate. This allows you to "sanity check" the script to make sure it corresponds with your expectations. If you and the tool both agree on what things should look like, then all is well and good; if not, your mappings may be wrong or there may be a subtle error in the way that you have related your data types.

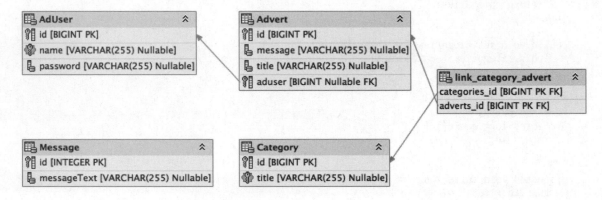

Figure 3-2. *The database entity relationships*

The script in Listing 3-14 is generated by the exportDDL task. It could easily have been written by hand, and it is easy to compare it against your prior expectations of the database schema (we have changed the formatting slightly, but otherwise this is identical to the output of the task).

Listing 3-14. *The Script Generated by the exportDDL Task*

```
alter table Advert
    drop constraint FK74A35BF4F310D740;

alter table link_category_advert
    drop constraint FKA7C387F06613C4A3;

alter table link_category_advert
    drop constraint FKA7C387F07F2F2556;

drop table AdUser if exists;
drop table Advert if exists;
drop table Category if exists;
drop table Message if exists;
drop table link_category_advert if exists;
```

```
create table AdUser (
    id bigint generated by default as identity (start with 1),
    name varchar(255),
    password varchar(255),
    primary key (id),
    unique (name)
);

create table Advert (
    id bigint generated by default as identity (start with 1),
    message varchar(255),
    title varchar(255),
    aduser bigint,
    primary key (id)
);

create table Category (
    id bigint generated by default as identity (start with 1),
    title varchar(255),
    primary key (id),
    unique (title)
);

create table Message (
    id integer generated by default as identity (start with 1),
    messageText varchar(255),
    primary key (id)
);

create table link_category_advert (
    categories_id bigint not null,
    adverts_id bigint not null,
    primary key (categories_id, adverts_id)
);

alter table Advert
    add constraint FK74A35BF4F310D740
    foreign key (aduser)
    references AdUser;

alter table link_category_advert
    add constraint FKA7C387F06613C4A3
    foreign key (categories_id)
    references Category;

alter table link_category_advert
    add constraint FKA7C387F07F2F2556
    foreign key (adverts_id)
    references Advert;
```

Note the foreign key constraints and the link table representing the many-to-many relationship.

Sessions

Chapter 4 will discuss the full life cycle of persistence objects in detail—but you need to understand the basics of the relationship between the session and the persistence objects if you are to build even a trivial application in Hibernate.

The Session and Related Objects

The session is always created from a `SessionFactory`. The `SessionFactory` is a heavyweight object, and there would normally be a single instance per application. In some ways, it is a little like a connection pool in a connected application. In a J2EE application, it would typically be retrieved as a JNDI resource. It is created from a `Configuration` object, which in turn acquires the Hibernate configuration information and uses this to generate an appropriate `SessionFactory` instance.

The session itself has a certain amount in common with a JDBC `Connection` object. To read an object from the database, you must use a session directly or indirectly. An example of a direct use of the session to do this would be, as in Chapter 1, calling the `session.get()` method, or creating a `Query` object from the session (a `Query` is very much like a `PreparedStatement`).

An indirect use of the session would be using an object itself associated with the session. For example, if we have retrieved a `Phone` object from the database using a session directly, we can retrieve a `User` object by calling `Phone`'s `getUser()` method, even if the associated `User` object has not yet been loaded (as a result of lazy loading).

An object that has not been loaded via the session can be explicitly associated with the session in several ways, the simplest of which is to call the `session.update()` method passing in the object in question.

The session does a lot more than this, however, as it provides some caching functionality, manages the lazy loading of objects, and watches for changes to associated objects (so that the changes can be persisted to the database).

A Hibernate transaction is typically used in much the same way as a JDBC transaction. It is used to batch together mutually dependent Hibernate operations, allowing them to be completed or rolled back atomically, and to isolate operations from external changes to the database. Hibernate can also take advantage of a transaction's scope to limit unnecessary JDBC "chatter," queuing SQL to be transmitted in a batch at the end of the transaction when possible.

We will discuss all of this in much greater detail in Chapter 4, but for now it suffices that we need to maintain a single `SessionFactory` for the entire application. However, a session should only be accessed within a single thread of execution. Because a session also represents information cached from the database, it is desirable to retain it for use within the thread until anything (specifically any Hibernate exception) causes it to become invalid.

We present in Listing 3-15 a pattern from which Data Access Objects (DAOs) can be derived, providing an efficient way for a thread to retrieve and (if necessary) create its sessions with a minimal impact on the clarity of the code. In this case, we are using a base DAO to manage the session, but we will not use individual DAOs for each entity. Our DAO encapsulates some of the Hibernate boilerplate code you need to manage sessions and transactions.

Listing 3-15. The Base Class Used to Manage the Session in the Example

```
package sample.dao;

import java.util.logging.Level;
import java.util.logging.Logger;

import org.hibernate.HibernateException;
import org.hibernate.Session;
import org.hibernate.SessionFactory;
import org.hibernate.cfg.AnnotationConfiguration;

public class DAO {

    protected DAO() {
    }

    public static Session getSession() {
        Session session = (Session) DAO.session.get();
        if (session == null) {
            session = sessionFactory.openSession();
            DAO.session.set(session);
        }
        return session;
    }

    protected void begin() {
        getSession().beginTransaction();
    }

    protected void commit() {
        getSession().getTransaction().commit();
    }

    protected void rollback() {
        try {
        getSession().getTransaction().rollback();
        } catch( HibernateException e ) {
            log.log(Level.WARNING,"Cannot rollback",e);
        }

        try {
            getSession().close();
        } catch( HibernateException e ) {
            log.log(Level.WARNING,"Cannot close",e);
        }
        DAO.session.set(null);
    }
```

```
    public static void close() {
       getSession().close();
       DAO.session.set(null);
    }

    private static final Logger log = Logger.getAnonymousLogger();

    private static final ThreadLocal session = new ThreadLocal();

    private static final SessionFactory sessionFactory =
       new AnnotationConfiguration().configure().buildSessionFactory();
}
```

Using the Session

The most common use cases for our POJOs will be to create them and delete them. In both cases, we want the change to be reflected in the database.

For example, we want to be able to create a user, specifying the username and password, and have this information stored in the database when we are done.

The logic to create a user (and reflect this in the database) is incredibly simple, as shown in Listing 3-16.

Listing 3-16. Creating a User Object and Reflecting This in the Database

```
try {
    begin();
    User user = new User(username,password);
    getSession().save(user);
    commit();
    return user;
} catch( HibernateException e ) {
    rollback();
    throw new Exception("Could not create user " + username,e);
}
```

We begin a transaction, create the new User object, ask the session to save the object, and then commit the transaction. If a problem is encountered (if, for example, a User entity with that username has already been created in the database), then a Hibernate exception will be thrown, and the entire transaction will be rolled back.

To retrieve the User object from the database, we will make our first excursion into HQL. HQL is somewhat similar to SQL, but you should bear in mind that it refers to the names used in the mapping files, rather than the table names and columns of the underlying database.

The appropriate HQL query to retrieve the users having a given name field is as follows:

```
from User where name= :username
```

where User is the class name and :username is the HQL named parameter that our code will populate when we carry out the query. This is remarkably similar to the SQL for a prepared statement to achieve the same end:

```
select * from user where name = ?
```

The complete code to retrieve a user for a specific username is shown in Listing 3-17.

Listing 3-17. Retrieving a User Object from the Database

```
try {
    begin();
    Query q = getSession().createQuery("from User where name = :username");
    q.setString("username",username);
    User user = (User)q.uniqueResult();
    commit();
    return user;
} catch( HibernateException e ) {
    rollback();
    throw new Exception("Could not get user " + username,e);
}
```

We begin a transaction, create a `Query` object (similar in purpose to `PreparedStatement` in connected applications), populate the parameter of the query with the appropriate username, and then list the results of the query. We extract the user (if one has been retrieved successfully) and commit the transaction. If there is a problem reading the data, the transaction will be rolled back.

The key line used to obtain the `User` entity is:

```
User user = (User)q.uniqueResult();
```

We use the `uniqueResult()`method because it is guaranteed to throw an exception if somehow our query identifies more than one `User` object for the given username. In principle, this could happen if the underlying database's constraints don't match our mapping constraint for a unique username field, and an exception is an appropriate way to handle the failure.

The logic to delete a user from the database (Listing 3-18) is even more trivial than that required to create one.

Listing 3-18. Deleting a User Object and Reflecting This in the Database

```
try {
    begin();
    getSession().delete(user);
    commit();
} catch( HibernateException e ) {
    rollback();
    throw new Exception("Could not delete user " + user.getName(),e);
}
```

We simply instruct the session to delete the `User` object from the database, and commit the transaction. The transaction will roll back if there is a problem—for example, if the user has already been deleted.

You have now seen all the basic operations that we want to perform on our data, so we will now put together an example application that uses our classes.

The Example Client

Listing 3-19 shows the example code tying this together. Of course, this isn't a full application, but this example gives a flavor of how our annotated Java classes can be used with the base DAO.

The code should be run with the tasks in the Ant script delivered in Listing 3-1. After running the exportDDL task to create the empty database, you should run the createUsers and createCategories tasks to provide initial users and categories, and then the postAdverts task to place advertisements in the database. Finally, run the listAdverts task to display the saved data.

The code invoking the annotated Java classes to perform the tasks in question is shown in Listing 3-19.

Listing 3-19. The Class to Create the Example Users

```java
package sample;

import org.hibernate.HibernateException;
import sample.dao.DAO;
import sample.entity.User;

public class CreateUser extends DAO {

    public static void main(String[] args) {

        if (args.length != 2) {
            System.out.println("params required: username, password");
            return;
        }
        String username = args[0];
        String password = args[1];

        try {
            CreateUser self = new CreateUser();
            System.out.println("Creating user " + username);
            self.create(username,password);
            System.out.println("Created user");
            DAO.close();
        } catch (Exception e) {
            System.out.println(e.getMessage());
        }

    }

    public User create(String username, String password)
            throws Exception
    {
        try
        {
            begin();
            User user = new User(username, password);
            getSession().save(user);
```

```
            commit();
            return user;
        }
        catch (HibernateException e)
        {
            throw new Exception("Could not create user " + username, e);
        }
    }
}
```

The `CreateUser` class uses the `DAO` class to create and persist an appropriate `User` object. The specifics of the (two) users created are drawn from the command-line parameters provided in the `createUsers` Ant task.

In Listing 3-20, we create `Category` objects via the `DAO` class with a similar pattern—and again we draw the specific details from the command line provided by the Ant script.

Listing 3-20. The Class to Create the Example Categories

```
package sample;

import org.hibernate.HibernateException;
import sample.dao.DAO;
import sample.entity.Category;

public class CreateCategory extends DAO {

    public static void main(String[] args) {

        if (args.length != 1) {
            System.out.println("param required: categoryTitle");
            return;
        }

        CreateCategory self = new CreateCategory();
        String title = args[0];
        try {
            System.out.println("Creating category " + title);
            self.create(title);
            System.out.println("Created category");
            DAO.close();
        } catch (Exception e) {
            System.out.println(e.getMessage());
        }

    }

    public Category create(String title)
            throws Exception {
```

```
        try {
            begin();
            Category category = new Category(title);
            getSession().save(category);
            commit();
            return category;
        } catch (HibernateException e) {
            throw new Exception("Could not create category " + title, e);
        }
    }
}
```

The code in Listing 3-21 allows us to create an advert for a preexisting user in a preexisting category. Note our use of the **Session** to obtain **User** and **Category** objects from the database. As with the user and category, the advert details are supplied by the Ant task.

Listing 3-21. The Class to Create the Example Adverts

```
package sample;

import org.hibernate.HibernateException;
import org.hibernate.Query;
import sample.dao.DAO;
import sample.entity.Advert;
import sample.entity.Category;
import sample.entity.User;

public class PostAdvert extends DAO {

    public static void main(String[] args) {

        if (args.length != 4) {
            System.out.println("params required: username, categoryTitle, title, message");
            return;
        }

        String username = args[0];
        String categoryTitle = args[1];
        String title = args[2];
        String message = args[3];

        try {

            PostAdvert self = new PostAdvert();

            System.out.println("Creating advert");
            Advert advert = self.create(username,categoryTitle,title, message);
            System.out.println("Created advert");
```

```
            DAO.close();
        } catch (Exception e) {
            e.printStackTrace();
        }

    }

    public Advert create(String username, String categoryTitle,
            String title, String message)
            throws Exception {
        try {
            begin();

            //get the user by username
            Query userQuery = getSession().createQuery(" from User where name = :username");
            userQuery.setString("username", username);
            User user = (User) userQuery.uniqueResult();

            //get the category by category title
            Query categoryQuery = getSession().createQuery(" from Category where title =
:categoryTitle");
            categoryQuery.setString("categoryTitle", categoryTitle);
            Category category = (Category) categoryQuery.uniqueResult();


            //create and save the new advert
            Advert advert = new Advert(title, message, user);
            getSession().save(advert);

            //add the advert to the category and save
            category.addAdvert(advert);
            getSession().save(category);

            commit();
            return advert;
        } catch (HibernateException e) {
            throw new Exception("Could not create advert " + title, e);
        }
    }
}
```

Finally, in Listing 3-22, we make use of the Session to iterate over the categories, and within these, the adverts drawn from the database. It is easy to see how this logic could now be incorporated into a web application or web service.

Listing 3-22. The Class to Display the Contents of the Database

```java
package sample;

import java.util.Iterator;
import java.util.List;

import sample.dao.CategoryDAO;
import sample.dao.DAO;
import sample.entity.Advert;
import sample.entity.Category;

public class ListAdverts {
    public static void main(String[] args) {
        try {
            List categories = new CategoryDAO().list();

            Iterator ci = categories.iterator();
            while(ci.hasNext()) {
                Category category = (Category)ci.next();
                System.out.println("Category: " + category.getTitle());
                System.out.println();
                Iterator ai = category.getAdverts().iterator();
                while(ai.hasNext()) {
                    Advert advert = (Advert)ai.next();
                    System.out.println();
                    System.out.println("Title: " + advert.getTitle());
                    System.out.println(advert.getMessage());
                    System.out.println(" posted by " + advert.getUser().getName());
                }
            }

            DAO.close();
        } catch( AdException e ) {
            System.out.println(e.getMessage());
        }


    }
}
```

When you run the example applications, you will see a considerable amount of "chatter" from the logging API, and from the Ant tool when you run these tasks, much of which can be controlled or eliminated in a production application. If the tasks all run correctly in order (exportDDL, createUsers, createCategories, postAdverts, and listAdverts), you should see output similar to Listing 3-23 in the output of the listAdverts task.

Listing 3-23. The Results of Listing the Adverts in the database.

```
[java] Category: retro
[java]
[java]
[java] Title: Sinclair Spectrum for sale
[java] 48k original box and packaging
[java]   posted by dave
[java]
[java] Title: Atari 2600 wanted
[java] Must have original joysticks.
[java]   posted by jeff
[java] Category: kitsch
[java]
[java]
[java] Title: Commemorative Plates
[java] Kitten and puppies design
[java]   posted by dave
[java]
[java] Title: Inflatable Sofa
[java] Leopard skin pattern. Nice.
[java]   posted by jeff
```

You will also notice that because you are starting each of these applications as new tasks (several times in the case of the tasks to create data), the tasks proceed relatively slowly. This is an artifact of the repeated creation of `SessionFactory`—a heavyweight object—from each invocation of the JVM from the Ant `java` task, and is not a problem in "real" applications.

Summary

In this chapter, we've shown how to acquire the Hibernate tools, how to create and run the example from Chapter 1, and how to create a slightly larger application from scratch, driving the database table generation from the `hbm2ddl` Ant task. All of the files described in this chapter and the others can be downloaded from the Apress web site (`www.apress.com`).

In the next chapter, we will look at the architecture of Hibernate and the lifecycle of a Hibernate-based application.

The Persistence Life Cycle

In this chapter, we discuss the life cycle of persistent objects in Hibernate. These persistent objects are POJOs without any special marker interfaces or inheritance related to Hibernate. Part of Hibernate's popularity comes from its ability to work with a normal object model.

We also discuss the methods of the Session interface that are used for creating, retrieving, updating, and deleting persistent objects from Hibernate.

Introduction to the Life Cycle

After adding Hibernate to your application, you do not need to change your existing Java object model to add persistence marker interfaces or any other type of hint for Hibernate. Instead, Hibernate works with normal Java objects that your application creates with the new operator, or that other objects create. For Hibernate's purposes, these can be drawn up into two categories: objects for which Hibernate has entity mappings, and objects that are not directly recognized by Hibernate. A correctly mapped entity object will consist of fields and properties that are mapped, and that are themselves either references to correctly mapped entities, references to collections of such entities, or "value" types (primitives, primitive wrappers, strings, or arrays of these).

Given an instance of an object that is mapped to Hibernate, it can be in any one of three different states: transient, persistent, or detached.

Transient objects exist in memory, as illustrated in Figure 4-1. Hibernate does not manage transient objects or persist changes to transient objects.

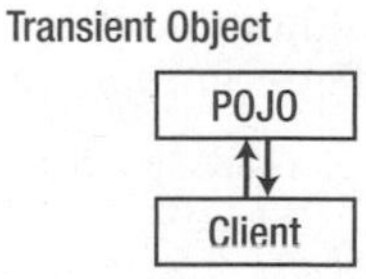

Transient Object

Figure 4-1. Transient objects are independent of Hibernate.

To persist the changes to a transient object, you would have to ask the session to save the transient object to the database, at which point Hibernate assigns the object an identifier.

Persistent objects exist in the database, and Hibernate manages the persistence for persistent objects. We show this relationship between the objects and the database in Figure 4-2. If fields or properties change on a persistent object, Hibernate will keep the database representation up-to-date.

Persistent Object

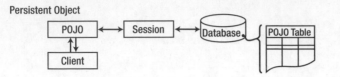

Figure 4-2. Persistent objects are maintained by Hibernate.

Detached objects have a representation in the database, but changes to the object will not be reflected in the database, and vice versa. This temporary separation of the object and the database is shown in Figure 4-3. A detached object can be created by closing the session that it was associated with, or by evicting it from the session with a call to the session's `evict()` method. One reason you might consider doing this would be to read an object out of the database, modify the properties of the object in memory, and then store the results some place other than your database. This would be an alternative to doing a deep copy of the object.

Detached Object

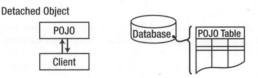

Figure 4-3. Detached objects exist in the database but are not maintained by Hibernate.

In order to persist changes made to a detached object, the application must reattach it to a valid Hibernate session. A detached instance can be associated with a new Hibernate session when your application calls one of the `load()`, `refresh()`, `merge()`, `update()`, or `save()` methods on the new session with a reference to the detached object. After the call, the detached object would be a persistent object managed by the new Hibernate session.

Versions prior to Hibernate 3 had support for the `Lifecycle` and `Validatable` interfaces. These allowed your objects to listen for `save`, `update`, `delete`, `load`, and `validate` events using methods on the object. In Hibernate 3, this functionality moved into events and interceptors, and the old interfaces were removed.

Entities, Classes, and Names

Entities represent Java objects with mappings that permit them to be stored in the database. The mappings indicate how the fields and properties of the object should be stored in the database tables. However, it is possible that you will want objects of a particular type to be represented in two different ways in the database. For instance, we could have one Java class for users, but two different tables in the database that store users. This may not be the best database design, but similar problems are common in legacy systems. Other systems that can't be easily modified may depend on the existing database design, and Hibernate is powerful enough to cover this scenario. In this case, how does Hibernate choose which to use?

An object representing an entity will have a normal Java class type. It will also have an entity name. By default, the name of the entity will be the same as the name of the class type. You have the option, however, to change this via the mappings, and thus distinguish between objects of the same type that are mapped to different tables. There are therefore methods in the Session API that require an entity name to be provided to determine the appropriate mapping. If this is omitted, it will either be because no such distinction is needed, or because, for convenience, the method assumes the most common case—in which the entity name is the same as the class name—and duplicates the functionality of another more specific method that permits the entity name to specified explicitly.

Identifiers

Hibernate requires all entities to have an identifier, which represents the primary key column(s) of the table to which it will be persisted. When an entity is persisted, a suitable identifier can be assigned to it automatically by Hibernate, or a suitable identifier may be explicitly assigned by the user (see Listing 4-1).

Listing 4-1. A Typical Identifier Field

```
public int id;
```

Usually, the entity will provide a suitable identifier field or property, and Hibernate will use this value to correlate entities in memory with those persisted to the tables of the database. However, if no such field or property is available (as will likely be the case with legacy code), then Hibernate itself can manage the identifier value internally. The type of the identifier must be defined in the mapping information.

Entities and Associations

Entities can contain references to other entities—either directly as a property or field, or indirectly via a collection of some sort (arrays, sets, lists, etc.). These associations are represented using foreign key relationships in the underlying tables.

When only one of the pair of entities contains a reference to the other, the association is unidirectional. If the association is mutual, then it is referred to as bidirectional.

■ **Tip** A common mistake when designing entity models using Hibernate is to try to make all associations bidirectional. Associations that are not a natural part of the object model should not be forced into it. Hibernate Query Language often presents a more natural way to access the same information.

If both ends of the association managed the foreign keys, then we would encounter a problem when client code called the appropriate set method on both ends of the association. Should two foreign key columns be maintained—one in each direction (risking circular dependencies)—or only one? (And if only one, should altering either side affect it, or only one?)

Ideally, we would like to dictate that only changes to one end of the relationship will result in any updates to the foreign key; and indeed, Hibernate allows us to do this by marking one end of the association as being managed by the other (in the XML mapping files, this is known as the "inverse" of the parent, whereas in the JPA terminology used by the annotation mappings, it is marked as being "mappedBy" the parent in the @OneToMany annotation).

■ **Caution** inverse and mappedBy are purely about how the foreign key relationships between entities are saved. They have nothing to do with saving the entities themselves. Despite this, they are often confused with the entirely orthogonal cascade functionality (described in the "Cascading Operations" section of this chapter).

While Hibernate lets us specify that changes to one association will result in changes to the database, it does *not* allow us to cause changes to one end of the association to be automatically reflected in the other end in the Java POJOs. For example, in a one-to-one bidirectional association between an Email class and a Message class, the code in Listing 4-2 is incomplete even if the Message entity is the inverse of the Email entity:

Listing 4-2. A Common Misconception About Bidirectional Associations

```
Email email = new Email("Test Email");
Message message = new Message("Test Message");
email.setMessage(message);
// Incorrectly managed
session.save(email);
session.save(message);
System.out.println(message.getEmail());
```

The final call to message.getEmail() will return null (assuming simple getters and setters are used). To get the desired effect, both entities must be updated—If the Email entity owns the association, this merely ensures the proper assignment of a foreign key column value. There is *no* implicit call of message.setEmail(email). This must be explicitly given as in Listing 4-3.

Listing 4-3. The Correct Maintenance of a Bidirectional Association

```
Email email = new Email("Test Email");
Message message = new Message("Test Message");
email.setMessage(message);
message.setEmail(email); // Correctly managed
session.save(email);
session.save(message);
System.out.println(message.getEmail());
```

It is common for users new to Hibernate to get confused about this point—the confusion arises from two origins, which are described in the following paragraphs.

The EJB 2 container-managed persistence (CMP) *does* work in this way—when a reference is assigned in one entity, the corresponding reference in the other entity will be updated to reflect this. Hibernate does not take this approach because it was designed to work in other environments and with POJOs from other bodies of code, where such behavior would be unexpected. If you pass a pair of objects to some third-party API, mysterious side effects should not occur. Since Hibernate is precisely that—a third-party API—from the perspective of most client code, Hibernate cannot safely cause their references to become connected in this way!

Though Hibernate does not produce this behavior automatically, there *is* a side effect of persistence to the database that can make it appear that it does (see Listing 4-4).

Listing 4-4. Misleading Behavior

```
openSession();
beginTransaction();

Email email = new Email("Test Email");
Message message = new Message("Test Message");
email.setMessage(message);

save(email,message);

System.out.println("Stored...");
System.out.println(email);
System.out.println(email.getMessage());
System.out.println(message);
System.out.println(message.getEmail());

Serializable emailPrimaryKey = session.getIdentifier(email);
Serializable messagePrimaryKey = session.getIdentifier(message);
endTransaction();

closeSession();

System.out.println();

openSession();

beginTransaction();

email = (Email)session.get(Email.class,emailPrimaryKey);
message = (Message)session.get(Message.class,messagePrimaryKey);

System.out.println("Retrieved...");
System.out.println(email);
System.out.println(email.getMessage());
```

```
System.out.println(message);
System.out.println(message.getEmail());
endTransaction();
closeSession();
```

If you run the code from Listing 4-4, you will see the following output:

```
Stored...
Test Email
Test Message
Test Message
null

Retrieved...
Test Email
Test Message
Test Message
Test Emails
```

When the entities are initially stored, the `Message` object's reference to its associated `Email` is `null`, even after Hibernate has stored the data. The entity in memory is not updated to reflect the change to the `Email` entity. However, after we have closed the session, opened a new one, and loaded the entities from the database, the entity has been updated.

Because the session has been closed, the session is forced to reload the entities from the database when we request them by primary key. Because the `Email` entity is the owner of the association, the association exists in the database purely in the form of a foreign key relationship from the `Email` table onto the `Message` table's primary key. When we altered the `Email` entity and saved it, this foreign key relationship was therefore updated. So, when we reload the entities, the `Message` entity's association details are (correctly) obtained from the same foreign key.

If we alter this code to make the association in the `Message` entity instead of the `Email` entity, but leave the `Email` entity the owner of the association, we will see the reverse effect, as follows:

```
Email email = new Email("Test Email");
Message message = new Message("Test Message");
//email.setMessage(message);
message.setEmail(email);
```

Because we have not made the association in the `Email` entity (the owner), the foreign key of the `Email` table is not pointed at the `Message` table. When we reload the entities, we do not see the "automatic" association behavior—quite the opposite:

```
Stored...
Test Email
null
Test Message
Test Email
```

```
Retrieved...
Test Email
null
Test Message
null
```

As you can see, although the two entities have been saved, the attempt to associate the `Email` with the `Message` entity by calling a method on the `Message` entity has not been honored in the database, because the `Message` entity does not own the association. The following list recaps the points made so far:

- You must explicitly manage both ends of an association.

- Only changes to the owner of an association will be honored in the database.

- When you load a detached entity from the database, it will reflect the foreign key relationships persisted into the database.

Table 4-1 shows how you can select the side of the relationship that should be made the owner of a bidirectional association. Remember that to make an association the owner, you must mark the *other* end as `inverse="true"` (the choice of terminology is poor, but entrenched).

Table 4-1. Marking the Owner of an Association

Type of Association	Options
One-to-one	Either end can be made the owner, but one (and only one) of them should be—if you don't specify this, you will end up with a circular dependency.
One-to-many	The *many* end must be made the owner of the association.
Many-to-one	This is the same as the one-to-many relationship, viewed from the opposite perspective, so the same rule applies—the *many* end must be made the owner of the association.
Many-to-many	Either end of the association can be made the owner.

If this all seems rather confusing, just remember that association ownership is concerned exclusively with the management of the foreign keys in the database, and things should become clearer as you use Hibernate further. Associations and mappings are discussed in detail in the next three chapters.

Saving Entities

Creating an instance of a class you mapped with a Hibernate mapping does not automatically persist the object to the database. Until you explicitly save the object with a valid Hibernate session, the object is transient, like any other Java object. In Hibernate, we use one of the `save()` methods on the `Session` interface to store a transient object in the database, as follows:

```
public Serializable save(Object object) throws HibernateException
```

```
public Serializable save(String entityName,Object object) throws HibernateException
```

Both save() methods take a transient object reference (which must not be null) as an argument. Hibernate expects to find a mapping (either annotations or an XML mapping) for the transient object's class—Hibernate cannot persist arbitrary unmapped objects. If you have mapped multiple entities to a Java class, you can specify which entity you are saving (Hibernate wouldn't know from just the Java class name) with the entityName argument.

The save() methods all create a new org.hibernate.event.SaveOrUpdateEvent event. We discuss events in more detail in Appendix A, although you do not have to worry about these implementation details to use Hibernate effectively.

At its simplest, we create a new object in Java, set a few of its properties, and then save it through the session, as follows:

```
Supplier superCorp = new Supplier();
superCorp.setName("SuperCorp");
session.save(superCorp);
```

It is not appropriate to save an object that has already been persisted. Equally, it is not appropriate to update a transient object. If it is impossible or inconvenient to determine the state of the object from your application code, you may use the saveOrUpdate() method. Hibernate uses the identifier of the object to determine whether to insert a new row into the database or update an existing row. The method signature is as follows:

```
public void saveOrUpdate(Object object) throws HibernateException
```

Once an object is in a persistent state, Hibernate manages updates to the database itself as you change the fields and properties of the object.

Object Equality and Identity

When we discuss persistent objects in Hibernate, we also need to consider the role that object equality and identity plays with Hibernate. When we have a persistent object in Hibernate, that object represents both an instance of a class in a particular Java virtual machine (JVM) and a row (or rows) in a database table (or tables).

Requesting a persistent object again from the same Hibernate session returns the same Java instance of a class, which means that you can compare the objects using the standard Java == equality syntax. If, however, you request a persistent object from more than one Hibernate session, Hibernate will provide distinct instances from each session, and the == operator will return false if you compare these object instances.

Taking this into account, if you are comparing objects in two different sessions, you will need to implement the equals() method on your Java persistence objects.

Loading Entities

Hibernate's `Session` interface provides several `load()` methods for loading entities from your database. Each `load()` method requires the object's primary key as an identifier.

In addition to the `id`, Hibernate also needs to know which class or entity name to use to find the object with that `id`. Last, you will need to cast the object returned by `load()` to the class you desire. The basic `load()` methods are as follows:

```
public Object load(Class theClass, Serializable id) throws HibernateException
public Object load(String entityName, Serializable id) throws HibernateException
public void load(Object object, Serializable id) throws HibernateException
```

The last `load()` method takes an object as an argument. The object should be of the same class as the object you would like loaded, and it should be empty. Hibernate will populate that object with the object you requested. We find this syntax to be somewhat confusing when put into applications, so we do not tend to use it ourselves.

The other `load()` methods take a lock mode as an argument. The lock mode specifies whether Hibernate should look into the cache for the object, and which database lock level Hibernate should use for the row (or rows) of data that represent this object. The Hibernate developers claim that Hibernate will usually pick the correct lock mode for you, although we have seen situations in which it is important to manually choose the correct lock. In addition, your database may choose its own locking strategy—for instance, locking down an entire table rather than multiple rows within a table. In order of least restrictive to most restrictive, the various lock modes you can use are as follows:

- **NONE:** Uses no row-level locking, and uses a cached object if available; this is the - Hibernate default.

- **READ:** Prevents other `SELECT` queries from reading data that is in the middle of a transaction (and thus possibly invalid) until it is committed.

- **UPGRADE:** Uses the `SELECT FOR UPDATE` SQL syntax to lock the data until the transaction is finished.

- **UPGRADE_NOWAIT:** Uses the `NOWAIT` keyword (for Oracle), which returns an error immediately if there is another thread using that row. Otherwise this is similar to `UPGRADE`.

- **FORCE:** Similar to `UPGRADE` but increments the version for objects with automatic versioning when loaded.

All of these lock modes are static fields on the `org.hibernate.LockMode` class. We discuss locking and deadlocks with respect to transactions in more detail in Chapter 8. The `load()` methods that use lock modes are as follows:

```
public Object load(Class theClass, Serializable id, LockMode lockMode)
        throws HibernateException

public Object load(String entityName, Serializable id, LockMode lockMode)
        throws HibernateException
```

You should not use a load() method unless you are sure that the object exists. If you are not certain, then use one of the get() methods. The load() methods will throw an exception if the unique id is not found in the database, whereas the get() methods will merely return a null reference.

Much like load(), the get() methods take an identifier and either an entity name or a class. There are also two get() methods that take a lock mode as an argument. The get() methods are as follows:

```
public Object get(Class clazz, Serializable id)
        throws HibernateException

public Object get(String entityName, Serializable id)
        throws HibernateException

public Object get(Class clazz, Serializable id, LockMode lockMode)
        throws HibernateException

public Object get(String entityName, Serializable id, LockMode lockMode)
        throws HibernateException
```

If you need to determine the entity name for a given object (by default, this is the same as the class name), you can call the getEntityName() method on the Session interface, as follows:

```
public String getEntityName(Object object) throws HibernateException
```

Using the get()and load() methods is straightforward. For the following code sample, we would be getting the Supplier id from another Java class. For instance, through a web application, someone may select a Supplier details page for the supplier with the id 1. If we are not sure that the supplier exists, we use the get() method, with which we could check for null, as follows:

```
// get an id from some other Java class, for instance, through a web application
Supplier supplier = (Supplier) session.get(Supplier.class,id);
if (supplier == null) {
    System.out.println("Supplier not found for id " + id);
    return;
}
```

We can also retrieve the entity name from Hibernate and use it with either the get() or load() method. The load() method will throw an exception if an object with that id cannot be found.

```
String entityName = session.getEntityName(supplier);
Supplier secondarySupplier = (Supplier) session.load(entityName,id);
```

Refreshing Entities

Hibernate provides a mechanism to refresh persistent objects from their database representation. Use one of the refresh() methods on the Session interface to refresh an instance of a persistent object, as follows:

```
public void refresh(Object object)
            throws HibernateException

public void refresh(Object object, LockMode lockMode)
            throws HibernateException
```

These methods will reload the properties of the object from the database, overwriting them. Hibernate usually does a very good job of taking care of this for you, so you do not have to use the refresh() method very often. There are instances where the Java object representation will be out of sync with the database representation of an object, however. For instance, if you use SQL to update the database, Hibernate will not be aware that the representation changed. You do not need to use this method regularly, though. Similar to the load() method, the refresh() method can take a lock mode as an argument. See the discussion of lock modes in the previous Loading Entities section.

Updating Entities

Hibernate automatically persists into the database changes made to persistent objects. If a property changes on a persistent object, the associated Hibernate session will queue the change for persistence to the database using SQL. From a developer's perspective, you do not have to do any work to store these changes, unless you would like to force Hibernate to commit all of its changes in the queue. You can also determine whether the session is dirty and changes need to be committed. When you commit a Hibernate transaction, Hibernate will take care of these details for you.

The flush() method forces Hibernate to flush the session, as follows:

```
public void flush() throws HibernateException
```

You can determine if the session is dirty with the isDirty() method, as follows:

```
public boolean isDirty() throws HibernateException
```

You can also instruct Hibernate to use a flushing mode for the session with the setFlushMode() method. The getFlushMode() method returns the flush mode for the current session, as follows:

```
public void setFlushMode(FlushMode flushMode)
public FlushMode getFlushMode()
```

The possible flush modes are the following:

- ALWAYS: Every query flushes the session before the query is executed This is going to be very slow.

- AUTO: Hibernate manages the query flushing to guarantee that the data returned by a query is up-to-date.

- COMMIT: Hibernate flushes the session on transaction commits.

- MANUAL: Your application needs to manage the session flushing with the flush() method. Hibernate never flushes the session itself.

By default, Hibernate uses the AUTO flush mode. Generally, you should use transaction boundaries to ensure that appropriate flushing is taking place, rather than trying to "manually" flush at the appropriate times.

Deleting Entities

In order to allow convenient removal of entities from the database, the Session interface provides a delete() method, as follows:

```
public void delete(Object object) throws HibernateException
```

This method takes a persistent object as an argument. The argument can also be a transient object with the identifier set to the id of the object that needs to be erased.

In the simplest form, in which you are simply deleting an object with no associations to other objects, this is straightforward; but many objects do have associations with other objects. To allow for this, Hibernate can be configured to allow deletes to cascade from one object to its associated objects.

For instance, consider the situation in which you have a parent with a collection of child objects, and you would like to delete them all. The easiest way to handle this is to use the cascade attribute on the collection's element in the Hibernate mapping. If you set the cascade attribute to delete or all, the delete will be cascaded to all of the associated objects. Hibernate will take care of deleting these for you—deleting the parent erases the associated objects.

Hibernate also supports bulk deletes (see Listing 4-5), where your application executes a DELETE HQL statement against the database. These are very useful for deleting more than one object at a time because each object does not need to be loaded into memory just to be deleted.

Listing 4-5. A Bulk Delete Using a Hibernate Query

```
session.createQuery("delete from User").executeUpdate();
```

Network traffic is greatly reduced, as are the memory requirements compared to those for individually issuing a delete() call against each entity identifier.

■ **Caution** Bulk deletes do not cause cascade operations to be carried out. If cascade behavior is needed, you will need to carry out the appropriate deletions yourself, or use the session's delete() method.

Cascading Operations

When you perform one of the operations described in this chapter on an entity, the operations will not be performed on the associated entities unless you explicitly tell Hibernate to perform them.

For example, the following code will fail when we try to commit the transaction because the message entity that is associated with the Email entity has not been persisted into the database—and so the Email entity cannot be accurately represented (with its foreign key onto the appropriate message row) in its table.

```
Session session = factory.openSession();
session.beginTransaction();

Email email = new Email("Email title");
Message message = new Message("Message content");
email.setMessage(message);
message.setEmail(email);

session.save(email);

session.getTransaction().commit();
session.close();

session = factory.openSession();
session.beginTransaction();
```

Ideally, we would like the save operation to be propagated from the Email entity to its associated Message object. We do this by setting the cascade operations for the properties and fields of the entity (or assigning an appropriate default value for the entity as a whole). So, the preceding code will perform correctly if at least the save cascade operation is set for the Email entity's message property. All of the basic life cycle operations discussed in this chapter have associated cascade values, as follows:

- create
- merge
- delete
- save-update
- evict
- replicate
- lock
- refresh

These values can be concatenated in a comma-separated list to allow cascading for any combination of these operations. When all operations should be cascaded, Hibernate provides a shortcut value named all that tells Hibernate to cascade all of these operations from the parent to each child object (for that relationship), except for delete-orphan, which we will discuss soon.

As part of the Hibernate mapping process, you can tell Hibernate to use one of these cascading types for a relationship between two objects (the parent and the child). On the collection or property element in the mapping file, set the cascade attribute to the type (or types) you would like to use.

By default, Hibernate does not cascade any operations—the default behavior can be overridden at the entity level via the XML mapping files using the default-cascade attribute on the <hibernate-mapping> XML element or in the annotated source files.

The last possible cascading type is delete-orphan. Use delete-orphan to remove a child object from the database when you remove the child from the parent's collection. This cascading type only works on one-to-many associations. The all cascading type does not include delete-orphan—you will have to use "all,delete-orphan", as in the following excerpt from a Hibernate mapping file:

```
<bag name="products" inverse="true" cascade="all,delete-orphan">
    <key column="supplierId"/>
    <one-to-many class="Product"/>
</bag>
```

Simply remove a child object from a parent object's collection after you have added the delete-orphan cascading type. Hibernate will remove the child object from the database itself, without any additional calls. The following example removes a child object from the collection:

```
supplier.getProducts().remove(product);
```

Lazy Loading, Proxies, and Collection Wrappers

Consider the stereotypical Internet web application: the online store. The store maintains a catalog of products. At the crudest level, this can be modeled as a catalog entity managing a series of product entities. In a large store, there may be tens of thousands of products grouped into various overlapping categories.

When a customer visits the store, the catalog must be loaded from the database. We probably don't want the implementation to load every single one of the entities representing the tens of thousands of products to be loaded into memory. For a sufficiently large retailer, this might not even be possible given the amount of physical memory available on the machine. Even if this were possible, it would probably cripple the performance of the site.

Instead, we want only the catalog to load, possibly with the categories as well. Only when the user drills down into the categories should a subset of the products in that category be loaded from the database.

To manage this problem, Hibernate provides a facility called lazy loading. When enabled (this is the default using XML mappings, but not when using annotations), an entity's associated entities will only be loaded when they are directly requested. For example, the following code loads only a single entity from the database:

```
Email email = (Email)session.get(Email.class,new Integer(42));
```

whereas if an association of the class is accessed, and lazy loading is in effect, the associations are pulled from the database as needed. For instance, in the following snippet, the associated Message object will be loaded since it is explicitly referenced.

```
Email email = (Email)session.get(Email.class,new Integer(42));
String text = email.getMessage().getContent();
```

The simplest way that Hibernate can force this behavior upon our entities is by providing a proxy implementation of them. Hibernate intercepts calls to the entity by substituting for it a proxy derived from the entity's class. Where the requested information is missing, it will be loaded from the database before control is ceded to the parent entity's implementation. Where the association is represented as a collection class, a wrapper (essentially a proxy for the collection, rather than for the entities that it contains) is created and substituted for the original collection.

Hibernate can only access the database via a session. If an entity is detached from the session when we try to access an association (via a proxy or collection wrapper) that has not yet been loaded, Hibernate throws an exception: the infamous LazyInitializationException. The cure is to either ensure that the entity is made persistent again by attaching it to a session or ensure that all of the fields that will be required are accessed *before* the entity is detached from the session.

If you need to determine whether a proxy, a persistence collection, or an attribute has been lazy loaded or not, you can call the `isInitialized(Object proxy)` and `isPropertyInitialized(Object proxy, String propertyName)` methods on the `org.hibernate.Hibernate` class. You can also force a proxy or collection to become fully populated by calling the `initialize(Obect proxy)` method on the `org.hibernate.Hibernate` class. If you initialize a collection using this method, you will also need to initialize each object contained in the collection, as only the collection is guaranteed to be initialized.

Querying Objects

Hibernate provides several different ways to query for objects stored in the database. The Criteria Query API is a Java API for constructing a query as an object. HQL is an object-oriented query language, similar to SQL, that you may use to retrieve objects that match the query. We discuss these further in Chapters 9 and 10. Hibernate provides a way to execute SQL directly against the database to retrieve objects—if you have legacy applications that use SQL or if you need to use SQL features that are not supported through HQL and the Criteria Query API (discussed in Chapter 11).

Summary

Hibernate provides a simple API for creating, retrieving, updating, and deleting objects from a relational database through the `Session` interface. Understanding the difference between transient, persistent, and detached objects in Hibernate will allow you to understand how changes to the objects update database tables.

We have touched upon the need to create mappings to correlate the database tables with the fields and properties of the Java objects that you want to persist. The next chapter covers these in detail, and discusses why they are required and what they can contain.

CHAPTER 5

■■■

An Overview of Mapping

The purpose of Hibernate is to allow you to treat your database as if it stores Java objects. However, databases in practice do not store objects—they store data in tables and columns. Unfortunately, there is no simple way to correlate the data stored in a database with the data represented by Java objects.

The difference between an object-oriented association and a relational one is fundamental. Consider a simple class to represent a user, and another to represent an e-mail address, as shown in Figure 5-1.

Figure 5-1. *An object-oriented association*

User objects contain fields referring to Email objects. The association has a direction—given a User object, you can determine its associated Email object. For example, consider Listing 5-1.

Listing 5-1. *Acquiring the Email Object from the User Object*

```
User user = ...
Email email = user.email;
```

The reverse, however, is not true. The natural way to represent this relationship in the database, as illustrated in Figure 5-2, is superficially similar.

Figure 5-2. A relational association

Despite that similarity, the direction of the association is effectively reversed. Given an Email row, you can immediately determine which User row it belongs to in the database; this relationship is mandated by a foreign key constraint. It is possible to reverse the relationship in the database world through suitable use of SQL—another difference.

Given the differences between the two worlds, it is necessary to manually intervene to determine how your Java classes should be represented in database tables.

Why Mapping Cannot Be Automated

It is not immediately obvious why you cannot create simple rules for storing your Java objects in the database so that they can be easily retrieved. For example, the most immediately obvious rule would be that a Java class must correlate to a single table. For example, instances of the User class defined in Listing 5-2 could surely be represented by a simple table like the one for a user shown in Figure 5-1.

Listing 5-2. A Simple User Class with a Password Field

```
public class User {
    String name;
    String password;
}
```

And indeed it could, but some questions present themselves:

- How many rows should you end up with if you save a user twice?

- Are you allowed to save a user without a name?

- Are you allowed to save a user without a password?

When you start to think about classes that refer to other classes, there are additional questions to consider. Have a look at the Customer and Email classes defined in Listing 5-3.

Listing 5-3. Customer and Email Classes

```
public class Customer {
    int customerId;
    int customerReference;
    String name;
    Email email;
}

public class Email {
    String address;
}
```

Based on this, the following questions arise:

- Is a unique customer identified by their customer ID, or their customer reference?

- Can an e-mail address be used by more than one customer?

- Should the relationship be represented in the `Customer` table?

- Should the relationship be represented in the `Email` table?

- Should the relationship be represented in some third (link) table?

Depending upon the answers to these questions, your database tables could vary considerably. You could take a stab at a reasonable design, such as that given in Figure 5-3, based upon your intuition about likely scenarios in the real world.

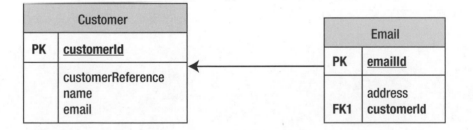

Figure 5-3. Tables in which the customer is identified by customerId. Here, e-mail address entities can only be used by a single customer, and the relationship is maintained by the Email table.

As soon as you take away the context provided by the variable and class names, it becomes much harder to form any useful decision about these classes (see Listing 5-4). It would be an impossible task to design an automated tool that could make this sort of decision.

Listing 5-4. A Class Identical in Structure to Listing 5-3, but with All Contextual Information Removed

```
public class Foo {
    int x;
    int y;
    String s;
    Bar bar;
}

public class Bar {
    String a;
}
```

Primary Keys

Most "relational" databases that provide SQL access are prepared to accept tables that have no predefined primary key. Hibernate is not so tolerant—even if your table has been created without a primary key, Hibernate will require you to specify one. This often seems perverse to users who are familiar with SQL and databases, but who are not familiar with ORM tools. As such, we will examine in more depth the problems that arise without a primary key.

Without a primary key, it is impossible to uniquely identify a row in a table. For example, consider Table 5-1.

Table 5-1. A Table in Which the Rows Cannot Be Uniquely Identified

User	Age
Dminter	35
Dminter	40
Dminter	55
Dminter	40
jlinwood	57

This table clearly contains information about users and their respective ages. However, there are four users with the same name (Dave Minter, Denise Minter, Daniel Minter, and Dashiel Minter). There is probably a way of distinguishing them somewhere else in the system—perhaps by an e-mail address or a user number. But if, for example, you want to know the ages of Dashiel Minter with user ID 32, there is no way to obtain it from Table 5-1.

While Hibernate will not let you omit the primary key, it will permit you to form the primary key from a collection of columns. For example, Table 5-2 could be keyed by Usernumber and User.

Table 5-2. A Table in Which the Rows Can Be Uniquely Identified

User	Usernumber	Age
Dminter	1	35
Dminter	2	40
Dminter	3	55
Dminter	32	42
Jlinwood	1	57

Neither User nor Usernumber contains unique entries, but in combination they uniquely identify the age of a particular user, and so they are acceptable to Hibernate as a primary key.

Why does Hibernate need to uniquely identify entries when SQL doesn't? Hibernate is representing Java objects, which are *always* uniquely identifiable. This is why the classic mistake made by new Java developers is to compare strings using the == operator instead of the equals() method. You can distinguish between references to two String objects that represent the same text and two references to the same String object. SQL has no such obligation, and there are arguably cases in which it is desirable to give up the ability to make the distinction.

If Hibernate could not uniquely identify an object with a primary key, then the following code could have several possible outcomes in the underlying table.

```
String customer = getCustomerFromHibernate("dcminter");
customer.setAge(10);
saveCustomerToHibernate(customer);
```

For example, let's say the table originally contained the data shown in Table 5-3.

Table 5-3. Updating an Ambiguous Table

User	Age
dcminter	30
dcminter	42

Which of the following should be contained in the resulting table?

- A single row for the user dcminter, with the age set to 10
- Two rows for the user, with both ages set to 10
- Two rows for the user, with one age set to 10 and the other to 42

- Two rows for the user, with one age set to 10 and the other to 30

- Three rows for the user, with one age set to 10 and the others to 30 and 42

In short, the Hibernate developers made a decision to enforce the use of primary keys when creating mappings so that this problem does not arise. Hibernate does provide facilities that will allow you to work around this if it is absolutely necessary (you can create views or stored procedures to "fake" the appropriate key, or you can use conventional JDBC to access the table data), but when using Hibernate, it is always more desirable to work with tables that have correctly specified primary keys if at all possible.

Lazy Loading

When you load classes into memory from the database, you don't necessarily want *all* the information to *actually* be loaded. To take an extreme example, loading a list of e-mails should not cause the full body text and attachments of every e-mail to be loaded into memory. First, they might demand more memory than is actually available. Second, even if they fit, it could take a long time for all of this information to be obtained.

If you were to tackle this problem in SQL, you would probably select a subset of the appropriate fields for the query to obtain the list; for example:

```
SELECT from, to, date, subject FROM email WHERE username = 'dcminter';
```

Hibernate will allow you to fashion queries that are rather similar to this, but it also offers a more flexible approach, known as *lazy loading*. Certain relationships can be marked as being "lazy," and they will not be loaded from disk until they are actually required.

The default in Hibernate 3 is that classes (including collections like `Set` and `Map`) should be lazily loaded. For example, when an instance of the `User` class given in the next listing is loaded from the database, the only fields initialized will be `userId` and `username`.

```
public class User {
    int userId;
    String username;
    EmailAddress emailAddress;
    Set roles;
}
```

However, as long as the object is still associated with Hibernate in the appropriate way (see Chapter 9), the appropriate objects for `emailAddress` and `roles` will be loaded from the database if they are accessed.

This is the default behavior only; the mapping file can be used to specify which classes and fields should behave in this way.

Associations

When we looked at why the mapping process could not be automated, we discussed the following example classes:

```
public class Customer {
    int customerId;
    int customerReference;
    String name;
    Email email;
}

public class Email {
    String address;
}
```

We also gave the following five questions that it raised:

- Is a unique customer identified by their customer ID, or their customer reference?

- Can a given e-mail address be used by more than one customer?

- Should the relationship be represented in the `Customer` table?

- Should the relationship be represented in the `Email` table?

- Should the relationship be represented in some third (link) table?

The first question can be answered simply—it depends on what column you specify as the primary key. The remaining four questions are related, and their answers depend upon the object relationships. Furthermore, if your `Customer` class represents the relationship with the `EmailAddress` using a `Collection` class or an array, it would be possible for a user to have multiple e-mail addresses.

```
public class Customer {
    int customerId;
    int customerReference;
    String name;
    Set email;
}
```

So, you should add another question: can a customer have more than one e-mail address? The set could contain a single entry, so you can't automatically infer that this is the case.

The key questions from the previous options are as follows:

- *Q1*: Can an e-mail address belong to more than one user?

- *Q2*: Can a customer have more than one e-mail address?

The answers to these questions can be formed into a truth table, as in Table 5-4.

Table 5-4. *Deciding the Cardinality of an Entity Relationship*

Q1 Answer	Q2 Answer	Relationship Between Customer and Email
No	No	One-to-one
Yes	No	Many-to-one
No	Yes	One-to-many
Yes	Yes	Many-to-many

These are the four ways in which the cardinality of the relationship between the objects can be expressed. Each relationship can then be represented within the mapping table(s) in various ways.

The One-to-One Association

A one-to-one association between classes can be represented in a variety of ways. At its simplest, the properties of both classes are maintained in the same table. For example, a one-to-one association between a User and an Email class might be represented as a single table, as in Table 5-5.

Table 5-5. *A Combined User/Email Table*

ID	Username	Email
1	dcminter	dcminter@example.com
2	jlinwood	jlinwood@example.com
3	tjkitchen	tjkitchen@example.com

The single database entity representing this combination of a User and an Email class is shown in Figure 5-4.

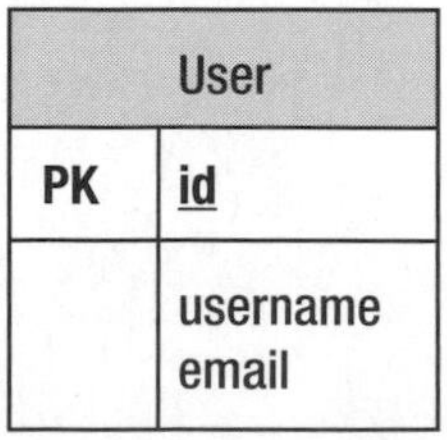

Figure 5-4. *A single entity representing a one-to-one relationship*

Alternatively, the entities can be maintained in distinct tables with identical primary keys, or with a key maintained from one of the entities into the other, as in Tables 5-6 and 5-7.

Table 5-6. *The User Table*

ID	Username
1	Dcminter
2	Jlinwood
3	Tjkitchen

Table 5-7. *The Email Table*

ID	Username
1	dcminter@example.com
2	jlinwood@example.com
3	tjkitchen@example.com

It is possible to create a mandatory foreign key relationship from one of the entities to the other, but this should not be applied in both directions because a circular dependency would be created. It is also possible to omit the foreign key relationships entirely (as shown in Figure 5-5) and rely upon Hibernate to manage the key selection and assignment.

Figure 5-5. *Entities related by primary keys*

If it is not appropriate for the tables to share primary keys, then a foreign key relationship between the two tables can be maintained, with a "unique" constraint applied to the foreign key column. For example, reusing the User table from Table 5-6, the Email table can be suitably populated, as shown in Table 5-8.

Table 5-8. An Email Table with a Foreign Key to the User Table

ID	Email	UserID (Unique)
34	dcminter@example.com	1
35	jlinwood@example.com	2
36	tjkitchen@example.com	3

This has the advantage that the association can easily be changed from one-to-one to many-to-one by removing the unique constraint. Figure 5-6 shows this type of relationship.

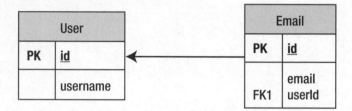

Figure 5-6. Entities related by a foreign key relationship

The One-to-Many and Many-to-One Association

A one-to-many association (or from the perspective of the other class, a many-to-one association) can most simply be represented by the use of a foreign key, with no additional constraints.

The relationship can also be maintained by the use of a link table. This will maintain a foreign key into each of the associated tables, which will itself form the primary key of the link table. An example of this is shown in Tables 5-9, 5-10, and 5-11.

Table 5-9. A Simple User Table

ID	Username
1	Dcminter
2	Jlinwood

Table 5-10. *A Simple Email Table*

ID	Email
1	dcminter@example.com
2	dave@example.com
3	jlinwood@example.com
4	jeff@example.com

Table 5-11. *A Link Table Joining User and Email in a One-to-Many Relationship*

UserID	EmailID
1	1
1	2
2	3
2	4

Additional columns can be added to the link table to maintain information on the ordering of the entities in the association.

A unique constraint must be applied to the "one" side of the relationship (the `userId` column of the `UserEmailLink` table in Figure 5-7); otherwise, the link table can represent the set of all possible relationships between `User` and `Email` entities—a many-to-many set association.

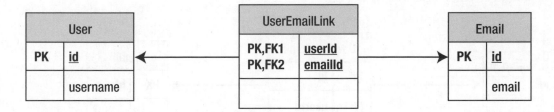

Figure 5-7. *A relationship represented by a link table (duplicates are not permitted because of the use of a compound primary key)*

The Many-to-Many Association

As noted at the end of the previous section, if a unique constraint is not applied to the "one" end of the relationship when using a link table, it becomes a limited sort of many-to-many relationship. All of the possible combinations of User and Email can be represented, but it is not possible for the same User to have the same e-mail address entity associated twice, because that would require the compound primary key to be duplicated.

If instead of using the foreign keys together as a compound primary key, we give the link table its own primary key (usually a surrogate key), the association between the two entities can be transformed into a full many-to-many relationship, as shown in Table 5-12.

Table 5-12. A Many-to-Many User/Email Link Table

ID	UserID	EmailID
1	1	1
2	1	2
3	1	3
4	1	4
5	2	1
6	2	2

Table 5-12 might describe a situation in which the user dcminter receives all e-mail sent to any of the four addresses, whereas jlinwood receives only e-mail sent to his own accounts.

When the link table has its own independent primary key, as with the association shown in Figure 5-8, thought should be given to the possibility that a new class should be created to represent the contents of the link table as an entity in its own right.

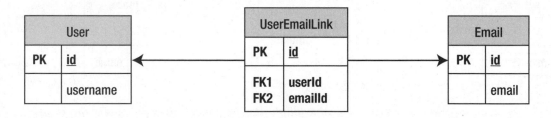

Figure 5-8. A many-to-many relationship represented by a link table (duplicates are permitted because of the use of a 0surrogate key)

Applying Mappings to Associations

The mappings are applied to express the various different ways of forming associations in the underlying tables—there is no automatically correct way to represent them.

In addition to the basic choice of the approach to take, the mappings are used to specify the minutiae of the tables' representations. While Hibernate tends to use sensible default values when possible, it is often desirable to override these. For example, the foreign key names generated automatically by Hibernate will be effectively random—whereas an informed developer can apply a name (e.g., FK_USER_EMAIL_LINK) to aid in the debugging of constraint violations at run time.

Other Information Represented in Mappings

While Hibernate can determine a lot of sensible default values for the mappings, most of these can be overridden by one or both of the annotation- and XML-based approaches. Some apply directly to mapping; others, such as the foreign key names, are really only pertinent when the mapping is used to create the database schema. Lastly, some mappings can also provide a place to configure some features that are perhaps not "mappings" in the purest sense. The final sections of this chapter discuss the features that Hibernate supports in addition to those already mentioned.

Specification of (Database) Column Types and Sizes

Java provides the primitive types and allows user declaration of interfaces and classes to extend these. Relational databases generally provide a small subset of "standard" types, and then provide additional proprietary types.

Restricting yourself to the proprietary types will still cause problems, as there are only approximate correspondences between these and the Java primitive types.

A typical example of a problematic type is java.lang.String (treated by Hibernate as if it were a primitive type since it is used so frequently), which by default will be mapped to a fixed-size character data database type. Typically, the database would perform poorly if a character field of unlimited size were chosen—but lengthy String fields will be truncated as they are persisted into the database. In most databases, you would choose to represent a lengthy String field as a VARCHAR type. This is one of the reasons why Hibernate can't do all the mapping for you and why you still need to understand some database fundamentals when you create an application that uses ORM.

By overriding the default type mappings, the developer can make appropriate trade-offs between storage space, performance, and fidelity to the original Java representation.

The Mapping of Inheritance Relationships to the Database

There is no SQL standard for representing inheritance relationships for the data in tables; and while some database implementations provide a proprietary syntax for this, not all do. Hibernate provides several configurable ways in which to represent inheritance relationships, and the mapping file permits users to select a suitable approach for their model.

Primary Key

Hibernate demands that a primary key be used to identify entities. The choice of a surrogate key, a key chosen from the business data, and/or a compound primary key can be made via the mapping file.

When a surrogate key is used, Hibernate also permits the key-generation technique to be selected—from a range of techniques that vary in portability and efficiency.

The Use of SQL Formula–Based Properties

It is sometimes desirable that a property of an entity should be maintained not as data directly stored in the database, but rather as a function performed on that data—for example, a subtotal field should not be managed directly by the Java logic, but instead maintained as an aggregate function of some other property.

Mandatory and Unique Constraints

As well as the implicit constraints of a primary or foreign key relationship, you can specify that a field must not be duplicated—for example, a `username` field should often be unique.

Fields can also be made mandatory—for example, requiring a message entity to have both a subject and message text.

The generated database schema will contain corresponding `NOT NULL` and `UNIQUE` constraints so that it is literally impossible to corrupt the table with invalid data (rather, the application logic will throw an exception if any attempt to do so is made).

Note that primary keys are implicitly both mandatory and unique.

Cascading of Operations

As alterations are made to the object model, operations on some objects should cascade through to related objects. For example, deleting a stocked item should perhaps cause any associated catalog entries to be deleted. The reverse—deleting a single catalog entry—should not necessarily cause the stocked item to be deleted from the database entirely!

It would be awkward to manage the appropriate cascading rules from code alone, so cascading rules can be specified at a fine level of detail within the mappings.

Summary

This chapter has given you an overview of the reason why mappings are needed, and what features they support beyond these absolute requirements. It has discussed the various types of associations, and the circumstances under which you would choose to use them.

The next two chapters look at how mappings are specified using annotations and XML files respectively.

■ ■ ■

## CHAPTER 6

Mapping with Annotations

In Chapter 5, we discussed the need to create mappings between the database model and the object model. Mappings can be created as separate XML files, or as annotations inline with the source code for your POJOs. In this chapter, we discuss the use of annotations, and in the next chapter, we will discuss the use of XML files.

Creating Hibernate Mappings with Annotations

Prior to annotations, the only way to create mappings was through XML files—although tools from Hibernate and third-party projects allowed part or all of these to be generated from Java source code. Although using annotations is the newest way to define mappings, it is not automatically the best way to do so. We will briefly discuss the drawbacks and benefits of annotations before discussing when and how to apply them.

Cons of Annotations

If you are migrating from a Hibernate 2 environment or an existing Hibernate 3 environment, you will already have XML-based mapping files to support your code base. All else being equal, you will not want to re-express these mappings using annotations just for the sake of it.

If you are migrating from a legacy environment, you may not want to alter the preexisting POJO source code, in order to avoid contaminating known-good code with possible bugs.

If you do not have the source code to your POJOs (because it has been lost, or because it was generated by an automated tool), you may prefer the use of external XML-based mappings to the decompilation of class files to obtain Java source code for alteration.

Maintaining the mapping information as external XML files allows the mapping information to be changed to reflect business changes or schema alterations without forcing you to rebuild the application as a whole.

Pros of Annotations

Having considered the drawbacks, there are some powerful benefits to contrast against them.

First, and perhaps most persuasively, we find annotations-based mappings to be far more intuitive than their XML-based alternatives, as they are immediately in the source code along with the properties that they are associated with.

Partly as a result of this, annotations are less verbose than their XML equivalents, as evidenced by the contrast between Listings 6-1 and 6-2.

Listing 6-1. A Minimal Class Mapped Using Annotations

```
import javax.persistence.Entity;
import javax.persistence.Id;

@Entity
public class Sample {
    @Id
    public Integer id;
    public String name;
}
```

Listing 6-2. A Minimal Class Mapped Using XML

```
<?xml version='1.0' encoding='utf-8'?>
<!DOCTYPE
    hibernate-mapping
    PUBLIC
    "-//Hibernate/Hibernate Mapping DTD//EN"
    "http://hibernate.sourceforge.net/hibernate-mapping-3.0.dtd">

<hibernate-mapping default-access="field">
    <class name="Sample">
        <id type="int" column="id">
            <generator class="native"/>
        </id>
        <property name="name" type="string"/>
    </class>
</hibernate-mapping>
```

Some of this verbosity is in the nature of XML itself (the tag names and the boilerplate document type declaration), and some of it is due to the closer integration of annotations with the source code. Here, for example, the XML file must explicitly declare that field access is used in place of property access (i.e., the fields are accessed directly rather than through their get/set methods), but the annotation infers this from the fact that it has been applied to the `id` field rather than the `getId()` method.

Hibernate uses and supports the JPA 2 persistence annotations. If you elect not to use Hibernate-specific features in your code and annotations, you will have the freedom to deploy your entities to environments using other ORM tools that support JPA 2.

Finally—and perhaps a minor point—because the annotations are compiled directly into the appropriate class files, there is less risk of a missing or stale mapping file causing problems at deployment (this point will perhaps prove most persuasive to those who already have some experience with this hazard of the XML technique).

Choosing Which to Use

When you are creating a Hibernate application that has complete or primary ownership of its database, and that is a new project, we would generally recommend the use of annotations.

If you intend to make your application portable to other JPA 2–compliant ORM applications, you *must* use annotations to represent the mapping information. Hibernate 3 XML file–based mapping is a proprietary format. However, you may lose this benefit if you rely upon any of the Hibernate 3–specific annotations (that is to say, annotations taken from the `org.hibernate` package tree rather than the `javax.persistence` package tree).

If you are migrating an existing application to Hibernate, or creating a new project reliant upon a database primarily owned by other applications, you can use the greater flexibility of XML-based mappings to ensure that your project will not be unduly inconvenienced by changes to the database schema.

Using Annotations in Your Application

Hibernate 3.5 now includes annotations as part of the core package; so unlike previous versions of Hibernate 3, you will not need to install any additional libraries to make annotations work.

If you are using a `hibernate.cfg.xml` file to establish the mapping configuration, you will need to provide the fully qualified name of the annotated class with the `<mapping>` element:

```
<mapping class="com.hibernatebook.annotations.Book"/>
```

When you are configuring the `SessionFactory`, you will need to make use of an -`AnnotationConfiguration` object instead of the `Configuration` object used with XML mappings, as follows:

```
SessionFactory factory =
    new AnnotationConfiguration().configure().buildSessionFactory();
```

If you prefer to configure the mappings manually rather than through the `hibernate.cfg.xml` file, you can do this through the `AnnotationConfiguration` object, as follows:

```
AnnotationConfiguration config = new AnnotationConfiguration();
config.addAnnotatedClass(Book.class);
SessionFactory factory = config.configure().buildSessionFactory();
```

If you need to use your annotated entities from within an EJB 3 container, you must use the standard `EntityManager` instead of the Hibernate-specific `Session`. Much like the annotations feature, Hibernate's `EntityManager` is now bundled with the core Hibernate package and is no longer an add on.

JPA 2 Persistence Annotations

When you develop using annotations, you start with a Java class, and then annotate the source code listing with metadata notations. The Java Runtime Environment (JRE) parses these annotations. Hibernate uses Java reflection to read the annotations and apply the mapping information. If you want to use the Hibernate tools to generate your database schema, you must compile your entity classes containing their annotations first.

In this section, we are going to introduce the significant core of the JPA 2 annotations alongside a simple set of classes to illustrate how they are applied.

The set of example classes represents a publisher's catalog of books. You'll start with a single class, Book, which has no annotations or mapping information. For this example's purposes, you do not have an existing database schema to work with, so you need to define your relational database schema as you go.

At the beginning of the example, the Book class is very simple. It has two fields, title and pages; and an identifier, id, which is an integer. The title is a String object, and pages is an integer. As we go through this example, we will add annotations, fields, and methods to the Book class. The complete source code listing for the Book and Author classes is given at the end of this chapter—the source files for the rest are available in the source code download for this chapter on the Apress web site (www.apress.com).

Listing 6-3 gives the source code of the Book class, in its unannotated form, as a starting point for the example.

Listing 6-3. The Book Class, Unannotated

```java
package com.hibernatebook.annotations;

public class Book {

    private String title;
    private int pages;
    private int id;

    // Getters...

    public int getId() {
        return id;
    }

    public String getTitle() {
        return title;
    }

    public int getPages() {
        return pages;
    }

    // Setters...

    public void setId(int id) {
        this.id = id;
    }

    public void setTitle(String title) {
        this.title = title;
    }
```

```
    public void setPages(int pages) {
        this.pages = pages;
    }
}
```

As you can see, this is a POJO. We are going to annotate this class as we go along, explaining the concepts behind annotation.

Entity Beans with @Entity

The first step is to annotate the Book class as a JPA 2 entity bean. We add the @Entity annotation to the Book class, as follows:

```
package com.hibernatebook.annotations;
import javax.persistence.*;

@Entity
public class Book
```

The JPA 2 standard annotations are contained in the javax.persistence package, so we import the appropriate annotations (here we will use wildcard imports to keep the listings short, but in the downloadable source code accompanying this chapter, we use explicit imports such as import javax.persistence.Entity;—annotations are imported in exactly the same way as the ordinary interfaces that they resemble).

The @Entity annotation marks this class as an entity bean, so it must have a no-argument constructor that is visible with at least protected scope. Hibernate supports package scope as the minimum, but you lose portability to other containers if you take advantage of this. Other JPA 2 rules for an entity bean class are that the class must not be final, and that the entity bean class must be concrete. Many of the rules for JPA 2 entity bean classes and Hibernate 3 persistent objects are the same—partly because the Hibernate team had much input into the JPA 2 design process, and partly because there are only so many ways to design a relatively unobtrusive object-relational persistence solution.

As you can see, although we did have to add the import statement and the annotations, we have not had to change the rest of the code. The POJO is essentially unchanged.

Primary Keys with @Id and @GeneratedValue

Each entity bean has to have a primary key, which you annotate on the class with the @Id annotation. Typically, the primary key will be a single field, though it can also be a composite of multiple fields.

The placement of the @Id annotation determines the default access strategy that Hibernate will use for the mapping. If the annotation is applied to a field as shown in Listing 6-4, then field access will be used.

Listing 6-4. A Class with Field Access

```
import javax.persistence.*;

@Entity
public class Sample {
    @Id
    int id;

    public int getId() {
        return this.id;
    }

    public void setId(int id) {
        this.id = id;
    }
}
```

If instead the annotation is applied to the getter for the field, as shown in Listing 6-5, then property access will be used.

Listing 6-5. The Same Class with Property Access

```
import javax.persistence.*;

@Entity
public class Sample {
    int id;

    @Id
    public int getId() {
        return this.id;
    }

    public void setId(int id) {
        this.id = id;
    }
}
```

Here you can see one of the strengths of the annotations approach—because the annotations are placed inline with the source code, information can be extracted from the context of the mapping in the code, allowing many mapping decisions to be inferred rather than stated explicitly—which helps to further reduce the verbosity of the annotations.

By default, the `@Id` annotation will automatically determine the most appropriate primary key generation strategy to use—you can override this by also applying the `@GeneratedValue` annotation. This takes a pair of attributes: `strategy` and `generator`. The `strategy` attribute must be a value from the `javax.persistence.GeneratorType` enumeration. If you do not specify a generator type, the default is `AUTO`. There are four different types of primary key generators on `GeneratorType`, as follows:

- **AUTO**: Hibernate decides which generator type to use, based on the database's support for primary key generation.

- **IDENTITY**: The database is responsible for determining and assigning the next primary key.

- **SEQUENCE**: Some databases support a **SEQUENCE** column type. See the "Generating Primary Key Values with **@SequenceGenerator**" section later in the chapter.

- **TABLE**: This type keeps a separate table with the primary key values. See the "Generating Primary Key Values with **@TableGenerator**" section later in the chapter.

You will notice that the available values for the **strategy** attribute do not exactly match the values for Hibernate's primary key generators for XML mapping. If you need to use Hibernate-specific primary key generation strategies, you can use some of the Hibernate extensions described at the end of this chapter—but as always, you risk forfeiting portability of your application to other JPA 2 environments when taking advantage of Hibernate-specific features.

For the **Book** class, we are going to use the default key generation strategy. Letting Hibernate determine which generator type to use makes your code portable between different databases. Because we want Hibernate to use property access to our POJO, we must annotate the getter method for the identifier, not the field that it accesses:

```
@Id
@GeneratedValue
public int getId() {
    return id;
}
```

Generating Primary Key Values with @SequenceGenerator

As noted in the section on the **@Id** tag, we can declare the primary key property as being generated by a database sequence. A sequence is a database object that can be used as a source of primary key values. It is similar to the use of an identity column type, except that a sequence is independent of any particular table and can therefore be used by multiple tables.

To declare the specific sequence object to use and its properties, you must include an @SequenceGenerator annotation on the annotated field. Here's an example:

```
@Id
@SequenceGenerator(name="seq1",sequenceName="HIB_SEQ")
@GeneratedValue(strategy=SEQUENCE,generator="seq1")
public int getId() {
    return id;
}
```

Here, a sequence generation annotation named **seq1** has been declared. This refers to the database sequence object called **HIB_SEQ**. The name **seq1** is then referenced as the generator attribute of the **@GeneratedValue** annotation.

Only the sequence generator name is mandatory—the other attributes will take sensible default values, but you should provide an explicit value for the **sequenceName** attribute as a matter of good practice anyway. If not specified, the **sequenceName** value to be used is selected by the persistence provider (i.e., Hibernate). The other (optional) attributes are `initialValue` (the generator starts with this number) and `allocationSize` (the number of ids in the sequence reserved at a time); these default to values of 1 and 50, respectively.

Generating Primary Key Values with @TableGenerator

The `@TableGenerator` annotation is used in a very similar way to the `@SequenceGenerator` annotation— but because `@TableGenerator` manipulates a standard database table to obtain its primary key values, instead of using a vendor-specific sequence object, it is guaranteed to be portable between database platforms.

■ **Note** For optimal portability *and* optimal performance, you should not specify the use of a table generator, but instead use the `@GeneratorValue(strategy=GeneratorType.AUTO)` configuration, which allows the persistence provider to select the most appropriate strategy for the database in use.

As with the sequence generator, the name attributes of `@TableGenerator` are mandatory and the other attributes are optional, with the table details being selected by the persistence provider.

```
@Id
@TableGenerator(name="tablegen",
                table="ID_TABLE",
                pkColumnName="ID",
                valueColumnName="NEXT_ID")
@GeneratedValue(strategy=TABLE,generator="tablegen")
public int getId() {
    return id;
}
```

The optional attributes are as follows:

- `allocationSize`: Allows the number of primary keys set aside at one time to be tuned for performance.

- `catalog`: Allows the catalog that the table resides within to be specified.

- `initialValue`: Allows the starting primary key value to be specified.

- `pkColumnName`: Allows the primary key column of the table to be identified. The table can contain the details necessary for generating primary key values for multiple entities.

- `pkColumnValue`: Allows the primary key for the row containing the primary key generation information to be identified.

- `schema`: Allows the schema that the table resides within to be specified.

- `table`: The name of the table containing the primary key values.

- **uniqueConstraints**: Allows additional constraints to be applied to the table for schema generation.

- **valueColumnName**: Allows the column containing the primary key generation information for the current entity to be identified.

Because the table can be used to contain the primary key values for a variety of entries, it is likely to contain a single row for each of the entities using it. It therefore needs its own primary key (pkColumnName), as well as a column containing the next primary key value to be used (pkColumnValue) for any of the entities obtaining their primary keys from it.

Compound Primary Keys with @Id, @IdClass, or @EmbeddedId

While the use of single column surrogate keys is advantageous for various reasons, you may sometimes be forced to work with business keys. When these are contained in a single column, you can use @Id without specifying a generation strategy (forcing the user to assign a primary key value before the entity can be persisted). However, when the primary key consists of multiple columns, you need to take a different strategy to group these together in a way that allows the persistence engine to manipulate the key values as a single object.

You must create a class to represent this primary key. It will not require a primary key of its own, of course, but it must be a public class, must have a default constructor, must be serializable, and must implement hashCode() and equals() methods to allow the Hibernate code to test for primary key collisions (i.e., they must be implemented with the appropriate database semantics for the primary key values).

Your three strategies for using this primary key class once it has been created are as follows:

- Mark it as @Embeddable and add to your entity class a normal property for it, marked with @Id.

- Add to your entity class a normal property for it, marked with @EmbeddableId.

- Add properties to your entity class for all of its fields, mark them with @Id, and mark your entity class with @IdClass, supplying the class of your primary key class.

All these techniques require the use of an id class because Hibernate must be supplied with a primary key object when various parts of its persistence API are invoked. For example, you can retrieve an instance of an entity by invoking the Session object's get() method, which takes as its parameter a single serializable object representing the entity's primary key.

The use of @Id with a class marked as @Embeddable, as shown in Listing 6-6, is the most natural approach. The @Embeddable tag can be used for non–primary key embeddable values anyway (@Embeddable is discussed in more detail later in the chapter). It allows you to treat the compound primary key as a single property, and it permits the reuse of the @Embeddable class in other tables.

Listing 6-6. Using the @Id and @Embeddable Annotations to Map a Compound Primary Key

```
package com.hibernatebook.annotations;

import javax.persistence.*;

@Entity
public class Account {
```

99

```java
    private String description;
    private AccountPk id;

    public Account (String description) {
        this.description = description;
    }

    protected Account() {
    }

    @Id
    public AccountPk getId() {
        return this.id;
    }

    public String getDescription() {
        return this.description;
    }

    public void setId(AccountPk id) {
        this.id = id;
    }

    public void setDescription(String description) {
        this.description = description;
    }

    @Embeddable
    public static class AccountPk {
        private String code;
        private Integer number;

        public AccountPk() {
        }

        public String getCode() {
            return this.code;
        }

        public Integer getNumber() {
            return this.number;
        }

        public void setNumber(Integer number) {
            this.number = number;
        }

        public void setCode(String code) {
            this.code = code;
        }
```

```
    public int hashCode() {
        int hashCode = 0;
        if( code != null ) hashCode ^= code.hashCode();
        if( number != null ) hashCode ^= number.hashCode();
        return hashCode;
    }

    public boolean equals(Object obj) {
        if( !(obj instanceof AccountPk) ) return false;
        AccountPk target = (AccountPk)obj;
        return ((this.code == null) ?
                (target.code == null) :
                    this.code.equals(target.code))
            && ((this.number == null) ?
                (target.number == null) :
                    this.number.equals(target.number));
    }
  }
}
```

The next most natural approach is the use of the @EmbeddedId tag. Here, the primary key class cannot be used in other tables since it is not an @Embeddable entity, but it does allow us to treat the key as a single attribute of the Account class (in Listings 6-7 and 6-8, the implementation of AccountPk is identical to that in Listing 6-6, and is thus omitted for brevity). Note that in Listings 6-7 and 6-8, the AccountPk class is *not* marked as @Embeddable.

Listing 6-7. Using the @EmbeddedId Annotation to Map a Compound Primary Key

```
package com.hibernatebook.annotations;

import javax.persistence.*;

@Entity
public class Account {
    private String description;
    private AccountPk id;

    public Account(String description) {
        this.description = description;
    }

    protected Account() {
    }

    @EmbeddedId
    public AccountPk getId() {
        return this.id;
    }
```

```
   public String getDescription() {
      return this.description;
   }

   public void setId(AccountPk id) {
      this.id = id;
   }

   public void setDescription(String description) {
      this.description = description;
   }

   public static class AccountPk {
      // ...
   }
}
```

Finally, the use of the **@IdClass** and **@Id** annotations allows us to map the compound primary key class using properties of the entity itself corresponding to the names of the properties in the primary key class. The names must correspond (there is no mechanism for overriding this), and the primary key class must honor the same obligations as with the other two techniques. The only advantage to this approach is its ability to "hide" the use of the primary key class from the interface of the enclosing entity. The **@IdClass** annotation takes a value parameter of **Class** type, which must be the class to be used as the compound primary key. The fields that correspond to the properties of the primary key class to be used must all be annotated with **@Id**—note in Listing 6-8 that the **getCode()** and **getNumber()** methods of the **Account** class are so annotated, and the **AccountPk** class is not mapped as **@Embeddable**, but it is supplied as the value of the **@IdClass** annotation.

Listing 6-8. Using the @IdClass and @Id Annotations to Map a Compound Primary Key

```
package com.hibernatebook.annotations;

import javax.persistence.*;

@Entity
@IdClass(Account.AccountPk.class)
public class Account {
   private String description;
   private String code;
   private Integer number;

   public Account(String description) {
      this.description = description;
   }

   protected Account() {
   }
```

```
@Id
public String getCode() {
    return this.code;
}

@Id
public Integer getNumber() {
    return this.number;
}

public String getDescription() {
    return this.description;
}

public void setDescription(String description) {
    this.description = description;
}

public void setNumber(Integer number) {
    this.number = number;
}

public void setCode(String code) {
    this.code = code;
}

public static class AccountPk {
    // ...
}
}
```

Regardless of which of these approaches we take to declare our compound primary key, the table that will be used to represent it will require the same set of columns. Listing 6-9 shows the DDL that will be generated from any of Listings 6-6, 6-7, or 6-8.

Listing 6-9. The DDL Generated from the Annotated Account Class (Regardless of the Approach Used)

```
create table Account (
    code varchar(255) not null,
    number integer not null,
    description varchar(255),
    primary key (code, number)
);
```

Database Table Mapping with @Table and @SecondaryTable

The @Table annotation allows you to specify the details of the table that will be used to persist the entity in the database. If you omit the annotation, Hibernate will default to using the class name for the table name, so you only need to provide this annotation if you want to override that behavior. The @Table annotation provides four attributes, allowing you to override the name of the table, its catalog, and its schema, and enforce unique constraints on columns in the table. Typically, you would only provide a substitute table name thus: @Table(name="ORDER_HISTORY"). The unique constraints will be applied if the database schema is generated from the annotated classes, and will supplement any column-specific constraints (see discussions of @Column and @JoinColumn later in this chapter). They are not otherwise enforced.

The @SecondaryTable annotation provides a way to model an entity bean that is persisted across several different database tables. Here, in addition to providing an @Table annotation for the primary database table, your entity bean can have an @SecondaryTable annotation, or an @SecondaryTables annotation in turn containing zero or more @SecondaryTable annotations. The @SecondaryTable annotation takes the same basic attributes as the @Table annotation, with the addition of the join attribute. The join attribute defines the join column for the primary database table. It accepts an array of javax.persistence.PrimaryKeyJoinColumn objects. If you omit the join attribute, then it will be assumed that the tables are joined on identically named primary key columns.

When an attribute in the entity is drawn from the secondary table, it must be marked with the @Column annotation, with a table attribute identifying the appropriate table. Listing 6-10 shows how a property of the Customer entity could be drawn from a second table mapped in this way.

Listing 6-10. An Example of a Field Access Entity Mapped Across Two Tables

```
package com.hibernatebook.annotations;

import javax.persistence.*;

@Entity
@Table(name="CUSTOMER")
@SecondaryTable(name="CUSTOMER_DETAILS")
public class Customer {

    @Id
    public int id;

    public String name;

    @Column(table="CUSTOMER_DETAILS")
    public String address;
}
```

Columns in the primary or secondary tables can be marked as having unique values within their tables by adding one or more appropriate @UniqueConstraint annotations to @Table or @SecondaryTable's uniqueConstraints attribute. You may also set uniqueness at the field level with the unique attribute on the @Column attribute. For example, to mark the name field in the preceding declaration as being unique, use the following:

```
@Entity
@Table(
    name="CUSTOMER",
    uniqueConstraints={@UniqueConstraint(columnNames="name")}
)
@SecondaryTable(name="CUSTOMER_DETAILS")
public class Customer {
    ...
}
```

Persisting Basic Types with @Basic

By default, properties and instance variables in your POJO are persistent—Hibernate will store their values for you. The simplest mappings are therefore for the "basic" types. These include primitives, primitive wrappers, arrays of primitives or wrappers, enumerations, and any types that implement `Serializable` but are not themselves mapped entities. These are all mapped implicitly—no annotation is needed. By default, such fields are mapped to a single column, and eager fetching is used to retrieve them (i.e., when the entity is retrieved from the database, all the basic fields and properties are retrieved). Also, when the field or property is not a primitive, it can be stored and retrieved as a null value.

This default behavior can be overridden by applying the `@Basic` annotation to the appropriate class member. This annotation takes two optional attributes, and is itself entirely optional. The first attribute is named `optional` and takes a `boolean`. Defaulting to `true`, this can be set to `false` to provide a hint to schema generation that the associated column should be created `NOT NULL`. The second is named `fetch` and takes a member of the enumeration `FetchType`. This is `EAGER` by default, but can be set to `LAZY` to permit loading on access of the value.

The use of lazy loading is unlikely to be valuable, except when large serializable objects have been mapped as basic types (rather than given entity mappings of their own) and retrieval time may become significant. While the (default) `EAGER` value must be honored, the `LAZY` flag is considered to be a hint, and can be ignored by the persistence engine.

The `@Basic` attribute is usually omitted, with the `@Column` attribute being used where the `@Basic` annotation's optional attribute might otherwise be used to provide the `NOT NULL` behavior.

Omitting Persistence with @Transient

Some fields, such as calculated values, may be used at run time only and they should be discarded from objects as they are persisted into the database. The EJB 3 specification provides the `@Transient` annotation for these transient fields. The `@Transient` annotation does not have any attributes—you just add it to the instance variable or the getter method as appropriate for the entity bean's property access strategy.

The `@Transient` annotation highlights one of the more important differences between using annotations with Hibernate and using XML mapping documents. With annotations, Hibernate will default to persisting all of the fields on a mapped object. When using XML mapping documents, Hibernate requires you to tell it explicitly which fields will be persisted.

For our example, we contrive to add a Date field named publicationDate, which will not be stored in the database to our Book class. We mark this field transient thus:

```
@Transient
public Date getPublicationDate() {
    return publicationDate;
}
```

Because we are using a property access strategy for our Book class, we must put the @Transient annotation on the getter method.

Mapping Properties and Fields with @Column

The @Column annotation is used to specify the details of the column to which a field or property will be mapped. Some of the details are schema related, and therefore apply only if the schema is generated from the annotated files. Others apply and are enforced at run time by Hibernate (or the JPA 2 persistence engine). It is optional, with an appropriate set of default behaviors, but is often useful when overriding default behavior, or when you need to fit your object model into a preexisting schema. It is more commonly used than the similar @Basic annotation, with the following attributes commonly being overridden:

name permits the name of the column to be explicitly specified—by default, this would be the name of the property. However, it is often necessary to override the default behavior when it would otherwise result in an SQL keyword being used as the column name (e.g., user).

length permits the size of the column used to map a value (particularly a String value) to be explicitly defined. The column size defaults to 255, which might otherwise result in truncated String data, for example.

nullable permits the column to be marked NOT NULL when the schema is generated. The default is that fields should be permitted to be null; however, it is common to override this when a field is, or ought to be, mandatory.

unique permits the column to be marked as containing only unique values. This defaults to false, but commonly would be set for a value that might not be a primary key but would still cause problems if duplicated (such as username).

We have marked up the title field of our Book entity using the @Column entity to show how three of these attributes would be applied:

```
@Column(name="working_title",length=200,nullable=false)
public String getTitle() {
    return title;
}
```

The remaining attributes, less commonly used, are as follows:

table is used when the owning entity has been mapped across one or more secondary tables. By default, the value is assumed to be drawn from the primary table, but the name of one of the secondary tables can be substituted here (see the @SecondaryTable annotation example earlier in this chapter).

insertable defaults to true, but if set to false, the annotated field will be omitted from insert statements generated by Hibernate (i.e., it won't be persisted).

updatable defaults to true, but if set to false, the annotated field will be omitted from update statements generated by Hibernate (i.e., it won't be altered once it has been persisted).

columnDefinition can be set to an appropriate DDL fragment to be used when generating the column in the database. This can only be used during schema generation from the annotated entity, and should be avoided if possible, since it is likely to reduce the portability of your application between database dialects.

precision permits the precision of decimal numeric columns to be specified for schema generation, and will be ignored when a non-decimal value is persisted. The value given represents the number of digits in the number (usually requiring a minimum length of n+1, where n is the scale).

scale permits the scale of decimal numeric columns to be specified for schema generation and will be ignored where a non-decimal value is persisted. The value given represents the number of places after the decimal point.

Modeling Entity Relationships

Naturally, annotations also allow you to model associations between entities. JPA 2 supports one-to-one, one-to-many, many-to-one, and many-to-many associations. Each of these has its corresponding annotation.

We discussed the various ways in which these mappings can be established in the tables in Chapter 5. In this section, we will show how the various mappings are requested using the annotations.

Mapping an Embedded (Component) One-to-One Association

When all the fields of one entity are maintained within the same table as another, the enclosed entity is referred to in Hibernate as a *component*. The JPA 2 standard refers to such an entity as being *embedded*.

The @Embedded and @Embeddable attributes are used to manage this relationship. In this book's database example, we associate an AuthorAddress class with an Author class in this way.

The AuthorAddress class is marked with the @Embeddable annotation. An embeddable entity must be composed entirely of basic fields and attributes. An embeddable entity can only use the @Basic, @Column, @Lob, @Temporal, and @Enumerated annotations. It cannot maintain its own primary key with the @Id tag because its primary key is the primary key of the enclosing entity.

The @Embeddable annotation itself is purely a marker annotation, and takes no additional attributes, as demonstrated in Listing 6-11. Typically, the fields and properties of the embeddable entity need no further markup.

Listing 6-11. Marking an Entity for Embedding Within Other Entities

```
@Embeddable
public class AuthorAddress {
...
}
```

The enclosing entity then marks appropriate fields or getters in entities, making use of the embeddable class with the @Embedded annotation, as shown in Listing 6-12.

Listing 6-12. Marking an Embedded Property

```
@Embedded
public AuthorAddress getAddress() {
    return this.address;
}
```

The @Embedded annotation draws its column information from the embedded type, but permits the overriding of a specific column or columns with the @AttributeOverride and @AttributeOverrides tags (the latter to enclose an array of the former if multiple columns are being overridden). For example, Listing 6-13 shows how to override the default column names of the address and country attributes of AuthorAddress with columns named ADDR and NATION.

Listing 6-13. Overriding Default Attributes of an Embedded Property

```
@Embedded
@AttributeOverrides({
    @AttributeOverride(name="address",column=@Column(name="ADDR")),
    @AttributeOverride(name="country",column=@Column(name="NATION"))
})
public AuthorAddress getAddress() {
    return this.address;
}
```

Neither Hibernate nor the JPA 2 standard supports mapping an embedded object across more than one table. In practice, if you want this sort of persistence for your embedded entity, you will usually be better off making it a first-class entity (i.e., *not* embedded) with its own @Entity marker and @Id annotations, and then mapping it via a conventional one-to-one association, as explained in the next section.

Mapping a Conventional One-to-One Association

There is nothing intrinsically wrong with mapping a one-to-one association between two entities where one is not a component of (i.e., embedded into) the other. The relationship is often somewhat suspect, however. You should give some thought to using the embedded technique described previously before using the @OneToOne annotation.

You can have a bidirectional relationship with a one-to-one association. One side will need to own the relationship and be responsible for updating a join column with a foreign key to the other side. The non-owning side will need to use the mappedBy attribute to indicate the entity that owns the relationship.

Assuming that you are resolute on declaring the association in this way (perhaps because you anticipate converting it to a one-to-many or many-to-one relationship in the foreseeable future), applying the annotation is quite simple—all of the attributes are optional. Listing 6-14 shows how simply a relationship like this might be declared.

Listing 6-14. Declaring a Simple One-to-One Relationship

```
@OneToOne
public Address getAddress() {
    return this.address;
}
```

The @OneToOne annotation permits the following optional attributes to be specified:

targetEntity can be set to the class of an entity storing the association. If left unset, the appropriate type will be inferred from the field type, or the return type of the property's getter.

cascade can be set to any of the members of the javax.persistence.CascadeType enumeration. It defaults to none being set. See the "Cascading Operations" sidebar for a discussion of these values.

fetch can be set to the EAGER or LAZY members of FetchType.

optional indicates whether the value being mapped can be null.

orphanRemoval indicates that if the value being mapped is deleted, this entity will also be deleted.

mappedBy indicates that a bidirectional one-to-one relationship is owned by the named entity.[1] The owning entity contains the primary key of the subordinate entity.

Mapping a Many-to-One or One-to-Many Association

A many-to-one association and a one-to-many association are the same association seen from the perspective of the owning and subordinate entities, respectively.

---

[1] An association is bidirectional if each entity maintains a property or field representing its end of the same relationship. For example, if our Address class maintained a reference to the Publisher located there, and the Publisher class maintained a reference to its Address, then the association would be bidirectional.

CASCADING OPERATIONS

When an association between two entities is established (such as a one-to-one association between Human and Pet or a one-to-many association between Customer and Orders), it is common to want certain persistence operations on one entity to also be applied to the entity that it is linked to. Take, for example, the following code:

```
Human dave = new Human("dave");
Pet cat = new PetCat("Tibbles");
dave.setPet(cat);
session.save(dave);
```

In the last line, highlighted in bold, we are likely to want to save the Pet object associated with the Human object. In a one-to-one relationship, we usually expect all operations on the owning entity to be propagated through—that is, to be *cascaded*—to the dependent entity. In other associations this is not true, and even in a one-to-one relationship we may have special reasons for wanting to spare the dependent entity from delete operations (perhaps for auditing reasons).

We are therefore able to specify the types of operations that should be cascaded through an association to another entity using the cascade annotation, which takes an array of members of the CascadeType enumeration. The members correspond with the names of the key methods of the EntityManager class used for EJB 3 persistence, and have the following rough correspondence with operations on entities:

- ALL requires all operations to be cascaded to dependent entities. This is the same as including MERGE, PERSIST, REFRESH, DETACH, and REMOVE.

- MERGE cascades updates to the entity's state in the database (i.e., UPDATE . . .).

- PERSIST cascades the initial storing of the entity's state in the database (i.e., INSERT. . .).

- REFRESH cascades the updating of the entity's state from the database (i.e., SELECT . . .).

- DETACH cascades the removal of the entity from the managed persistence context.

- REMOVE cascades deletion of the entity from the database (i.e., DELETE . . .).

- If no cascade type is specified, no operations will be cascaded through the association.

In the light of these options, the appropriate annotation for the relationship between a publisher and its address would be as follows:

```
@OneToOne(cascade=CascadeType.ALL)
public Address getAddress() {
return this.address;
}
```

The simplest way to maintain a many-to-one relationship between two entities is by managing the foreign key of the entity at the "one" end of the one-to-many relationship as a column in the "many" entity's table.

The @OneToMany annotation can be applied to a field or property value for a collection or an array representing the mapped "many" end of the association.

COLLECTION ORDERING

An ordered collection can be persisted in Hibernate or JPA 2 using the @OrderColumn annotation to maintain the order of the collection. You can also order the collection at retrieval time by means of the @OrderBy annotation. For example, if you were to retrieve a list ordered by the books' names in ascending order, you could annotate a suitable method.

The following code snippet specifies a retrieval order for an ordered collection:

```
@OneToMany(cascade = ALL, mappedBy = "publisher"
@OrderBy("name ASC")
public List<Book> getBooks() {
return books
}
```

The value of the @OrderBy annotation is an ordered list of the field names to sort by, each one optionally appended with ASC (for ascending order, as in the preceding code) or DESC (for descending order). If neither ASC nor DESC is appended to one of the field names, the order will default to ascending. @OrderBy can be applied to any collection-valued association.

The mappedBy attribute is mandatory on a bidirectional association and optional (being implicit) on a unidirectional association.

cascade is optional, taking a member of the javax.persistence.CascadeType enumeration and dictating the cascade behavior of the mapped entity.

targetEntity is optional, as it can usually be deduced from the type of the field or property, as in Listing 6-15, where the property represents a Set of Book entities, making the target entity implicitly Book. However, if necessary (if generics are not being used, for example), the class of the target entity can be provided here.

fetch is optional, allowing lazy or eager fetching to be specified as a member of the javax.persistence.FetchType enumeration.

Listing 6-15. Mapping a One-to-Many Relationship from the Book Entity to the Publisher Entity

```
@OneToMany(cascade = ALL,mappedBy = "publisher")
public Set<Book> getBooks() {
    return books;
}
```

The many-to-one end of this relationship is expressed in similar terms to the one-to-many end, as shown in Listing 6-16.

Listing 6-16. Mapping a Many-to-One Relationship from the Publisher Entity to the Book Entity

```
@ManyToOne
@JoinColumn(name = "publisher_id")
public Publisher getPublisher() {
    return publisher;
}
```

The @ManyToOne annotation takes a similar set of attributes to @OneToMany. The following list describes the attributes, all of which are optional.

cascade indicates the appropriate cascade policy for operations on the association; it defaults to none.

fetch indicates the fetch strategy to use; it defaults to LAZY.

optional indicates whether the value can be null; it defaults to true.

targetEntity indicates the entity that stores the primary key—this is normally inferred from the type of the field or property (Publisher in the preceding example).

We have also supplied the optional @JoinColumn attribute to name the foreign key column required by the association something other than the default (publisher)—this is not necessary, but it illustrates the use of the annotation.

When a unidirectional one-to-many association is to be formed, it is possible to express the relationship using a link table. This is achieved by adding the @JoinTable annotation as shown in Listing 6-17.[2]

Listing 6-17. A Simple Unidirectional One-to-Many Association with a Join Table

```
@OneToMany(cascade = ALL)
@JoinTable
public Set<Book> getBooks() {
    return books;
}
```

---

[2] When a join table is being used, the foreign key relationship is maintained within the join table itself—it is therefore not appropriate to combine the mappedBy attribute of the @OneToMany annotation with the use of an @JoinTable annotation.

The `@JoinTable` annotation provides attributes that allow various aspects of the link table to be controlled. These attributes are as follows:

name is the name of the join table to be used to represent the association.

catalog is the name of the catalog containing the join table.

schema is the name of the schema containing the join table.

joinColumns is an array of `@JoinColumn` attributes representing the primary key of the entity at the "one" end of the association.

inverseJoinColumns is an array of `@JoinColumn` attributes representing the primary key of the entity at the "many" end of the association.

Listing 6-18 shows a fairly typical application of the `@JoinTable` annotation to specify the name of the join table and its foreign keys into the associated entities.

Listing 6-18. A Unidirectional One-to-Many Association with a More Fully Specified Join Table

```
@OneToMany(cascade = ALL)
@JoinTable(
        name="PublishedBooks",
        joinColumns = { @JoinColumn( name = "publisher_id") },
        inverseJoinColumns = @JoinColumn( name = "book_id")
)
public Set<Book> getBooks() {
    return books;
}
```

Mapping a Many-to-Many Association

When a many-to-many association does not involve a first-class entity joining the two sides of the relationship, a link table must be used to maintain the relationship. This can be generated automatically, or the details can be established in much the same way as with the link table described in the "Mapping a Many-to-One or One-to-Many Association" section of the chapter.

The appropriate annotation is naturally `@ManyToMany`, and takes the following attributes:

mappedBy is the field that owns the relationship—this is only required if the association is bidirectional. If an entity provides this attribute, then the other end of the association is the owner of the association, and the attribute must name a field or property of that entity.

targetEntity is the entity class that is the target of the association. Again, this may be inferred from the generic or array declaration, and only needs to be specified if this is not possible.

cascade indicates the cascade behavior of the association, which defaults to none.

fetch indicates the fetch behavior of the association, which defaults to LAZY.

The example maintains a many-to-many association between the Book class and the Author class. The Book entity owns the association, so its getAuthors() method must be marked with an appropriate @ManyToMany attribute, as shown in Listing 6-19.

Listing 6-19. The Book Side of the Many-to-Many Association

```
@ManyToMany(cascade = ALL)
public Set<Author> getAuthors() {
    return authors;
}
```

The Author entity is managed by the Book entity. The link table is not explicitly managed, so, as shown in Listing 6-20, we mark it with a @ManyToMany annotation and indicate that the foreign key is managed by the authors attribute of the associated Book entity.

Listing 6-20. The Author Side of the Many-to-Many Association

```
@ManyToMany(mappedBy = "authors")
public Set<Book> getBooks() {
    return books;
}
```

Alternatively, we could specify the link table in full, as in Listing 6-21.

Listing 6-21. Specifying the Link Table in Full Using the Book Entity Annotations

```
@ManyToMany(cascade = ALL)
@JoinTable(
        name="Books_to_Author",
        joinColumns={@JoinColumn(name="book_ident")},
        inverseJoinColumns={@JoinColumn(name="author_ident")}
)
public Set<Author> getAuthors() {
    return authors;
}
```

Inheritance

The JPA 2 standard and Hibernate both support three approaches to mapping inheritance hierarchies into the database. These are as follows:

- Single table (SINGLE_TABLE): One table for each class hierarchy

- Joined (JOINED): One table for each subclass (including interfaces and abstract classes)

- Table-per-class (TABLE_PER_CLASS): One table for each concrete class implementation

Persistent entities that are related by inheritance must be marked up with the @Inheritance annotation. This takes a single strategy attribute, which is set to one of three javax.persistence. InheritanceType enumeration values corresponding to these approaches (shown in brackets in the preceding bulleted list).

Single Table

The single table approach manages one class for the superclass and all its subtypes. There are columns for each mapped field or property of the superclass, and for each distinct field or property of the derived types. When following this strategy, you will need to ensure that columns are appropriately renamed when any field or property names collide in the hierarchy.

To determine the appropriate type to instantiate when retrieving entities from the database, an @DiscriminatorColumn annotation should be provided in the root (and only in the root) of the persistent hierarchy.[3] This defines a column containing a value that distinguishes between each of the types used. The attributes permitted by the @DiscriminatorColumn annotation are as follows:

> name is the name of the discriminator column.

> discriminatorType is the type of value to be stored in the column as selected from the javax.persistence.DiscriminatorType enumeration of STRING, CHAR, or INTEGER.

> columnDefinition is a fragment of DDL defining the column type. Using this is liable to reduce the portability of your code across databases.

> length is the column length of STRING discriminator types. It is ignored for CHAR and INTEGER types.

All of these (and the annotation itself) are optional, but we recommend supplying at least the name attribute. If no @DiscriminatorColumn is specified in the hierarchy, a default column name of DTYPE and type of STRING will be used.

Hibernate will supply an appropriate discriminator value for each of your entities. For example, if the STRING discriminator type is used, the value this column contains will be the name of the entity (which defaults to the class name). You can also override this behavior with specific values using the @DiscriminatorValue annotation. If the discriminator type is INTEGER, any value provided via the @DiscriminatorValue annotation must be convertible directly into an integer.

In Listing 6-22, we specify that an INTEGER discriminator type should be stored in the column named DISCRIMINATOR. Rows representing Book entities will have a value of 1 in this column, whereas the following mapping in Listing 6-23 requires that rows representing ComputerBook entities should have a value of 2 in the same column.

---

[3] That is to say, the highest class in the hierarchy that is mapped to the database as an entity should be annotated in this way.

Listing 6-22. The Root of the Inheritance Hierarchy Mapped with the SINGLE_TABLE Strategy

```
@Entity
@Inheritance(strategy = SINGLE_TABLE)
@DiscriminatorColumn(
    name="DISCRIMINATOR",
    discriminatorType=INTEGER
)
@DiscriminatorValue("1")
public class Book {
...
}
```

Listing 6-23. A Derived Entity in the Inheritance Hierarchy

```
@Entity
@DiscriminatorValue("2")
public class ComputerBook extends Book {
...
}
```

Joined

An alternative to the monolithic single table approach is the otherwise similar joined table approach. Here a discriminator column is used, but the fields of the various derived types are stored in distinct tables. Other than the differing strategy, this inheritance type is specified in the same way (as shown in Listing 6-24).

Listing 6-24. The Root of the Inheritance Hierarchy Mapped with the JOINED Strategy

```
@Entity
@Inheritance(strategy = JOINED)
@DiscriminatorColumn(
    name="DISCRIMINATOR"
)
public class Book {
...
}
```

Table per Class

Finally, there is the table-per-class approach, in which all of the fields of each type in the inheritance hierarchy are stored in distinct tables. Because of the close correspondence between the entity and its table, the @DiscriminatorColumn annotation is not applicable to this inheritance strategy. Listing 6-25 shows how our Book class could be mapped in this way.

Listing 6-25. The Root of the Inheritance Hierarchy Mapped with the TABLE_PER_CLASS Strategy

```
@Entity
@Inheritance(strategy = TABLE_PER_CLASS)
public class Book {
...
}
```

Choosing Between Inheritance Types When Modeling Inheritance

Each of these different inheritance types has tradeoffs. When you create a database schema that models a class hierarchy, you have to weigh performance and database maintainability to decide which inheritance type to use.

It is easiest to maintain your database when using the joined table approach. If fields are added or removed from any class in the class hierarchy, only one database table needs to be altered to reflect the changes. In addition, adding new classes to the class hierarchy only requires that a new table be added, eliminating the performance problems of adding database columns to large datasets. With the table-per-class approach, a change to a column in a parent class requires that the column change be made in all child tables. The single table approach can be messy, leading to many columns in the table that aren't used in every row, as well as a rapidly horizontally growing table.

Read performance will be best with the single table approach. A select query for any class in the hierarchy will only read from one table, with no joins necessary. The table-per-class type has great performance if you only work with the leaf nodes in the class hierarchy. Any queries related to the parent classes will require joins on a number of tables to get results. The joined table approach will also require joins for any select query, so this will affect performance. The number of joins will be related to the size of the class hierarchy—large, deep class hierarchies may not be good candidates for the joined table approach.

We recommend using the joined table approach unless performance could be a problem because of the size of the dataset and the depth of the class hierarchy.

Other JPA 2 Persistence Annotations

Although we have now covered most of the core JPA 2 persistence annotations, there are a few others that you will encounter fairly frequently. We cover some of these in passing in the following sections.

Temporal Data

Fields or properties of an entity that have `java.util.Date` or `java.util.Calendar` types represent temporal data. By default, these will be stored in a column with the `TIMESTAMP` data type, but this default behavior can be overridden with the `@Temporal` annotation.

The annotation accepts a single `value` attribute from the `javax.persistence.TemporalType` enumeration. This offers three possible values: `DATE`, `TIME`, and `TIMESTAMP`. These correspond respectively to `java.sql.Date`, `java.sql.Time`, and `java.sql.Timestamp`. The table column is given the appropriate data type at schema generation time. Listing 6-26 shows an example mapping a `java.util.Date` property as a `TIME` type—the `java.sql.Date` and `java.sql.Time` classes are both derived from the `java.util.Date` class, so confusingly, both are capable of representing dates *and* times!

Listing 6-26. A Date *Property Mapped as a* Time *Temporal Field*

```
@Temporal(TIME)
public java.util.Date getStartingTime() {
    return this.startingTime;
}
```

Element Collections

In addition to mapping collections using one-to-many mappings, JPA 2 introduced an
@ElementCollection annotation for mapping collections of basic or embeddable classes. You can use the
@ElementCollection annotation to simplify your mappings. Listing 6-27 shows an example where you
use the @ElementCollection annotation to map a `java.util.List` collection of string objects.

Listing 6-27. An Example of ElementCollections

```
@ElementCollection
public List<String> getPasswordHints {
    return this.passwordHints;
}
```

There are two attributes on the @ElementCollection annotation: targetClass and fetch. The
targetClass attribute tells Hibernate which class is stored in the collection. If you use generics on your
collection, you do not need to specify targetClass because Hibernate will infer the correct class. The
fetch attribute takes a member of the enumeration, FetchType. This is EAGER by default, but can be set to
LAZY to permit loading when the value is accessed.

Large Objects

A persistent property or field can be marked for persistence as a database-supported large object type by
applying the @Lob annotation.

The annotation takes no attributes, but the underlying large object type to be used will be inferred
from the type of the field or parameter. String- and character-based types will be stored in an
appropriate character-based type. All other objects will be stored in a BLOB. Listing 6-28 maps a String
into a large object column type.

Listing 6-28. An Example of a Large Object Property

```
@Lob
public String getTitle() {
    return this.title;
}
```

The @Lob annotation can be used in combination with the @Basic or the @ElementCollection
annotation.

Mapped Superclasses

A special case of inheritance occurs when the root of the hierarchy is not itself a persistent entity, but various classes derived from it are. Such a class can be abstract or concrete. The `@MappedSuperclass` annotation allows you to take advantage of this circumstance.

The class marked with `@MappedSuperclass` is not an entity, and is not queryable (it cannot be passed to methods that expect an entity in the `Session` or `EntityManager` objects). It cannot be the target of an association.

The mapping information for the columns of the superclass will be stored in the same table as the details of the derived class (in this way, the annotation resembles the use of the an `@Inheritance` tag with the `SINGLE_TABLE` strategy).

In other respects, the superclass can be mapped as a normal entity, but the mappings will apply to the derived classes only (since the superclass itself does not have an associated table in the database). When a derived class needs to deviate from the superclass's behavior, the `@AttributeOverride` annotation can be used (much as with the use of an embeddable entity).

For example, if in our example model `Book` was a superclass of `ComputerBook`, but `Book` objects themselves were never persisted directly, then `Book` could be marked as `@MappedSuperclass`, as in Listing 6-29.

Listing 6-29. Marking the `Book` Class As a Mapped Superclass

```
@Entity
@MappedSuperclass
public class Book {
...
}
```

The fields of the `ComputerBook` entity derived from `Book` would then be stored in the `ComputerBook` entity class's table. Classes derived directly from `Book` but not mapped as entities in their own right, such as a hypothetical `MarketingBook` class, would not be persistable. In this respect alone, the mapped superclass approach behaves differently from the conventional `@Inheritance` approach with a `SINGLE_TABLE` strategy.

Ordering Collections with @OrderColumn

While `@OrderBy` allows data to be ordered once it has been retrieved from the database, JPA 2 also provides an annotation that allows the ordering of appropriate collection types (e.g., `List`) to be maintained in the database; it does so by maintaining an order column to represent that order. Here's an example:

```
@OneToMany
@OrderColumn(
    name="employeeNumber"
)
public List<Employee> getEmployees() {
    return this.employees;
}
```

Here, we are declaring that an `employeeNumber` column will maintain a value, starting at 0 and incrementing as each entry is added to the list. The default starting value can be overridden by the `base` attribute. By default, the column can contain null (unordered) values. The nullability can be overridden by setting the `nullable` attribute to `false`. By default, when the schema is generated from the annotations, the column is assumed to be an `integer` type; however, this can be overridden by supplying a `columnDefinition` attribute specifying a different column definition string.

Named Queries (HQL or JPQL)

`@NamedQuery` and `@NamedQueries` allow one or more Hibernate Query Language or Java Persistence Query Language (JPQL) queries to be associated with an entity. The required attributes are as follows:

> `name` is the name by which the query is retrieved.

> `query` is the JPQL (or HQL) query associated with the name.

Listing 6-30 shows an example associating a named query with the `Author` entity. The query would retrieve `Author` entities by name, so it is natural to associate it with that entity—however, there is no actual requirement that a named query be associated in this way with the entity that it concerns.

Listing 6-30. A JPQL Named Query Annotation

```
@Entity
@NamedQuery(
        name="findAuthorsByName",
        query="from Author where name = :author"
)
public class Author {
...
}
```

There is also a `hints` attribute, taking a `QueryHint` annotation name/value pair, which allows caching mode, timeout value, and a variety of other platform-specific tweaks to be applied (this can also be used to comment the SQL generated by the query).

You do not need to directly associate the query with the entity against which it is declared, but it is normal to do so. If a query has no natural association with any of the entity declarations, it is possible to make the `@NamedQuery` annotation at the package level.

There is no natural place to put a package-level annotation, so Java annotations allow for a specific file, called `package-info.java`, to contain them. Listing 6-31 gives an example of this.

Listing 6-31. A package-info.java File

```
@javax.annotations.NamedQuery(
    name="findAuthorsByName",
    query="from Author where name = :author"
)
package com.hibernatebook.annotations;
```

Hibernate's session allows named queries to be accessed directly, as shown in Listing 6-32.

Listing 6-32. Invoking a Named Query via the Session

```
Query query = session.getNamedQuery("findAuthorsByName");
query.setParameter("author", "Dave");
List booksByDave = query.list();
System.out.println("There is/are " + booksByDave.size()
        + " author(s) called Dave in the catalog");
```

If you have multiple @NamedQuery annotations to apply to an entity, they can be provided as an array of values of the @NamedQueries annotation.

Named Native Queries (SQL)

Hibernatealso allows the database's native query language (usually a dialect of SQL) to be used in place of HQL or JPQL. You risk losing portability here if you use a database-specific feature, but as long as you use reasonably generic SQL, you should be OK. The @NamedNativeQuery annotation is declared in almost exactly the same manner as the @NamedQuery annotation. The following block of code shows a simple example of the use of a named native query.

```
@NamedNativeQuery(
    name="nativeFindAuthorNames",
    query="select name from author"
)
```

Multiple @NamedNativeQuery annotations can be grouped with the @NamedNativeQueries annotation.

Configuring the Annotated Classes

Once you have an annotated class, you will need to provide the class to your application's Hibernate configuration, just as if it were an XML mapping. With annotations, you can use either the declarative configuration in the hibernate.cfg.xml XML configuration document, or you can programmatically add annotated classes to Hibernate's org.hibernate.cfg.AnnotationConfiguration object. Your application may use both annotated entities and XML mapped entities in the same configuration.

To provide declarative mapping, we use a normal hibernate.cfg.xml XML configuration file and add the annotated classes to the mapping using the mapping element (see Listing 6-33). Notice that we have specified the name of the annotated class as a mapping.

Listing 6-33. A Hibernate XML Configuration File with an Annotated Class

```
<?xml version='1.0' encoding='utf-8'?>
<!DOCTYPE hibernate-configuration PUBLIC
    "-//Hibernate/Hibernate Configuration DTD//EN"
    "http://hibernate.sourceforge.net/hibernate-configuration-3.0.dtd">
<hibernate-configuration>
    <session-factory>
```

```
    <property name="connection.driver_class">
        org.hsqldb.jdbcDriver
    </property>
    <property name="connection.url">
        jdbc:hsqldb:file:annotationsdb;shutdown=true
    </property>
    <property name="connection.username">sa</property>
    <property name="connection.password"></property>
    <property name="hibernate.connection.pool_size">0</property>
    <property name="show_sql">false</property>
    <property name="dialect">
        org.hibernate.dialect.HSQLDialect
    </property>

    <!-- Mapping files -->
    <mapping class="com.hibernatebook.annotations.Author"/>
    <mapping class="com.hibernatebook.annotations.AuthorAddress"/>
    <mapping class="com.hibernatebook.annotations.Book"/>
    <mapping class="com.hibernatebook.annotations.Address"/>
    <mapping class="com.hibernatebook.annotations.Publisher"/>
    <mapping class="com.hibernatebook.annotations.ComputerBook"/>

    </session-factory>
</hibernate-configuration>
```

You can also add an annotated class to your Hibernate configuration programmatically. The annotations toolset comes with an **org.hibernate.cfg.AnnotationConfiguration** object that extends the base Hibernate **Configuration** object for adding mappings. The methods on **AnnotationConfiguration** for adding annotated classes to the configuration are as follows:

```
addAnnotatedClass(Class persistentClass) throws MappingException
addAnnotatedClasses(List<Class> classes)
addPackage(String packageName) throws MappingException
```

Using these methods, you can add one annotated class, a list of annotated classes, or an entire package (by name) of annotated classes. As with the Hibernate XML configuration file, the annotated entities are interoperable with XML mapped entities.

Hibernate 3–Specific Persistence Annotations

We will now look at some of these Hibernate-specific annotations in more detail—however, bear in mind that using any of this functionality potentially reduces the portability of your application to other JPA 2 solutions.

Annotations that are not recognized by an JPA 2 environment will be ignored, rather than causing a runtime exception directly—however, this may result in different runtime application behavior that may not be desirable. In some cases, Hibernate 3 annotations can be used to prepare resources that are referenced by standard JPA 2 annotations, in which case the application will fail when the JPA 2 environment attempts to use the missing resource.

■ **Tip** It is possible to overstate the importance of portability—most bespoke applications are never deployed to an environment other than the one for which they were originally developed. As a mature product, Hibernate 3 has numerous features to offer above and beyond the base JPA 2specification. You should not waste too much time trying to achieve a portable solution in preference to these proprietary features unless you have a definite requirement for portability.

@Entity

The Hibernate-specific `@Entity` annotation extends the basic details of the `@javax.persistence.Entity` annotation, but is otherwise used in the same contexts. It allows the following additional attributes to be specified:

> `dynamicInsert` is used to flag that insert statements should be generated at run time (not at startup), allowing only the altered columns to be inserted. By default this is disabled.

> `dynamicUpdate` is used to flag that update statements should be generated at run time, allowing only the altered columns to be updated. By default this is disabled.

> `mutable` is `true` by default, but if set to `false`, it allows the persistence engine to cache the values read from the database, and the persistence engine will make no attempt to update them in response to changes (changes that should not be made if this flag is set to `false`).

> `optimisticLock` allows an optimistic lock strategy to be selected from the -`OptimisticLockType` enumeration values of `ALL`, `DIRTY`, `NONE`, and `VERSION`. This defaults to `VERSION`.

> `persister` allows a persister class other than the default Hibernate one to be selected for the entity (for example, allowing serialization to be used instead of relational persistence).

> `polymorphism` allows the polymorphism strategy to be selected from the `PolymorphismType` enumeration values of `EXPLICIT` and `IMPLICIT`. This defaults to `IMPLICIT`.

> `selectBeforeUpdate` allows the user to request that a `SELECT` be performed to retrieve the entity before any potential update.

Sorting Collections with @Sort

The Hibernate-specific `@Sort` annotation allows a collection managed by Hibernate to be sorted by a standard Java comparator. The following code gives an example.

```
@javac.persistence.OneToMany
@org.hibernate.annotations.Sort(
   type=org.hibernate.annotations.SortType.COMPARATOR,
   comparator=EmployeeComparator.class
)
public Set<Employee> getEmployees() {
   return this.employees;
}
```

Applying Indexes with @Table and @Index

The Hibernate-specific @Table annotation supplements the standard table annotation and allows additional index hints to be provided to Hibernate. These will be used at schema generation time to apply indexes to the columns specified. The following code gives an example.

```
// Standard persistence annotations:
@javax.persistence.Entity
@javax.persistence.Table(name="FOO")

// Hibernate-specific table annotation:
@Table(
   appliesTo="FOO", indexes = {
      @Index(name="FOO_FROM_TO_IDX",columnNames={"FIRST","LAST"}),
      @Index(name="FOO_EMPLOYEE_IDX",columnNames={"EMPLOYEE_NUM"}))
public class Foo {
...
}
```

Restricting Collections with @Where

The contents of a collection that will be retrieved from the database can be restricted with a Hibernate-specific @Where annotation from the @org.hibernate.annotations package. This simply adds a Where clause to the query that will be used to obtain the entities contained within the collection. Here's an example:

```
@javax.persistence.OneToMany
@org.hibernate.annotations.Where(clause="grade > 2")
public Set<Employee> getEmployees() {
   return this.employees;
}
```

Alternative Key Generation Strategies with @GenericGenerator

As mentioned in the "Primary Keys with @Id and @GeneratedValue" section, the full gamut of Hibernate primary key value generators is not supported by the standard set of annotations. Hibernate therefore supplies the @GenericGenerator annotation to fill the void.

The attributes that can be supplied to the annotation are as follows:

name is mandatory, and is used to identify the generic generator in the @GeneratedValue annotation.

strategy is mandatory, and determines the generator type to be used. This can be a standard Hibernate generator type or the name of a class implementing the org.hibernate.id.IdentifierGenerator interface.

parameters is a list of @Parameter annotations defining any parameter values required by the generator strategy.

The available standard Hibernate strategies are increment, identity, sequence, hilo, seqhilo, uuid, guid, native, assigned, select, and foreign. For example, the non-standard uuid strategy for a primary key is configured as follows:

```
@Id
@GenericGenerator(name="unique_id",strategy="uuid")
@GeneratedValue(generator="unique_id")
public String getId() {
    return this.id;
}
```

Alternatively, to configure the sequence strategy (equivalent to specifying a strategy of SEQUENCE in the @GeneratedValue annotation), you can supply the following parameters:

```
@Id
@GenericGenerator(name="seq_id",strategy="sequence",
    parameters= {
        @Parameter(name="sequence",value="HIB_SEQ")
    }
)
@GeneratedValue(generator="seq_id")
public Integer getId() {
    return this.id;
}
```

Using Ant with Annotation-Based Mappings

When using the Hibernate Ant tasks in conjunction with the annotation-based mappings, you operate under one important constraint: the Ant task cannot read the mapping information from the raw source files. The annotated files must be compiled before you can perform any operations on them (including schema generation). You should therefore ensure that any Hibernate Ant tasks are granted a dependency upon the compile task for the entities.

The Ant task will also need access to the classes via the configuration object—you will therefore need to explicitly include any annotated classes in the hibernate.cfg.xml file as described in the first part of the previous "Configuring the Annotated Classes" section. You cannot use programmatic configuration of the classes in conjunction with tasks such as hbm2ddl, so this is an important step.

The various Hibernate JAR files, including hibernate-annotations.jar, will need to be in the classpath of the task definition.

Finally, you will need to specify an `<annotationconfiguration .../>` element, rather than the usual `<configuration .../>` element. An example Ant target to build a DDL script from annotated classes is shown in Listing 6-34.

Listing 6-34. A Sample Excerpt from this Chapter's Task to Perform Schema Generation

```
<target name="exportDDL" depends="compile">
    <mkdir dir="${sql}"/>
    <htools destdir="${sql}">
        <classpath refid="classpath.tools"/>
        <annotationconfiguration
            configurationfile="${src}/hibernate.cfg.xml"/>
        <hbm2ddl
            create="true"
            drop="true"
            format="true"
            export="true"
            outputfilename="${ant.project.name}.dll"/>
    </htools>
</target>
```

A full Ant script is provided with the online source code for this chapter (at www.apress.com).

Code Listings

Listings 6-35 and 6-36 contain the completed annotated source code for the **Author** and **Book** classes described in this chapter. The database schema also follows in Listing 6-36.

Listing 6-35 illustrates use of the **@Entity**, **@Inheritance**, **@Id**, **@GeneratedValue**, **@Column**, **@Transient**, **@ManyToOne**, **@JoinColumn**, and **@ManyToMany** annotations.

Listing 6-35. The Fully Annotated Book Class

```
package com.hibernatebook.annotations;

import static javax.persistence.CascadeType.ALL;
import static javax.persistence.InheritanceType.JOINED;

import java.util.*;
import javax.persistence.*;

@Entity
@Inheritance(strategy = JOINED)
public class Book {

    private String title;
    private Publisher publisher;
    private Set<Author> authors = new HashSet<Author>();
    private int pages;
    private int id;
```

```java
protected Date publicationDate;

// Constructors...

protected Book() {
}

public Book(String title, int pages) {
    this.title = title;
    this.pages = pages;
}

// Getters...

@Id
@GeneratedValue
public int getId() {
    return id;
}

@Column(name = "working_title", length = 200, nullable = false)
public String getTitle() {
    return title;
}

public int getPages() {
    return pages;
}

@Transient
public Date getPublicationDate() {
    return publicationDate;
}

@ManyToOne
@JoinColumn(name = "publisher_id")
public Publisher getPublisher() {
    return publisher;
}

@ManyToMany(cascade = ALL)
public Set<Author> getAuthors() {
    return authors;
}

// Setters...

public void setId(int id) {
    this.id = id;
}
```

```
    public void setTitle(String title) {
        this.title = title;
    }

    public void setPages(int pages) {
        this.pages = pages;
    }

    public void setPublicationDate(Date publicationDate) {
        this.publicationDate = publicationDate;
    }

    public void setPublisher(Publisher publisher) {
        this.publisher = publisher;
    }

    public void setAuthors(Set<Author> authors) {
        this.authors = authors;
    }

    // Helpers...
    public void addAuthor(Author author) {
        authors.add(author);
    }
}
```

Listing 6-36 demonstrates the use of the @NamedQuery, @Embedded, @AttributeOverrides, and @AttributeOverride annotations.

Listing 6-36. *The Fully Annotated Author Class*

```
package com.hibernatebook.annotations;

import java.util.HashSet;
import java.util.Set;

import javax.persistence.*;

@Entity
@NamedQuery(
  name="findAuthorsByName",
  query="from Author where name = :author"
)
public class Author {

    private int id;
    private String name;
    private Set<Book> books = new HashSet<Book>();
    private AuthorAddress address;
```

```java
// Constructors...

protected Author() {
}

public Author(String name, AuthorAddress address) {
    this.name = name;
    this.address = address;
}

// Getters...

@Id
@GeneratedValue
public int getId() {
    return id;
}

public String getName() {
    return name;
}

@ManyToMany(mappedBy = "authors")
public Set<Book> getBooks() {
    return books;
}

@Embedded
@AttributeOverrides({
    @AttributeOverride(name="address",column=@Column(name="ADDR")),
    @AttributeOverride(name="country",column=@Column(name="NATION"))
})
public AuthorAddress getAddress() {
    return this.address;
}

// Setters...

public void setId(int id) {
    this.id = id;
}

public void setName(String name) {
    this.name = name;
}

public void setBooks(Set<Book> books) {
    this.books = books;
}
```

```
    public void setAddress(AuthorAddress address) {
        this.address = address;
    }
}
```

Finally, Listing 6-37 shows the database schema for the classes supporting this chapter, as generated by the Ant `hbm2ddl` export task for the HSQL database. You will note that we are unable to control the names selected for the foreign key relationships. This is one area in which the Hibernate XML mapping files are superior to the JPA 2 annotations.

Listing 6-37. The Database Schema for the Example

```
create table Address (
    id integer not null,
    city varchar(255),
    country varchar(255),
    primary key (id)
);

create table Author (
    id integer generated by default as identity (start with 1),
    ADDR varchar(255),
    NATION varchar(255),
    name varchar(255),
    primary key (id)
);

create table Book (
    id integer generated by default as identity (start with 1),
    pages integer not null,
    working_title varchar(200) not null,
    publisher_id integer,
    primary key (id)
);

create table Book_Author (
    books_id integer not null,
    authors_id integer not null,
    primary key (books_id, authors_id)
);

create table ComputerBook (
    BOOK_ID integer not null,
    softwareName varchar(255),
    primary key (BOOK_ID)
);
```

```
create table Publisher (
    id integer generated by default as identity (start with 1),
    name varchar(255),
    address_id integer,
    primary key (id)
);

alter table Book
    add constraint FK1FAF0990BF1C70
    foreign key (publisher_id)
    references Publisher;

alter table Book_Author
    add constraint FK1A9A0FA1B629DD87
    foreign key (authors_id)
    references Author;

alter table Book_Author
    add constraint FK1A9A0FA1D3BA8BC3
    foreign key (books_id)
    references Book;

alter table ComputerBook
    add constraint FK98D97CC4600B1724
    foreign key (BOOK_ID)
    references Book;

alter table Publisher
    add constraint FKCDB7C1DC158ECEF0
    foreign key (address_id)
    references Address;
```

Summary

In this chapter, we used JPA 2 annotations to add metadata to our POJOs for Hibernate, and we looked at the Hibernate-specific annotations that can enhance these at the cost of reduced portability.

In the next chapter, we discuss the alternative approach of using XML mapping documents to express the mapping requirements.

CHAPTER 7

■ ■ ■

Creating Mappings with Hibernate XML Files

In addition to annotations, Hibernate supports the use of XML mapping files to describe the relationship between the object model and the database. A mapping file can map a single class or multiple classes to the database. The mapping can also describe standard queries (in HQL and SQL) and filters.

If you are creating a new application that uses Hibernate, we recommend using annotations for mapping relationships. However, there are many applications that use XML mapping files that are already in existence, and XML mapping files are a perfectly valid way of organizing your application. We have found that annotations lead to less cluttered applications. We have also found that annotations are also easier to understand when we read other developers' code, because we don't have to refer to two different files to figure out how a Java class is mapped.

Hibernate Types

Although we have referred to the Hibernate types in passing, we have not discussed the terminology in any depth. In order to express the behavior of the mapping file elements, we need to make these fine distinctions explicit.

Hibernate types fall into three broad categories: entities, components, and values.

Entities

Generally, an entity is a POJO class that has been mapped into the database using the `<class>` or `<subclass>` elements.

An entity can also be a dynamic map (actually a `Map` of `Maps`). These are mapped against the database in the same way as a POJO, but with the default entity mode of the `SessionFactory` set to `dynamic-map`.

The advantage of POJOs over the `dynamic-map` approach is that compile-time type safety is retained. Conversely, dynamic maps are a quick way to get up and running when building prototypes.

It is also possible to represent your entities as Dom4J `Document` objects. This is a useful feature when importing and exporting data from a preexisting Hibernate database, but it is not really central to the everyday use of Hibernate.

We recommend that you use the standard entity mode unless you need to sacrifice accuracy for timeliness, so the alternate approaches are not discussed in this chapter—however, we give some simple examples of the Map-based mappings in Appendix A.

Components

Lying somewhere between entities and values are component types. When the class representation is simple and its instances have a strong one-to-one relationship with instances of another class, then it is a good candidate to become a component of that other class.

The component will normally be mapped as columns in the same table that represents most of the other attributes of the owning class, so the strength of the relationship must justify this inclusion. In the following code, the MacAddress class might a good candidate for a component relationship.

```java
public class NetworkInterface {
    public int id;
    public String name;
    public String manufacturer;
    public MacAddress physicalAddress;
}
```

The advantage of this approach is that it allows you to dispense with the primary key of the component and the join to its containing table. If a poor choice of component is made (for example, when a many-to-one relationship actually holds), then data will be duplicated unnecessarily in the component columns.

Values

Everything that is not an entity or a component is a value. Generally, these correspond to the data types supported by your database, the collection types, and, optionally, some user-defined types.

The details of these mappings will be vendor-specific, so Hibernate provides its own value type names; the Java types are defined in terms of these (see Table 7-1).

Table 7-1. *The Standard Hibernate 3 Value Names*

Hibernate 3 Type	Corresponding Java Type
Primitives and Wrappers	
integer	int, java.lang.Integer
long	long, java.lang.Long
short	short, java.lang.Short
float	float, java.lang.Float

Hibernate 3 Type	Corresponding Java Type
double	double, java.lang.Double
character	char, java.lang.Character
byte	byte, java.lang.Byte
boolean, yes_no, true_false	boolean, java.lang.Boolean
Other Classes	
string	java.lang.String
date, time, timestamp	java.util.Date
calendar, calendar_date	java.util.Calendar
big_decimal	java.math.BigDecimal
big_integer	java.math.BigInteger
Locale	java.util.Locale
timezone	java.util.TimeZone
currency	java.util.Currency
class	java.lang.Class
Binary	byte[]
text	java.lang.String
serializable	java.io.Serializable
clob	java.sql.Clob
blob	java.sql.Blob

In addition to these standard types, you can create your own. Your user type class should implement either the `org.hibernate.usertype.UserType` interface or the `org.hibernate.usertype.CompositeUserType` interface. Once implemented, a custom type can behave identically to the standard types; though depending on your requirements, it may be necessary to specify multiple column names to contain its values, or to provide initialization parameters for your implementation.

For one-off cases, we recommend that you use components—these have similar behavior, but they can be "created" in the mapping file without needing to write Hibernate-specific code. Unless you propose to make substantial use of a custom type throughout your application, it will not be worth the effort. We do not discuss this feature further in this book.

The Anatomy of a Mapping File

A mapping file is a normal XML file. It is validated against a DTD, which can be downloaded from `http://hibernate.sourceforge.net/hibernate-mapping-3.0.dtd`.

The terminology used in the naming of elements and attributes is somewhat confusing at first because it is the point of contact between the jargon of the object-oriented and relational worlds.

The <hibernate-mapping> Element

The root element of any mapping file is `<hibernate-mapping>`. As the top-level element, its attributes mostly define default behaviors and settings to apply to the child elements (see Table 7-2).

Table 7-2. The `<hibernate-mapping>` Attributes

Attribute	Values	Default	Description
auto-import	true, false	True	By default, allows you to use the unqualified class names in Hibernate queries. You would normally only set this to false if the class name would otherwise be ambiguous.
catalog			The database catalog against which queries should apply.
default-access		Property	The default access type. If set to property, then get and set methods are used to access the data. If set to field, then the data is accessed directly. Alternatively, you can provide the class name of a PropertyAccessor implementation defining any other access mechanism.
default-cascade			Defines how (and whether) direct changes to data should affect dependent data by default.
default-lazy	true, false	True	Defines whether lazy instantiation is used by default. Generally, the performance benefits are such that you will want to use lazy instantiation whenever possible.

Attribute	Values	Default	Description
package			The package from which all implicit imports are considered to occur.
schema			The database schema against which queries should apply.

The default cascade modes available for the `default-cascade` attribute (and for the cascade attributes in all other elements) are as follows:

```
create, merge, delete, save-update, evict, replicate, lock, refresh
```

These correspond to the various possible changes in the lifestyle of the parent object. When set (you can include combinations of them as comma-separated values), the relevant changes to the parent will be cascaded to the relation. For example, you may want to apply the `save-update` cascade option to a class that includes `Set` attributes, so that when new persistent classes are added to these, they will not have to be saved explicitly in the session.

There are also three special options:

```
all, delete-orphan, none
```

`all` specifies that all changes to the parent should be propagated to the relation, and `none` specifies that none should. `delete-orphan` applies only to one-to-many associations, and specifies that the relation should be deleted when it is no longer referenced by the parent.

The required order and cardinality of the child elements of `<hibernate-mapping>` are as follows:

```
(meta*,
 typedef*,
 import*,
 (class | subclass | joined-subclass | union-subclass)*,
 (query | sql-query)*,
 filter-def*)
```

The Order and Cardinality Information from the DTD

The mapping files used by Hibernate have a great many elements and are somewhat self-referential. For example, the `<component>` element permits you to include within it further `<component>` elements, and within those further `<component>` elements—and so on, ad infinitum.

While we do not quote exhaustively from the mapping file's DTD, we sometimes quote the part of it that specifies the permitted ordering and cardinality (number of occurrences) of the child elements of a given element.

The cardinality is expressed by a symbol after the end of the name of the element: * means "zero or more occurrences," ? means "zero or one occurrences," and no trailing symbol means "exactly one occurrence."

The elements can be grouped using brackets, and where the elements are interchangeable, | (the pipe symbol) means "or."

In practical terms, this allows us to tell from the order and cardinality information quoted for the hibernate-mapping file that all of the elements immediately below it are, in fact, optional. We can also see that there is no limit to the number of <class> elements that can be included.

You can look up this ordering and cardinality information in the DTD for the mapping file for all the elements, including the ones that we have omitted from this chapter. You will also find within the DTD the specification of which attributes are permitted to each element, the values they may take (when they are constrained), and their default values when provided. We recommend that you look at the DTD for enlightenment whenever you are trying to work out whether a specific mapping file should be syntactically valid.

Throughout this book, we have assumed that the mappings are defined in one mapping file for each significant class that is to be mapped to the database. We suggest that you follow this practice in general, but there are some exceptions to this rule. You may, for instance, find it useful to place query and sql-query entries into an independent mapping file, particularly when they do not fall clearly into the context of a single class.

The <class> Element

The child element that you will use most often—indeed, in nearly all of your mapping files—is <class>. As you have seen in earlier chapters, we generally describe the relationships between Java objects and database entities in the body of the <class> element. The <class> element permits the following attributes to be defined (see Table 7-3).

Table 7-3. The <class> Attributes

Attribute	Values	Default	Description
abstract	true, false	false	The flag that should be set if the class being mapped is abstract.
batch-size		1	Specifies the number of items that can be batched together when retrieving instances of the class by identifier.
catalog			The database catalog against which the queries should apply.
check			Defines an additional row-level check constraint, effectively adding this as a SQL CHECK(...) clause during table generation (for example, check="salary < 1000000").

Attribute	Values	Default	Description
discriminator-value			A value used to distinguish between otherwise identical subclasses of a common type persisted to the same table. `is null` and `is not null` are permissible values. To distinguish between a `Cat` and a `Dog` derivative of the `Mammal` abstract class, for example, you might use discriminator values of `C` and `D`, respectively.
dynamic-insert	true, false	false	Indicates whether all columns should appear in `INSERT` statements. If the attribute is set to `true`, null columns will not appear in generated `INSERT` commands. On very wide tables, this may improve performance; but because insert statements are cached, `dynamic-insert` can easily produce a performance hit.
dynamic-update	true, false	false	Indicates whether all columns should appear in `UPDATE` statements. If the attribute is set to `true`, unchanged columns will not appear in generated `UPDATE` commands. As with `dynamic-insert`, this can be tweaked for performance reasons. You must enable `dynamic-update` if you want to use version-based optimistic locking (discussed in Appendix A).
entity-name			The name of the entity to use in place of the class name (therefore required if dynamic mapping is used).
lazy	true, false		Used to disable or enable lazy fetching against the enclosing mapping's default.
mutable	true, false	true	Used to flag that a class is immutable (allowing Hibernate to make some performance optimizations when dealing with these classes).
name			The fully qualified Java name, or optionally unqualified if the `<hibernate-mapping>` element declares a package attribute, of the class (or interface) that is to be made persistent.
node			If using XML relational persistence (in place of or in addition to relational database persistence), specifies the name of the XML element or attribute that maps to this class.
optimistic-lock	none, version	version	Specifies the optimistic locking `dirty`, `all` strategy to use. The strategy applies at a class level, but in Hibernate 3 can also be specified (or overridden) at an attribute level. Optimistic locking is discussed in Appendix A.

Continued

Attribute	Values	Default	Description
persister			Allows a custom **ClassPersister** object to be used when persisting the entity.
polymorphism	implicit, explicit	implicit	Determines how polymorphism is to be used. The default implicit behavior will return instances of the class if superclasses or implemented interfaces are named in the query, and will return subclasses if the class itself is named in the query.
proxy			Specifies a class or an interface to use as the proxy for lazy initialization. Hibernate uses runtime-generated proxies by default, but you can specify your own implementation of **org.hibernate.HibernateProxy** in their place.
rowid			Flags that row IDs should be used (a database-implementation detail allowing Hibernate to optimize updates).
schema			Optionally overrides the schema specified by the **<hibernate-mapping>** element.
select-before-update	true, false	false	Flags that Hibernate should carry out extra work to avoid issuing unnecessary **UPDATE** statements. If set to **true**, Hibernate issues a **SELECT** statement before attempting to issue an **UPDATE** statement in order to ensure that the **UPDATE** statement is actually required (i.e., that columns have been modified). While this is likely to be less efficient, it can prevent database triggers from being invoked unnecessarily.
subselect			A subselection of the contents of the underlying table. A class can only use a **subselect** if it is immutable and read-only (because the SQL defined here cannot be reversed). Generally, the use of a database view is preferable.
table			The table name associated with the class (if unspecified, the unqualified class name will be used).
where			An arbitrary SQL **where** condition to be used when retrieving objects of this class from the table.

Many of these attributes in the **<class>** element are designed to support preexisting database schemas. In practice, the **name** attribute is very often the only one set.

In addition to the attributes on the `<class>` element, the `<class>` element also has several child elements, which we discuss throughout the rest of this chapter. The required order and cardinality of the child elements of `<class>` are as follows:

```
(meta*,
 subselect?,
 cache?,
 synchronize*,
 comment?,
 tuplizer*,
 (id | composite-id),
 discriminator?,
 (version | timestamp)?,
 (property | many-to-one | one-to-one | component | dynamic-component |
  properties | any | map | set | list | bag | idbag |
  array | primitive-array)*,
 ((join*, subclass*) | joined-subclass* | union-subclass*),
 loader?,
 sql-insert?,
 sql-update?,
 sql-delete?,
 filter*
 resultset,
 (query | sql-query)
)
```

The <id> Element

All entities need to define their primary key in some way. Any class directly defined by the `<class>` element (not a derived or component class) must therefore have an `<id>` or a `<composite-id>` element to define this (see Table 7-4). Note that while it is not a requirement that your class implementation itself should implement the primary key attribute, it is certainly advisable. If you cannot alter your class design to accommodate this, you can instead use the `getIdentifier()` method on the `Session` object to determine the identifier of a persistent class independently.

Table 7-4. The `<id>` Attributes

Attribute	Values	Default	Description
access			Defines how the properties should be accessed: through `field` (directly), through `property` (calling the get/set methods), or through the name of a `PropertyAccessor` class to be used. The value from the `<hibernate-mapping>` element will be inherited if this is not specified.
column			The name of the column in the table containing the primary key. The value given in the `name` attribute will be used if this is not specified.

Continued

Attribute	Values	Default	Description
length			The column length to be used.
name			The name of the attribute in the class representing this primary key. If this is omitted, it is assumed that the class does not have an attribute directly representing this primary key. Naturally, the `column` attribute must be provided if the `name` attribute is omitted.
node			Specifies the name of the XML element or attribute that should be used by the XML relational persistence features.
type			The Hibernate type of the column.
unsaved-value			The value that the attribute should take when an instance of the class has been created but not yet persisted to the database. This attribute is mandatory.

The `<id>` element requires a `<generator>` element to be specified, which defines how to generate a new primary key for a new instance of the class. The generator takes a `class` attribute, which defines the mechanism to be used. The class should be an implementation of `org.hibernate.id.IdentifierGenerator`. Optional `<param>` elements can be provided if the identifier needs additional configuration information, each having the following form:

```
<param name="parameter name">parameter value</param>
```

Hibernate provides several default `IdentifierGenerator` implementations, which can be referenced by convenient short names, as shown in Table 7-5. These are fairly comprehensive, so you are unlikely to need to implement your own `IdentifierGenerator`.

Table 7-5. The Default IdentifierGenerator Implementations

Short Name	Description
guid	Uses a database-generated "globally" unique identifier. This is not portable to databases that do not have a `guid` type. The specific implementation, and hence the quality of the uniqueness of this key, may vary from vendor to vendor.
hilo	Uses a database table and column to efficiently and portably maintain and generate identifiers that are unique to that database. The Hibernate `int`, `short`, and `long` types are supported.
identity	Supports the `identity` column type available in some, but not all, databases. This is therefore not a fully portable option. The Hibernate `int`, `short`, and `long` types are supported.

Short Name	Description
increment	Generates a suitable key by adding 1 to the current highest key value. Can apply to int, short, or long hibernate types. This only works if other processes are not permitted to update the table at the same time. If multiple processes are running, then depending on the constraints enforced by the database, the result may be an error in the application(s) or data corruption.
native	Selects one of sequence, identity, or hilo, as appropriate. This is a good compromise option since it uses the innate features of the database and is portable to most platforms. This is particularly appropriate if your code is likely to be deployed to a number of database implementations with differing capabilities.
seqhilo	Uses a sequence to efficiently generate identifiers that are unique to that database. The Hibernate int, short, and long types are supported. This is not a portable technique (see sequence, following).
sequence	Supports the sequence column type (essentially a database-enforced increment) available in some, but not all, databases. This is, therefore, not a fully portable option. The Hibernate int, short, and long types are supported.
uuid	Attempts to portably generate a (cross-database) unique primary key. The key is composed of the local IP address, the startup time of the JVM (accurate to ¼ of a second), the system time, and a counter value (unique within the JVM). This cannot guarantee absolutely that a given key is unique, but it will be good enough for most clustering purposes.

The child elements of the `<id>` element are as follows:

`(meta*, column*, type?, generator?)`

While this is all rather complex, Listing 7-1 shows a typical `<id>` element from Chapter 3, which illustrates the simplicity of the usual case.

Listing 7-1. A Typical `<id>` Element

```
<id name="id" type="long" column="id">
    <generator class="native"/>
</id>
```

■ **Note** When the `<id>` element cannot be defined, a compound key can instead be defined using the `<composite-id>` element. This is provided purely to support existing database schemas. A new Hibernate project with a clean database design does not require this.

143

In addition to using the standard and custom generator types, you have the option of using the special `assigned` generator type. This allows you to explicitly set the identifier for the entities that you will be persisting—Hibernate will not then attempt to assign any identifier value to such an entity. If you use this technique, you will not be able to use the `saveOrUpdate()` method on a transient entity—instead, you will have to call the appropriate `save()` or `update()` method explicitly.

The <property> Element

While it is not absolutely essential, almost all classes will also maintain a set of properties in the database in addition to the primary key. These must be defined by a `<property>` element (see Table 7-6).

Table 7-6. The `<property>` Attributes

Attribute	Values	Default	Description
access			Defines how the properties should be accessed: through `field` (directly), through `property` (calling the get/set methods), or through the name of a `PropertyAccessor` class to be used. The value from the `<class>` element or `<hibernate-mapping>` element will be inherited if this is not specified.
column			The column in which the property will be maintained. If omitted, this will default to the name of the attribute; or it can be specified with nested `<column>` elements (see Listing 7-2).
formula			An arbitrary SQL query representing a computed property (i.e., one that is calculated dynamically, rather than represented in a column).
index			The name of an index to be maintained for the column.
insert	true, false	true	Specifies whether creation of an instance of the class should result in the column associated with this attribute being included in `insert` statements.
lazy	true, false	false	Defines whether lazy instantiation is used by default for this column.
length			The column length to be used.
name			The (mandatory) name of the attribute. This should start with a lowercase letter.
node			Specifies the name of the XML element or attribute that should be used by the XML relational persistence features.

Attribute	Values	Default	Description
not-null	true, false	false	Specifies whether the column is permitted to contain null values.
optimistic -lock	true, false	true	Determines whether optimistic locking should be used when the attribute has been updated.
precision			Allows the precision (the number of digits) to be specified for numeric data.
scale			Allows the scale (the number of digits to the right of the decimal point) to be specified for numeric data.
type			The Hibernate type of the column.
unique	true, false	false	Indicates whether duplicate values are permitted for this column/attribute.
unique-kcy			Groups the columns together by this attribute value. Represents columns across which a unique key constraint should be generated (not yet supported in the schema generation).
update	true, false	true	Specifies whether changes to this attribute in instances of the class should result in the column associated with this attribute being included in update statements.

The child elements of the `<property>` element are as follows:

```
(meta*, (column | formula)*, type?)
```

Any element accepting a `column` attribute, as is the case for the `<property>` element, will also accept `<column>` elements in its place. For an example, see Listing 7-2.

Listing 7-2. Using the `<column>` Element

```
<property name="message"/>
    <column name="message" type="string"/>
</property>
```

This particular example does not really give us anything beyond the use of the `column` attribute directly; but the `<column>` element comes into its own with custom types and some of the more complex mappings that we will be looking into later in the chapter.

The <component> Element

The <component> element is used to map classes that will be represented as extra columns within a table describing some other class. We have already discussed how components fit in as a compromise between full entity types and mere value types.

The <component> element can take the attributes listed in Table 7-7.

Table 7-7. The <component> *Attributes*

Attribute	Values	Default	Description
access			Defines how the properties should be accessed: through field (directly), through property (calling the get/set methods), or through the name of a PropertyAccessor class to be used
class			The class that the parent class incorporates by composition
insert	true, false	True	Specifies whether creation of an instance of the class should result in the column associated with this attribute being included in insert statements
lazy	true, false	False	Defines whether lazy instantiation is used by default for this mapped entity
name			The name of the attribute (component) to be persisted
node			Specifies the name of the XML element or attribute that should be used by the XML relational persistence features
optimistic-lock	true, false	true	Specifies the optimistic locking strategy to use
unique	true, false	False	Indicates that the values that represent the component must be unique within the table
update	true, false	True	Specifies whether changes to this attribute in instances of the class should result in the column associated with this attribute being included in update statements

The child elements of the `<component>` element are as follows:

```
(meta*,
 tuplizer*,
 parent?,
 (property | many-to-one | one-to-one |
  component | dynamic-component | any |
  map | set | list | bag |
  array | primitive-array)* )
```

We provide a full example of the use of the `<component>` element in the "Mapping Composition" section later in this chapter.

The <one-to-one> Element

The `<one-to-one>` element expresses the relationship between two classes, where each instance of the first class is related to a single instance of the second, and vice versa. Such a one-to-one relationship can be expressed either by giving each of the respective tables the same primary key values, or by using a foreign key constraint from one table onto a unique identifier column of the other. Table 7-8 shows the attributes that apply to the `<one-to-one>` element.

Table 7-8. The `<one-to-one>` Attributes

Attribute	Values	Default	Description
access			Specifies how the class member should be accessed: `field` for direct field access or `attribute` for access via the get and set methods.
cascade			Determines how changes to the parent entity will affect the linked relation.
check			The SQL to create a multirow check constraint for schema generation.
class			The property type of the `attribute` or `field` (if omitted, this will be determined by reflection).
constrained	true, false		Indicates that a foreign key constraint on the primary key of this class references the table of the associated class.
embed-xml	true, false		When using XML relational persistence, indicates whether the XML tree for the associated entity itself, or only its identifier, will appear in the generated XML tree.
entity-name			The entity name of the associated class.

Continued

Attribute	Values	Default	Description
fetch	join, select		The mode in which the element will be retrieved (outer join, a series of selects, or a series of subselects). Only one member of the enclosing class can be retrieved by outer join.
foreign-key			The name to assign to the foreign key enforcing the relationship.
formula			Allows the value to which the associated class maps its foreign key to be overridden using an SQL formula.
lazy	true, false		Overrides the entity-loading mode.
name			Assigns a name to the entity (required in dynamic mappings).
node			Specifies the name of the XML element or attribute that should be used by the XML relational persistence features.
outer join	true, false, auto		Specifies whether an outer join should be used.
property-ref			Specifies the column in the target entity's table that the foreign key references. If the referenced table's foreign key does not reference the primary key of the "many" end of the relationship, then property-ref can be used to specify the column that it references. This should only be the case for legacy designs—when creating a new schema, your foreign keys should always reference the primary key of the related table.

You would select a primary key association when you do not want an additional table column to relate the two entities. The master of the two entities takes a normal primary key generator, and its one-to-one mapping entry will typically have the attribute name and associated class specified only. The slave entity will be mapped similarly, but must have the constrained attribute setting applied to ensure that the relationship is recognized.

Because the slave class's primary key must be identical to that allocated to the master, it is given the special id generator type of foreign. On the slave end, the <id> and <one-to-one> elements will therefore look like this:

```
<id name="id" column="product">
   <generator class="foreign">
      <param name="property">campaign</param>
   </generator>
</id>

<one-to-one name="campaign"
   class="com.hibernatebook.xmlmapping.Campaign"
   constrained="true"/>
```

There are some limitations to this approach: it cannot be used on the receiving end of a many-to-one relationship (even when the "many" end of the association is limited by a unique constraint), and the slave entity cannot be the slave of more than one entity.

In these circumstances, you will need to declare the master end of the association as a uniquely constrained one-to-many association. The slave entity's table will then need to take a foreign key column associating it with the master's primary key. The `property-ref` attribute setting is used to declare this relationship, like so:

```
<one-to-one
   name="campaign"
   class="com.hibernatebook.xmlmapping.Campaign"
   property-ref="product"/>
```

The format used in this example is the most common. The body of the element consists of an infrequently used optional element:

```
(meta* | formula*)
```

We discuss the `<many-to-many>` element and the alternative approach of composition in some detail in the "Mapping Collections" section later in this chapter.

The <many-to-one> Element

The many-to-one association describes the relationship in which multiple instances of one class can reference a single instance of another class. This enforces a relational rule for which the "many" class has a foreign key into the (usually primary) unique key of the "one" class. Table 7-9 shows the attributes permissible for the `<many-to-one>` element.

Table 7-9. The `<many-to-one>` Attributes

Attribute	Values	Default	Description
access			Specifies how the class member should be accessed: `field` for direct field access, or `attribute` for access via the get and set methods.
cascade			Determines how changes to the parent entity will affect the linked relation.
class			The property type of the attribute or field (if omitted, this will be determined by reflection).
column			The column containing the identifier of the target entity (i.e., the foreign key from this entity into the mapped one).
embed-xml	true, false		When using XML relational persistence, indicates whether the XML tree for the associated entity itself, or only its identifier, will appear in the generated XML tree.
entity-name			The name of the associated entity.
fetch	join, select		The mode in which the element will be retrieved (`outer join`, a series of `select`s, or a series of `subselect`s). Only one member of the enclosing class can be retrieved by `outer join`.
foreign-key			The name of the foreign key constraint to generate for this association.
formula			An arbitrary SQL expression to use in place of the normal primary key relationship between the entities.
index			The name of the index to be applied to the foreign key column in the parent table representing the "many" side of the association.
insert	true, false	true	Indicates whether the field can be persisted. When set to `false`, this prevents inserts if the field has already been mapped as part of a `composite` identifier or some other attribute.
lazy	false, proxy, noproxy		Overrides the entity-loading mode.

Attribute	Values	Default	Description
name			The (mandatory) name of the attribute. This should start with a lowercase letter.
node			Specifies the name of the XML element or attribute that should be used by the XML relational persistence features.
not-found	exception, ignore	exception	The behavior to exhibit if the related entity does not exist (either throw an exception or ignore the problem).
not-null	true, false	false	Specifies whether a `not-null` constraint should be applied to this column.
optimistic-lock	true, false	true	Specifies whether optimistic locking should be used.
outer-join	true, false, auto		Specifies whether an outer join should be used.
property-ref			Specifies the column in the target entity's table that the foreign key references. If the referenced table's foreign key does not reference the primary key of the "many" end of the relationship, then `property-ref` can be used to specify the column that it references. This should only be the case for legacy designs—when creating a new schema, your foreign keys should always reference the primary key of the related table.
unique	true, false	false	Specifies whether a `unique` constraint should be applied to the column.
unique-key			Groups the columns together by this attribute value. Represents columns across which a unique key constraint should be generated (not yet supported in the schema generation).
update	true, false	true	When set to `false`, prevents updates if the field has already been mapped elsewhere.

If a `unique` constraint is specified on a many-to-one relationship, it is effectively converted into a one-to-one relationship. This approach is preferred over creating a one-to-one association, both because it results in a simpler mapping and because it requires less intrusive changes to the database should it become desirable to relax the one-to-one association into a many-to-one.

This element has a small number of optional daughter elements—the `<column>` element will be required when a composite key has to be specified:

```
(meta*, (column | formula)*)
```

The following mapping from the `User` class XML file illustrates the creation of a simple many-to-one association between a `User` class and an `Email` class: each user can have only one e-mail address—but an e-mail address can belong to more than one user.

```
<many-to-one
    name="email"
    class="com.hibernatebook.xmlmapping.Email"
    column="email"
    cascade="all" unique="true"/>
```

The simplest approach to creating a many-to-one relationship, as shown in the previous example, requires two tables and a foreign key dependency. An alternative is to use a link table to combine the two entities. The link table contains the appropriate foreign keys referencing the two tables associated with both of the entities in the association. The following code shows the mapping of a many-to-one relationship via a link table.

```
<join table="link_email_user" inverse="true" optional="false">
    <key column="user_id"/>
    <many-to-one name="email" column="email_id" not-null="true"/>
</join>
```

The disadvantage of the link table approach is its slightly poorer performance (it requires a join of three tables to retrieve the associations, rather than one). Its benefit is that it requires less extreme changes to the schema if the relationship is modified—typically, changes would be made to the link table, rather than to one of the entity tables.

The Collection Elements

These are the elements that are required for you to include an attribute in your class that represents any of the collection classes. For example, if you have an attribute of type **Set**, then you will need to use a `<bag>` or `<set>` element to represent its relationship with the database.

Because of the simplicity of the object-oriented relationship involved, where one object has an attribute capable of containing many objects, it is a common fallacy to assume that the relationship must be expressed as a one-to-many. In practice, however, this will almost always be easiest to express as a many-to-many relationship, where an additional link table closely corresponds with the role of the collection itself. See the "Mapping Collections" section later in this chapter for a more detailed illustration of this.

All the collection mapping elements share the attributes shown in Table 7-10.

Table 7-10. *The Attributes Common to the Collection Elements*

Attribute	Values	Default	Description
Access			Specifies how the class member should be accessed: `field` for direct field access or `attribute` for access via the get and set methods.
batch-size			Specifies the number of items that can be batched together when retrieving instances of the class by identifier.
cascade			Determines how changes to the parent entity will affect the linked relation.
catalog			The database catalog against which the queries should apply.
collection-type			When using a collection class other than one of the standard Java collection classes, specify an implementation of the `UserCollectionType` class describing the collection type to be used in place of the defaults.
check			The SQL to create a multirow check constraint for schema generation.
embed-xml	true, false		When using XML relational persistence, indicates whether the XML tree for the associated entity itself, or only its identifier, will appear in the generated XML tree.
fetch	join, select		The mode in which the element will be retrieved (`outer-join`, a series of `select`s, or a series of `subselect`s). Only one member of the enclosing class can be retrieved by `outer-join`.
lazy	true, false		Can be used to disable or enable lazy fetching against the enclosing mapping's default.
mutable	true, false	true	Can be used to flag that a class is mutable (allowing Hibernate to make some performance optimizations when dealing with these classes).
name			The (mandatory) name of the attribute. This should start with a lowercase letter.

Continued

Attribute	Values	Default	Description
node			Specifies the name of the XML element or attribute that should be used by the XML relational persistence features.
optimistic-lock	true, false	true	Specifies the optimistic locking strategy to use.
outer-join	true, false, auto		Specifies whether an outer join should be used.
persister			Allows a custom `ClassPersister` object to be used when persisting this class.
schema			The database schema against which queries should apply.
subselect			A query to enforce a subselection of the contents of the underlying table. A class can only use a `subselect` if it is immutable and read-only (because the SQL defined here cannot be reversed). Generally, the use of a database view is preferable.
table			The name of the table in which the associated entity is stored.
where			An arbitrary SQL `where` clause limiting the linked entities.

The set Collection

A `set` collection allows collection attributes derived from the `Set` interface to be persisted.

In addition to the common collection mappings, the `<set>` element offers the `inverse`, `order-by`, and `sort` attributes, as shown in Table 7-11.

Table 7-11. *The Additional* `<set>` *Attributes*

Attribute	Values	Default	Description
inverse	true, false	false	Specifies that an entity is the opposite navigable end of a relationship expressed in another entity's mapping.
order-by			Specifies an arbitrary SQL `order by` clause to constrain the results returned by the SQL query that populates the `set` collection.
sort			Specifies the collection class sorting to be used. The value can be `unsorted`, `natural`, or any `Comparator` class.

The child elements of the `<set>` element are as follows:

```
(meta*,
 subselect?,
 cache?,
 synchronize*,
 comment?,
 key,
 (element | one-to-many | many-to-many |
  composite-element | many-to-any),
 loader?,
 sql-insert?,
 sql-update?,
 sql-delete?,
 sql-delete-all?,
 filter*)
```

The following code shows an implementation of mapping a set of strings into a property called `titles`:

```
<set name="titles" table="nameset">
   <key column="titleid"/>
   <element type="string" column="name" not-null="true"/>
</set>
```

A typical implementation, however, also maps other entity model classes from your application into the collection. Here we map **Phone** entities from the "many" side of a one-to-many association into a **Set** property, called **phoneNumbers**, that belongs to a **User** entity:

```
<set name="phoneNumbers">
   <key column="aduser"/>
   <one-to-many class="sample.Phone"/>
</set>
```

If the Phone class contains a reference to a User object, it is not automatically clear whether this constitutes a pair of unrelated associations or two halves of the same association—a bidirectional association. When a bidirectional association is to be established, one side must be selected as the owner (in a one-to-many or many-to-one association, it must always be the "many" side), and the other will be marked as being the inverse half of the relationship. See the discussion of unidirectional and bidirectional associations at the end of Chapter 4. The following code shows a mapping of a one-to-many relationship as a reverse association.

```
<set name="phoneNumbers" inverse="true">
    <key column="aduser"/>
    <one-to-many class="sample.Phone"/>
</set>
```

The list Collection

A list collection allows collection attributes derived from the List interface to be persisted.

In addition to the common collection mappings, the <list> element offers the inverse attribute, as shown in Table 7-12.

Table 7-12. The Additional <list> Attribute

Attribute	Values	Default	Description
inverse	true, false	false	Specifies that an entity is the opposite navigable end of a relationship expressed in another entity's mapping

The child elements of the <list> element are as follows:

```
(meta*,
 subselect?,
 cache?,
 synchronize*,
 comment?,
 key,
 (index | list-index),
 (element | one-to-many | many-to-many |
  composite-element | many-to-any),
 loader?,
 sql-insert?,
 sql-update?,
 sql-delete?,
 sql-delete-all?,
 filter*)
```

A typical implementation of a `list` mapping is as follows:

```
<list name="list" table="namelist">
   <key column="fooid"/>
   <index column="position"/>
   <element type="string" column="name" not-null="true"/>
</list>
```

The idbag Collection

An `idbag` collection allows for appropriate use of collection attributes derived from the `List` interface. A `bag` data structure permits unordered storage of unordered items, and permits duplicates. Because the collection classes do not provide a native `bag` implementation, classes derived from the `List` interface tend to be used as a substitute. The imposition of ordering imposed by a `list` is not itself a problem, but the implementation code can become dependent upon the ordering information.

`idbag` usually maps to a `List`. However, by managing its database representation with a surrogate key, you can make the performance of updates and deletions of items in a collection defined with `idbag` dramatically better than with an unkeyed `bag` (described at the end of this section). Hibernate does not provide a mechanism for obtaining the identifier of a row in the `bag`.

In addition to the common collection mappings, the `<idbag>` element offers the `order-by` element, as shown in Table 7-13.

Table 7-13. The Additional `<idbag>` Attribute

Attribute	Values	Default	Description
order-by			Specifies an arbitrary SQL `order by` clause to constrain the results returned by the SQL query that populates the collection

The child elements of the `<idbag>` element are as follows:

```
(meta*,
 subselect?,
 cache?,
 synchronize*,
 comment?,
 collection-id,
 key,
 (element | many-to-many |
  composite-element | many-to-any),
 loader?,
 sql-insert?,
 sql-update?,
 sql-delete?,
 sql-delete-all?,
 filter*)
```

A typical implementation of an **idbag** mapping is as follows:

```
<idbag name="idbag" table="nameidbag">
   <collection-id column="id" type="int">
      <generator class="native"/>
   </collection-id>

   <key column="fooid"/>
   <element type="string" column="name" not-null="true"/>
</idbag>
```

The map Collection

A map collection allows collection attributes derived from the Map interface to be persisted.

In addition to the common collection mappings, the <map> element offers the inverse, order-by, and sort attributes, as shown in Table 7-14.

Table 7-14. The Additional <map> Attributes

Attribute	Values	Default	Description
inverse	true, false	false	Specifies that this entity is the opposite navigable end of a relationship expressed in another entity's mapping
order-by			Specifies an arbitrary SQL order by clause to constrain the results returned by the SQL query that populates the map
sort		unsorted	Specifies the collection class sorting to be used. The value can be unsorted, natural, or any Comparator class

The child elements of the <map> element are as follows:

```
(meta*,
 subselect?,
 cache?,
 synchronize*,
 comment?,
 key,
 (map-key | composite-map-key | map-key-many-to-many |
  index | composite-index | index-many-to-many |
  index-many-to-any),
 (element | one-to-many | many-to-many | composite-element |
  many-to-any),
 loader?,
 sql-insert?,
 sql-update?,
```

```
 sql-delete?,
 sql-delete-all?,
 filter*)
```

A typical implementation of the mapping is as follows:

```
<map name="map" table="namemap">
   <key column="fooid"/>
   <index column="name" type="string"/>
   <element column="value" type="string" not-null="true"/>
</map>
```

The bag Collection

If your class represents data using a class derived from the List interface, but you do not want to maintain an index column to keep track of the order of items, you can optionally use the bag collection mapping to achieve this. The order in which the items are stored and retrieved from a bag is completely ignored.

Although the bag's table does not contain enough information to determine the order of its contents prior to persistence into the table, it *is* possible to apply an order by clause to the SQL used to obtain the contents of the bag so that it has a natural sorted order as it is acquired. This will not be honored at other times during the lifetime of the object.

If the <bag> elements lack a proper key, there will be a performance impact that will manifest itself when update or delete operations are performed on the contents of the bag.

In addition to the common collection mappings, the <bag> element therefore offers the order-by as well as the inverse attribute, as shown in Table 7-15.

Table 7-15. The Additional <bag> Attributes

Attribute	Values	Default	Description
inverse	true, false	false	Specifies that an entity is the opposite navigable end of a relationship expressed in another entity's mapping
order-by			Specifies an arbitrary SQL order by clause to constrain the results returned by the SQL query that populates the collection

The child elements of the <bag> element are as follows:

```
(meta*,
 subselect?,
 cache?,
 synchronize*,
 comment?,
 key,
 (element | one-to-many | many-to-many |
  composite-element | many-to-any),
```

```
loader?,
sql-insert?,
sql-update?,
sql-delete?,
sql-delete-all?,
filter*)
```

A typical implementation of a **bag** mapping is as f is as follows:

```
<bag name="bag" table="namebag">
   <key column="fooid"/>
   <element column="value" type="string" not-null="true"/>
</bag>
```

Mapping Simple Classes

Figure 7-1 shows the class diagram and entity relationship diagram for a simple class. They are as straightforward as you would expect.

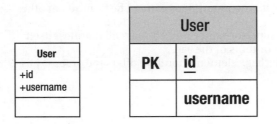

Figure 7-1. *Representing a simple class*

The elements discussed so far are sufficient to map a basic class into a single table, as shown in Listing 7-3.

Listing 7-3. *A Simple Class to Represent a User*

```
package com.hibernatebook.xmlmapping;

public class User {

   public User(String username) {
      this.username = username;
   }

   User() {
   }
```

```java
public int getId() {
   return id;
}

public String getUsername() {
   return username;
}

public void setId(int id) {
   this.id = id;
}

public void setUsername(String username) {
   this.username = username;
}

// We will map the id to the table's primary key
private int id = -1;

// We will map the username into a column in the table
private String username;
}
```

It's pretty easy to see that we might want to represent the class in Listing 7-3 in a table with the format shown in Table 7-16.

Table 7-16. Mapping a Simple Class to a Simple Table

Column	Type
Id	Integer
Username	Varchar(32)

The mapping between the two is, thus, similarly straightforward:

```xml
<?xml version='1.0' encoding='utf-8'?>
<!DOCTYPE hibernate-mapping
   PUBLIC "-//Hibernate/Hibernate Mapping DTD//EN"
   "http://hibernate.sourceforge.net/hibernate-mapping-3.0.dtd">

<hibernate-mapping>
   <class name="book.hibernatebook.chapter06.User">

      <id name="id" type="int">
         <generator class="native"/>
      </id>
```

```
    <property name="username" type="string" length="32"/>

  </class>
</hibernate-mapping>
```

Aside from the very limited number of properties maintained by the class, this is a pretty common mapping type, so it is reassuring to see that it can be managed with a minimal number of elements (`<hibernate-mapping>`, `<class>`, `<id>`, `<generator>`, and `<property>`).

Mapping Composition

Figure 7-2 shows the class diagram and the entity relationship diagram for a composition relationship between two classes. Here, the `Advert` class is composed of a `Picture` class in addition to its normal value types.

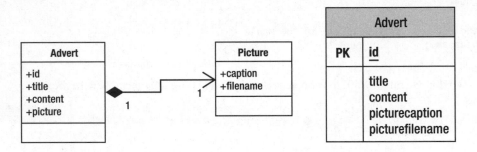

Figure 7-2. Representing composition

Composition is the strongest form of aggregation—in which the life cycle of each object is dependent upon the life cycle of the whole. Although Java does not make the distinction between other types of aggregation and composition, it becomes relevant when we choose to store the components in the database, because the most efficient and natural way to do this is to store them in the same table.

In our example, we will look at an `Advert` class that has this relationship with a `Picture` class. The idea is that our advert is always going to be associated with a picture (see Listings 7-4 and 7-5). In these circumstances, there is a clear one-to-one relationship that could be represented between two distinct tables, but which is more efficiently represented with one.

Listing 7-4. The Class Representing the Picture

```
package com.hibernatebook.xmlmapping;

public class Picture {
    public Picture(String caption, String filename) {
        this.caption = caption;
        this.filename = filename;
    }
```

```
    Picture() {
    }

    public String getCaption() {
        return this.caption;
    }

    public String getFilename() {
        return this.filename;
    }

    public void setCaption(String title) {
        this.caption = title;
    }

    public void setFilename(String filename) {
        this.filename = filename;
    }

    private String caption;
    private String filename;
}
```

Listing 7-5. The Class Representing the Advert

```
package com.hibernatebook.xmlmapping;

public class Advert {
    public Advert(String title, String content, Picture picture) {
        this.title = title;
        this.content = content;
        this.picture = picture;
    }

    Advert() {
    }

    public int getId() {
        return id;
    }

    public String getTitle() {
        return this.title;
    }

    public String getContent() {
        return this.content;
    }
```

```java
    public Picture getPicture() {
        return this.picture;
    }

    public void setId(int id) {
        this.id = id;
    }

    public void setTitle(String title) {
        this.title = title;
    }

    public void setContent(String content) {
        this.content = content;
    }

    public void setPicture(Picture picture) {
        this.picture = picture;
    }

    private int id = -1;
    private String title;
    private String content;
    private Picture picture;
}
```

Again, Hibernate manages to express this simple relationship with a correspondingly simple mapping file. We introduce the **component** entity for this association. Here it is in use:

```xml
<?xml version='1.0' encoding='utf-8'?>
<!DOCTYPE hibernate-mapping
    PUBLIC "-//Hibernate/Hibernate Mapping DTD//EN"
    "http://hibernate.sourceforge.net/hibernate-mapping-3.0.dtd">

<class name="com.hibernatebook.xmlmapping.Advert">
    <id name="id" type="int">
        <generator class="native"/>
    </id>
    <property name="title" type="string" length="255"/>
    <property name="content" type="text"/>
    <component name="picture" class="com.hibernatebook.xmlmapping.Picture">
        <property name="caption" type="string" length="255"/>
        <property name="filename" type="string" length="32"/>
    </component>
</class>
```

In this example, we use the `<property>` element to describe the relationship between `Picture` and its attributes. In fact, this is true of all of the rest of the elements of `<class>`—a `<component>` element can even contain more `<component>` elements. Of course, this makes perfect sense, since a component usually corresponds with a Java class.

Mapping Other Associations

In Figure 7-3, the `Advert` class includes an instance of a `Picture` class. The relationship in the tables is represented with the `Picture` table having a foreign key onto the `Advert` table.

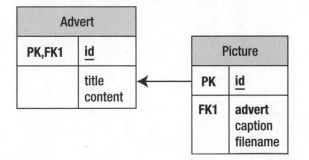

Figure 7-3.Mapping an aggregation or composition relationship

A one-to-one correspondence does not absolutely require you to incorporate both parties into the same table. There are often good reasons not to. For instance, in the `Picture` example, it is entirely possible that while the initial implementation will permit only one `Picture` per `Advert`, a future implementation will relax this relationship. Consider this scenario from the perspective of the database for a moment (see Table 7-17).

Table 7-17. The `Advert` Table

Id	Title	Contents	PictureCaption	PictureFilename
1	Bike	Bicycle for sale	My bike (you can ride it if you like)	advert001.jpg
2	Sofa	Sofa, comfy but used	Chesterfield sofa	advert002.jpg
3	Car	Shabby MGF for sale	MGF VVC (BRG)	advert003.jpg

If we want to allow the advert for the sofa to include another picture, we would have to duplicate some of the data, or include null columns. It would probably be preferable to set up a pair of tables: one to represent the adverts, and one to represent the distinct tables (as shown in Tables 7-18 and 7-19).

Table 7-18. The Refined Advert Table

Id	Title	Contents
1	Bike	Bicycle for sale
2	Sofa	Sofa, comfy but used
3	Car	Shabby MGF for sale

Table 7-19. The Picture Table

Id	Advert	Caption	Filename
1	1	My bike (you can ride it if you like)	advert001.jpg
2	2	Chesterfield sofa	advert002.jpg
3	3	MGF VVC (BRG)	advert003.jpg

If we decide (considering the database only) to allow additional pictures, we can then include extra rows in the Picture table without duplicating any data unnecessarily (see Table 7-20).

Table 7-20. The Picture Table with Multiple Pictures per Advert

Id	Advert	Caption	Filename
1	1	My bike (you can ride it if you like)	advert001.jpg
2	2	Chesterfield sofa	advert002.jpg
3	2	Back of sofa	advert003.jpg
4	3	MGF VVC (BRG)	advert004.jpg

With the single Advert table, the query to extract the data necessary to materialize an instance of the Advert consists of something like this:

```
select id,title,contents,picturecaption,picturefilename from advert where id = 1
```

It is obvious here that a single row will be returned, since we are carrying out the selection on the primary key.

Once we split things into two tables, we have a slightly more ambiguous pair of queries:

```
select id,title,contents from advert where id = 1
select id,caption,filename from picture where advert = 1
```

While Hibernate is not under any particular obligation to use this pair of SQL instructions to retrieve the data (it could reduce it to a join on the table pair), it is the easiest way of thinking about the data we are going to retrieve. While the first query of the two is required to return a single row, this is not true for the second query—if we have added multiple pictures, we will get multiple rows back.

In these circumstances, there is very little difference between a one-to-one relationship and a one-to-many relationship, except from a business perspective. That is to say, we choose not to associate an advert with multiple pictures, even though we have that option.

This, perhaps, explains why the expression of a one-to-one relationship in Hibernate is usually carried out via a many-to-one mapping. If you do not find that persuasive, remember that a foreign key relationship, which is the relationship that the `advert` column in the `Picture` table has with the `id` column in the `Advert` table, is a many-to-one relationship between the entities.

In our example, the `Picture` table will be maintaining the `advert` column as a foreign key into the `Advert` table, so this must be expressed as a many-to-one relationship with the `Advert` object (see Listing 7-6).

Listing 7-6. The New Picture Mapping

```xml
<?xml version='1.0' encoding='utf-8'?>
<!DOCTYPE hibernate-mapping
    PUBLIC "-//Hibernate/Hibernate Mapping DTD//EN"
    "http://hibernate.sourceforge.net/hibernate-mapping-3.0.dtd">

<class name="com.hibernatebook.xmlmapping.Picture">
    <id name="id" type="int">
        <generator class="native"/>
    </id>
    <many-to-one
      name="advert"
      class="com.hibernatebook.xmlmapping.Advert"
      column="advert"/>
    <property name="caption" type="string" length="255"/>
    <property name="filename" type="string" length="32"/>
</class>
```

If you still object to the many-to-one relationship, you will probably find it cathartic to note that we have explicitly constrained this relationship with the `unique` attribute. You will also find it reassuring that in order to make navigation possible directly from the `Advert` to its associated `Picture`, we can in fact use a one-to-one mapping entry. We need to be able to navigate in this direction because we expect to retrieve adverts from the database, and then display their associated pictures (see Listing 7-7).

Listing 7-7. The Revised Advert Mapping

```xml
<?xml version='1.0' encoding='utf-8'?>
<!DOCTYPE hibernate-mapping
    PUBLIC "-//Hibernate/Hibernate Mapping DTD//EN"
    "http://hibernate.sourceforge.net/hibernate-mapping-3.0.dtd">

<class name="com.hibernatebook.xmlmapping.Advert">
    <id name="id" type="int">
        <generator class="native"/>
    </id>
    <property name="title" type="string" length="255"/>
    <property name="content" type="text"/>
    <one-to-one name="picture"
                class="com.hibernatebook.xmlmapping.Picture"
                property-ref="picture">
</class>
```

Now that we have seen how one-to-one and many-to-one relationships are expressed, we will see how a many-to-many relationship can be expressed.

Mapping Collections

In Figure 7-4, we show the **User** objects as having an unknown number of **Advert** instances. In the database, this is then represented with three tables, one of which is a link table between the two entity tables.

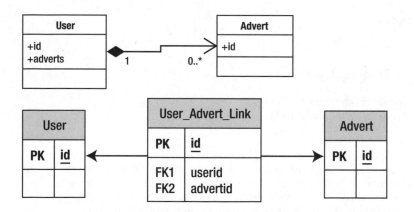

Figure 7-4. Mapping collections

The Java collection classes provide the most elegant mechanism for expressing the "many" end of a many-to-many relationship in our own classes:

```
public Set getAdverts();
```

If we use generics, we can give an even more precise specification:

```
public Set<Advert> getAdverts();
```

■ **Note** A lot of legacy code will not use generics. However, if you have the opportunity you should do so, as it allows you to make this sort of distinction clear at the API level, instead of at the documentation level. Hibernate 3 is compatible with generics.

Of course, we can place values (of `Object` type) into collections as well as entities, and Java 5 introduced autoboxing so that we have the illusion of being able to place primitives into them as well.

```
List<Integer> ages = getAges();
int first = ages.get(0);
```

The only catch with collection mapping is that an additional table may be required to correctly express the relationship between the owning table and the collection. Table 7-21 shows how it should be done; the entity table contains only its own attributes.

Table 7-21. The `Entity` Table

Id	Name
1	Entity 1

A separate collection table, on the other hand, contains the actual values (see Table 7-22). In this case, we are linking a `List` to the owning entity, so we need to include a column to represent the position of the values in the list, as well as the foreign key into the owning entity and the column for the actual values that are contained within the collection.

Table 7-22. `ListTable`

entityid	positionInList	listValue
1	1	Good
1	2	Bad
1	3	Indifferent

In a legacy schema, you may quite often encounter a situation in which all the values have been retained within a single table (see Table 7-23).

Table 7-23. EntityTable

Id	Name	positionInList	listValue
1	Entity 1	1	Good
1	Entity 1	2	Bad
1	Entity 1	3	Indifferent

It should be obvious that this is not just poor design from Hibernate's perspective—it's also bad relational design. The values in the entity's name attribute have been duplicated needlessly, so this is not a properly normalized table. We also break the foreign key of the table, and need to form a compound key of id and positionInList. Overall, this is a poor design, and we encourage you to use a second table if at all possible. If you must work with such an existing design, see Chapter 13 for some techniques for approaching this type of problem.

If your collection is going to contain entity types instead of value types, the approach is essentially the same, but your second table will contain keys into the second entity table instead of value types. This changes the combination of tables into the situation shown in the entity relationship diagram (see Figure 7-4), in which we have a link table joining two major tables into a many-to-many relationship. This is a very familiar pattern in properly normalized relational schemas.

The following code shows a mapping of a Set attribute representing the adverts with which the User class is associated:

```
<set name="adverts"
     table="user_advert_link"
     cascade="save-update">
  <key column="userid"/>
  <many-to-many
     class="com.hibernatebook.xmlmapping.Advert"
     column="advertid"/>
</set>
```

Hibernate's use of collections tends to expose the lazy loading issues more than most other mappings. If you enable lazy loading, the collection that you retrieve from the session will be a proxy implementing the relevant collection interface (in our example, Set), rather than one of the usual Java concrete collection implementations.

This allows Hibernate to retrieve the contents of the collection only as they are required by the user. If you load an entity, consult a single item from the collection, and then discard it, often only a handful of SQL operations will be required. If the collection in question represents hundreds of entity instances, the performance advantages of lazy loading (compared with the massive task of reading in *all* of the entities concerned) are massive.

However, you will need to ensure that you do not try to access the contents of a lazily loaded collection at a time when it is no longer associated with the session, unless you can be certain that the contents of the collection that you are accessing have already been loaded.

Mapping Inheritance Relationships

Figure 7-5 shows a simple class hierarchy. The superclass is `Advert`, and there are two classes derived from this: a `Personal` class to represent personal advertisements and a `Property` class to represent property advertisements.

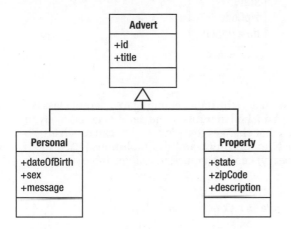

Figure 7-5. *A simple inheritance hierarchy*

Hibernate can represent inheritance relationships in a relational schema in three ways, each mapped in a slightly different way. These are as follows:

- One table for each concrete class implementation

- One table for each subclass (including interfaces and abstract classes)

- One table for each class hierarchy

Each of these techniques has different costs and benefits, so we will show you an example mapping from each and discuss some of these issues.

One Table per Concrete Class

This approach is the easiest to implement. You map each of the concrete classes as normal, writing mapping elements for each of its persistent properties (including those that are inherited). No mapping files are required for interfaces and abstract classes.

Figure 7-6 shows the schema required to represent the hierarchy from Figure 7-5 using this technique.

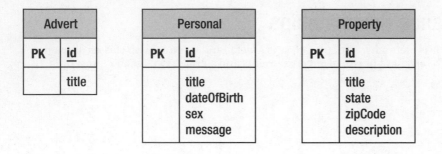

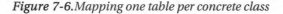

Figure 7-6. Mapping one table per concrete class

While this is easy to create, there are several disadvantages; the data belonging to a parent class is scattered across a number of different tables, so a query couched in terms of the parent class is likely to cause a large number of select operations. It also means that changes to a parent class can touch an awful lot of tables. We suggest that you file this approach under "quick-and-dirty solutions."

Listing 7-8 demonstrates how a derived class (**Property**) can be mapped to a single table independently of its superclass ((**Advert**).

Listing 7-8. Mapping a **Property** *Advert with the One-Table-per-Concrete-Class Approach*

```
<hibernate-mapping>
    <class name="com.hibernatebook.xmlmapping.Property">
        <id name="id" type="int">
            <generator class="native"/>
        </id>
        <property name="title" type="string" length="255"/>
        <property name="state" type="string"/>
        <property name="zipCode" type="string"/>
        <property name="description" type="string"/>
    </class>
</hibernate-mapping>
```

One Table per Subclass

A slightly more complex mapping is to provide one table for each class in the hierarchy, including the abstract and interface classes. The pure "is a" relationship of our class hierarchy is then converted into a "has a" relationship for each entity in the schema.

Figure 7-7 shows the schema required to represent the hierarchy from Figure 7-5 using this technique.

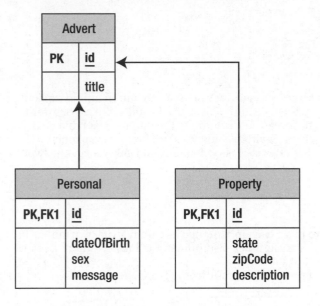

Figure 7-7.Mapping one table per subclass

We like this approach, as it is conceptually easy to manage, does not require complex changes to the schema when a single parent class is modified, and is similar to how most JVMs manage the same data behind the scenes.

The disadvantage of this approach is that while it works well from an object-oriented point of view, and is correct from a relational point of view, it can result in poor performance. As the hierarchy grows, the number of joins required to construct a leaf class also grows.

The technique works well for shallow inheritance hierarchies. Deep inheritance hierarchies are often a symptom of poorly designed code, so you may want to reconsider your application architecture before abandoning this technique. In our opinion, it should be preferred until performance issues are substantially proven to be an issue.

Listing 7-9 shows how you can map a derived class (**Property**) as a table joined to another representing the superclass (**Advert**).

*Listing 7-9. Mapping a **Property** Advert with the One-Table-per-Subclass Approach*

```
<hibernate-mapping>
    <joined-subclass
        name="com.hibernatebook.xmlmapping.Property"
        extends="com.hibernatebook.xmlmapping.Advert">

        <key column="advertid"/>
```

```
        <property name="state" type="string"/>
        <property name="zipCode" type="string"/>
        <property name="description" type="string"/>
    </joined-subclass>
</hibernate-mapping>
```

Note in the mapping that we replace `class` with `joined-subclass` to associate our mapping explicitly with the parent. You specify the entity that is being extended and replace the `id` and `title` classes from the subclass with a single key element that maps the foreign key column to the parent class table's primary key. Otherwise, the `<joined-subclass>` element is virtually identical to the `<class>` element. Note, however, that a `<joined-subclass>` cannot contain `<subclass>` elements and vice versa—the two strategies are not compatible.

One Table per Class Hierarchy

The last of the inheritance mapping strategies is to place each inheritance hierarchy in its own table. The fields from each of the child classes are added to this table, and a discriminator column contains a key to identify the base type represented by each row in the table.

Figure 7-8 shows the schema required to represent the hierarchy from Figure 7-5 using this technique.

Advert	
PK	<u>id</u>
	title advertType dateOfBirth sex message state zipCode description

Figure 7-8. *Mapping one table per hierarchy*

This technique offers the best performance—for simple queries on simple classes even in the deepest of inheritance hierarchies, a single select may suffice to gather all the fields to populate the entity.

Conversely, this is not a satisfying representation of the attribute. Changes to members of the hierarchy will usually require a column to be altered, added, or deleted from the table. This will often be a very slow operation. As the hierarchy grows (horizontally as well as vertically), so too will the number of columns required by this table.

Each mapped subclass must specify the class that it extends and a value that can be used to discriminate this subclass from the other classes held in the same table. Thus, this is known as the discriminator value, and is mapped with a `discriminator-value` attribute in the `<subclass>` element (see Listing 7-10).

Listing 7-10. Mapping a `Property` Advert with the One-Table-per-Class-Hierarchy Approach

```
<hibernate-mapping>
  <subclass
     name="com.hibernatebook.xmlmapping.Property"
     extends="com.hibernatebook.xmlmapping.Advert"
     discriminator-value="property">

     <property name="state" type="string"/>
     <property name="zipCode" type="string"/>
     <property name="description" type="string"/>
  </subclass>
</hibernate-mapping>
```

Note that this also requires the specification of a discriminator column for the root of the class hierarchy, from which the discriminator values identifying the types of the child classes can be obtained (see Listing 7-11).

Listing 7-11. The Addition to `Advert.hbm.xml` Required to Support a One-Table-per-Class-Hierarchy Approach

```
<discriminator column="advertType" type="string"/>
```

A subclass mapping cannot contain `<joined-subclass>` elements and vice versa—the two strategies are not compatible.

More Exotic Mappings

The Hibernate mapping DTD is large. We have discussed the core set of mappings that you will use on a day-to-day basis; but before we move on, we will take a very quick tour around four of the more interesting remaining mapping types.

The any Tag

The any tag represents a polymorphic association between the attribute and several entity classes. The mapping is expressed in the schema with a column to specify the type of the related entity, and then columns for the identifier of the related entity.

Because a proper foreign key cannot be specified (being dependent upon multiple tables), this is not the generally recommended technique for making polymorphic associations. When possible, use the techniques described in the previous "Mapping Inheritance Relationships" section.

The array Tag

The **array** tag represents the innate array feature of the Java language. The syntax of this is virtually identical to that used for the **List** collection class, and we recommend the use of **List** except when primitive values are to be stored, or when you are constrained by an existing application architecture to work with arrays.

The <dynamic-component> Element

While the full-blown **dynamic** class approach (discussed briefly in the "Entities" section at the beginning of the chapter) is really only suitable for prototyping exercises, the dynamic component technique allows some of that flexibility in a package that reflects some legitimate techniques.

The **<dynamic-component>** element permits you to place any of the items that can be mapped with the normal **<component>** element into a map with a given key. For example, we could obtain and combine several items of information relating to an entity's ownership into a single **Map** with named elements, as follows:

```
<dynamic-component name="ownership">
    <property name="user" type="string" column="user"/>
    <many-to-one
        name="person"
        class="com.hibernatebook.xmlmapping.Person"
        column="person_id"/>
</dynamic-component>
```

The code to access this information in the entity is then very familiar:

```
Map map = entity.getOwnership();
System.out.println(map.get("user"));
System.out.println(map.get("person"));
```

The output would then be as follows:

```
dcminter
person: { "Dave Minter", 33, "5'10" }
```

Summary

This chapter has covered the data types supported by Hibernate 3: entities, values, and components. You have seen how all three can be expressed in a mapping file, and how each relates to the underlying database schema. We have listed the attributes available to the major mapping elements, and we have discussed some detailed examples of the elements that you will use most frequently when working with Hibernate.

In the next chapter, we will look at how a client application communicates with the database representation of the entities by using the **Session** object.

CHAPTER 8

■ ■ ■

Using the Session

You may have noticed that the Session object is the central point of access to Hibernate functionality. We will now look at what it embodies and what that implies about how you should use it.

Sessions

From the examples in the earlier chapters, you will have noticed that a small number of classes dominate our interactions with Hibernate. Of these, Session is the linchpin.

The Session object is used to create new database entities, read in objects from the database, update objects in the database, and delete objects from the database. It allows you to manage the transaction boundaries of database access, and (in a pinch) it allows you to obtain a traditional JDBC connection object so that you can do things to the database that the Hibernate developers have not already considered in their existing design (precious little).

If you are familiar with the JDBC approach, it helps to think of a Session object as being somewhat like a JDBC connection, and the SessionFactory, which provides Session objects, as being somewhat like a ConnectionPool, which provides Connection objects. These similarities in roles are illustrated in Figure 8-1.

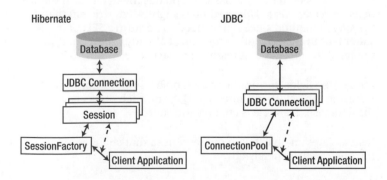

Figure 8-1. Similarities between Hibernate and JDBC objects

SessionFactory objects are expensive objects—needlessly duplicating them will cause problems quickly, and creating them is a relatively time-consuming process. Ideally, you should have a single SessionFactory for each database your application will access. SessionFactory objects are threadsafe, so it is not necessary to obtain one for each thread. However, you will create numerous Session objects—at least one for each thread using Hibernate. Sessions in Hibernate are not threadsafe, so sharing Session objects between threads could cause data loss or deadlock. In fact, you will often want to create multiple Session instances even during the lifetime of a specific thread (see the "Threads" section for concurrency issues).

■ **Caution** The analogy between a Hibernate session and a JDBC connection only goes so far. One important difference is that if a Hibernate Session object throws an exception of any sort, you must discard it and obtain a new one. This prevents data in the session's cache from becoming inconsistent with the database.

We've already covered the core methods in Chapter 4, so we won't discuss all the methods available to you through the Session interface. For an exhaustive look at what's available, you should read the API documentation on the Hibernate web site or in the Hibernate 3 download. Table 8-1 gives an overview of the various categories of methods available to you.

Table 8-1. Hibernate Method Summary

Method	Description
Create, Read, Update, and Delete	
save()	Saves an object to the database. This should not be called for an object that has already been saved to the database.
saveOrUpdate()	Saves an object to the database, or updates the database if the object already exists. This method is slightly less efficient than the save() method since it may need to perform a SELECT statement to check whether the object already exists, but it will not fail if the object has already been saved.
merge()	Merges the fields of a nonpersistent object into the appropriate persistent object (determined by ID). If no such object exists in the database, then one is created and saved.
persist()	Reassociates an object with the session so that changes made to the object will be persisted.
get()	Retrieves a specific object from the database by the object's identifier.

Method	Description
getEntityName()	Retrieves the entity name (this will usually be the same as the fully qualified class name of the POJO).
getIdentifier()	Determines the identifier—the object(s) representing the primary key—for a specific object associated with the session.
load()	Loads an object from the database by the object's identifier (you should use the get() methods if you are not certain that the object is in the database).
refresh()	Refreshes the state of an associated object from the database.
update()	Updates the database with changes to an object.
delete()	Deletes an object from the database.
createFilter()	Creates a filter (query) to narrow operations on the database.
enableFilter()	Enables a named filter in queries produced by createFilter().
disableFilter()	Disables a named filter.
getEnabledFilter()	Retrieves a currently enabled filter object.
createQuery()	Creates a Hibernate query to be applied to the database.
getNamedQuery()	Retrieves a query from the mapping file.
cancelQuery()	Cancels execution of any query currently in progress from another thread.
createCriteria()	Creates a criteria object for narrowing search results.

Transactions and Locking

Method	Description
beginTransaction()	Begins a transaction.
getTransaction()	Retrieves the current transaction object. This does not return null when no transaction is in progress. Instead, the active property of the returned object is false.
lock()	Gets a database lock for an object (or can be used like persist() if LockMode.NONE is given).

Continued

Method	Description
<u>Managing Resources</u>	
contains()	Determines whether a specific object is associated with the database.
clear()	Clears the session of all loaded instances and cancels any saves, updates, or deletions that have not been completed. Retains any iterators that are in use.
evict()	Disassociates an object from the session so that subsequent changes to it will not be persisted.
flush()	Flushes all pending changes into the database—all saves, updates, and deletions will be carried out; essentially, this synchronizes the session with the database.
isOpen()	Determines whether the session has been closed.
isDirty()	Determines whether the session is synchronized with the database.
getCacheMode()	Determines the caching mode currently employed.
setCacheMode()	Changes the caching mode currently employed.
getCurrentLockMode()	Determines the locking mode currently employed.
setFlushMode()	Determines the approach to flushing currently used. The options are to flush after every operation, flush when needed, never flush, or flush only on commit.
setReadOnly()	Marks a persistent object as read-only (or as writable). There are minor performance benefits from marking an object as read-only, but changes to its state will be ignored until it is marked as writable.
close()	Closes the session, and hence, the underlying database connection; releases other resources (such as the cache). You must not perform operations on the Session object after calling close().
getSessionFactory()	Retrieves a reference to the SessionFactory object that created the current Session instance.

Method	Description
The JDBC Connection	
connection()	Retrieves a reference to the underlying database connection.
disconnect()	Disconnects the underlying database connection.
reconnect()	Reconnects the underlying database connection.
isConnected()	Determines whether the underlying database connection is connected.

Transactions and Locking

Transactions and locking are intimately related—the locking techniques chosen to enforce a transaction can determine both the performance and likelihood of success of the transaction. The type of transaction selected dictates, to some extent, the type of locking that it must use.

You are not obliged to use transactions if they do not suit your needs, but there is rarely a good reason to avoid them. If you decide to avoid them, you will need to invoke the **flush()** method on the session at appropriate points to ensure that your changes are persisted to the database.

Transactions

A transaction is a unit of work guaranteed to behave as if you have exclusive use of the database. If you wrap your work in a transaction, the behavior of other system users will not affect your data. A transaction can be started, committed to write data to the database, or rolled back to remove all changes from the beginning onward (usually as the result of an error). To achieve this, you obtain a **Transaction** object from the database (beginning the transaction) and manipulate the session as shown in the following code:

```
Session session = factory.openSession();
try {
  session.beginTransaction();

  // Normal session usage here...

  session.getTransaction().commit();
} catch (HibernateException e) {
  Transaction tx = session.getTransaction();
  if (tx.isActive()) tx.rollback();
} finally {
  session.close();
}
```

In the real world, it's not actually desirable for all transactions to be fully ACID (see the sidebar entitled "The ACID Tests") because of the performance problems that this can cause.

Different database suppliers support and permit you to break the ACID rules to a lesser or greater extent, but the degree of control over the isolation rule is actually mandated by the SQL-92 standard. There are important reasons that you might want to break this rule, so both JDBC and Hibernate also make explicit allowances for it.

The Acid Tests

- *Atomicity*: A transaction should be all or nothing. If it fails to complete, the database will be left as if none of the operations had ever been performed—this is known as a *rollback*.

- *Consistency*: A transaction should be incapable of breaking any rules defined for the database. For example, foreign keys must be obeyed. If for some reason this is impossible, the transaction will be rolled back.

- *Isolation*: The effects of the transaction will be completely invisible to all other transactions until it has completed successfully. This guarantees that the transaction will always see the data in a sensible state. For example, an update to a user's address should only contain a correct address (i.e., it will never have the house name for one location but the ZIP code for another); without this rule, a transaction could easily see when another transaction had updated the first part but had not yet completed.

- *Durability*: The data should be retained intact. If the system fails for any reason, it should always be possible to retrieve the database up to the moment of the failure.

The isolation levels permitted by JDBC and Hibernate are listed in Table 8-2.

Table 8-2. JDBC Isolation Levels

Level	Name	Transactional Behavior
0	None	Anything is permitted; the database or driver does not support transactions.
1	Read Uncommitted	Dirty, nonrepeatable, and phantom reads are permitted.
2	Read Committed	Nonrepeatable reads and phantom reads are permitted.
4	Repeatable Read	Phantom reads are permitted.
8	Serializable	The rule must be obeyed absolutely.

A *dirty read* may see the in-progress changes of an uncommitted transaction. As with the isolation example discussed in the preceding sidebar, it could see the wrong ZIP code for an address.

A *nonrepeatable read* sees different data for the same query. For example, it might determine a specific user's ZIP code at the beginning of the transaction and again at the end, and get a different answer both times without making any updates.

A *phantom read* sees different numbers of rows for the same query. For example, it might see 100 users in the database at the beginning of the query and 105 at the end without making any updates.

Hibernate treats the isolation as a global setting—you apply the configuration option `hibernate.connection.isolation` in the usual manner, setting it to one of the values permitted in Table 8-2. This is not always ideal. You will sometimes want to treat one particular transaction at a high level of isolation (usually Serializable), while permitting lower degrees of isolation for others. To do so, you will need to obtain the JDBC connection directly, alter the isolation level, begin the transaction, roll back or clean up the transaction as appropriate, and reset the isolation level back to its original value before releasing the connection for general usage. Hibernate does not provide a more direct way to alter the isolation level of the connection in a localized way. The implementation of the `createUser()` method, shown in Listing 8-1, demonstrates the additional complexity that the connection-specific transaction isolation involves.

Listing 8-1. Using a Specific Isolation Level

```
public static void createUser(String username)
   throws HibernateException
{
   Session session = factory.openSession();
   int isolation = -1;
   try {
      isolation = session.connection().getTransactionIsolation();
      session.connection().setTransactionIsolation(
         Connection.TRANSACTION_SERIALIZABLE);
      session.beginTransaction();

      // Normal usage of the Session here...
      Publisher p = new Publisher(username);
      Subscriber s = new Subscriber(username);
      session.saveOrUpdate(p);
      session.saveOrUpdate(s);

      // Commit the transaction
      session.getTransaction().commit();
   } catch (SQLException e1) {
      rollback(session);
      throw new HibernateException(e1);
   } catch (HibernateException e1) {
      rollback(session);
      throw e1;
   } finally {
      // reset isolation
      reset(session,isolation);
```

```
        // Close the session
        close(session);
    }
}
```

Fortunately, the normal case for a transaction using the global isolation level is much simpler. We provide a more standard implementation of the **createUser()** method for comparison in Listing 8-2.

Listing 8-2. Using the Global (Default) Isolation Level

```
public static void createUser(String username) throws HibernateException {
    Session session = factory.openSession();
    try {
        session.beginTransaction();

        // Normal usage of the Session here...
        Publisher p = new Publisher(username);
        Subscriber s = new Subscriber(username);
        session.saveOrUpdate(p);
        session.saveOrUpdate(s);

        // Commit the transaction
        session.getTransaction().commit();
    } catch (HibernateException e1) {
        rollback(session);
        throw e1;
    } finally {
        // Close the session
        close(session);
    }
}
```

Locking

A database can conform to these various levels of isolation in a number of ways, and you will need a working knowledge of locking to elicit the desired behavior and performance from your application in all circumstances.

To prevent simultaneous access to data, the database itself will acquire a lock on that data. This can be acquired for the momentary operation on the data only, or it can be retained until the end of the transaction. The former is called *optimistic locking* and the latter is called *pessimistic locking*.

The Read Uncommitted isolation level always acquires optimistic locks, whereas the Serializable isolation level will only acquire pessimistic locks. Some databases offer a feature that allows you to append the FOR UPDATE query to a select operation, which requires the database to acquire a pessimistic lock even in the lower isolation levels.

Hibernate provides some support for this feature when it is available, and takes it somewhat further by adding facilities that describe additional degrees of isolation obtainable from Hibernate's own cache.

The LockMode object controls this fine-grained isolation (see Table 8-3). It is only applicable to the get() methods, so it is limited—however, when possible, it is preferable to the direct control of isolation mentioned previously.

Table 8-3. *Lock Modes*

Mode	Description
NONE	Reads from the database only if the object is not available from the caches.
READ	Reads from the database regardless of the contents of the caches.
UPGRADE	Obtains a dialect-specific upgrade lock for the data to be accessed (if this is available from your database).
UPGRADE_NOWAIT	Behaves like UPGRADE, but when support is available from the database and dialect, the method will fail with a locking exception immediately. Without this option, or on databases for which it is not supported, the query must wait for a lock to be granted (or for a timeout to occur).

An additional lock mode, WRITE, is acquired by Hibernate automatically when it has written to a row within the current transaction. This mode cannot be set explicitly, but calls to getLockMode may return it.

Having discussed locking in general, we need to touch on some of the problems that locks can cause.

Deadlocks

Even if you have not encountered a deadlock (sometimes given the rather louche name of "deadly embrace") in databases, you have probably encountered the problem in multithreaded Java code. The problem arises from similar origins.

Two threads of execution can get into a situation in which each is waiting for the other to release a resource that it needs. The most common way to create this situation in a database is shown in Figure 8-2.

Each thread obtains a lock on its table when the update begins. Each thread proceeds until the table held by the other user is required. Neither thread can release the lock on its own table until the transaction completes—so something has to give.

A deadlock can also occur when a single thread of execution is carrying out an equivalent sequence of operations using two Session objects connected to the same database. In practice, the multiple-thread scenario is more common.

Fortunately, a database management system (DBMS) can detect this situation automatically, at which point the transaction of one or more of the offending processes will be aborted by the database. The resulting deadlock error will be received and handled by Hibernate as a normal HibernateException. Now you must roll back your transaction, close the session, and then (optionally) try again.

Listing 8-3 demonstrates how four updates from a pair of sessions can cause a deadlock. If you look at the output from the threads, you will see that one of them completes while the other fails with a deadlock error.

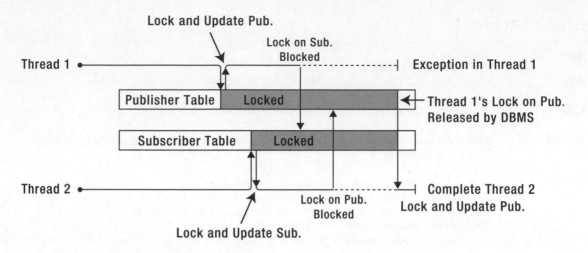

Figure 8-2. *The anatomy of a deadlock*

Looking at the database after completion, you will see that the **test** user has been replaced with either **jeff** or **dave** in both tables (you will never see **dave** from one thread and **jeff** from the other). Though it is not necessary here, because we close the session regardless, in a more extensive application it is important to ensure that the session associated with a deadlock or any other Hibernate exception is closed and never used again because the cache may be left in a corrupted state.

It is worth building and running Listing 8-3 to ensure that you are familiar with the symptoms of a deadlock when they occur.

Listing 8-3. Code to Generate a Deadlock

```
package com.hibernatebook.session.deadlock;

import java.sql.Connection;
import java.sql.SQLException;

import org.hibernate.HibernateException;
import org.hibernate.Query;
import org.hibernate.Session;
import org.hibernate.SessionFactory;
import org.hibernate.Transaction;
import org.hibernate.cfg.Configuration;

public class GenerateDeadlock {

    private static SessionFactory factory = new Configuration().configure()
            .buildSessionFactory();

    public static void createUser(String username) throws HibernateException {
        Session session = factory.openSession();
        try {
```

```
        session.beginTransaction();

        // Normal usage of the Session here...
        Publisher p = new Publisher(username);
        Subscriber s = new Subscriber(username);
        session.saveOrUpdate(p);
        session.saveOrUpdate(s);

        // Commit the transaction
        session.getTransaction().commit();
    } catch (HibernateException e1) {
        rollback(session);
        throw e1;
    } finally {
        // Close the session
        close(session);
    }
}

public static void reset(Session session, int isolation) {
    if (isolation >= 0) {
        try {
            session.connection().setTransactionIsolation(isolation);
        } catch (SQLException e) {
            System.err.println("Could not reset the isolation level: " + e);
        } catch (HibernateException e) {
            System.err.println("Could not reset the isolation level: " + e);
        }
    }
}

public static void close(Session session) {
    try {
        session.close();
    } catch (HibernateException e) {
        System.err.println("Could not close the session: " + e);
    }
}

public static void rollback(Session session) {
    try {
        Transaction tx = session.getTransaction();
        if (tx.isActive())
            tx.rollback();
    } catch (HibernateException e) {
        System.err.println("Could not rollback the session: " + e);
    }
}

public static void main(String[] argv) {
```

```
System.out.println("Creating test user...");
createUser("test");

System.out.println("Proceeding to main test...");
Session s1 = factory.openSession();
Session s2 = factory.openSession();

try {
    s1.beginTransaction();
    s2.beginTransaction();

    System.out.println("Update 1");
    Query q1 = s1.createQuery("from Publisher");
    Publisher pub1 = (Publisher) q1.uniqueResult();
    pub1.setUsername("jeff");
    s1.flush();

    System.out.println("Update 2");
    Query q2 = s2.createQuery("from Subscriber");
    Subscriber sub1 = (Subscriber) q2.uniqueResult();
    sub1.setUsername("dave");
    s2.flush();

    System.out.println("Update 3");
    Query q3 = s1.createQuery("from Subscriber");
    Subscriber sub2 = (Subscriber) q3.uniqueResult();
    sub2.setUsername("jeff");
    s1.flush();

    System.out.println("Update 4");
    Query q4 = s2.createQuery("from Publisher");
    Publisher pub2 = (Publisher) q4.uniqueResult();
    pub2.setUsername("dave");
    s2.flush();

    s1.getTransaction().commit();
    s2.getTransaction().commit();

} catch (RuntimeException e1) {
    e1.printStackTrace();
    // Run the boilerplate to roll back the sessions
    rollback(s1);
    rollback(s2);
    throw e1;
} finally {
    // Run the boilerplate to close the sessions
    close(s1);
    close(s2);
}
}
}
```

Caching

Accessing a database is an expensive operation, even for a simple query. The request has to be sent (usually over the network) to the server. The database server may have to compile the SQL into a query plan. The query plan has to be run and is limited largely by disk performance. The resulting data has to be shuttled back (again, usually across the network) to the client, and only then can the application program begin to process the results.

Most good databases will cache the results of a query if it is run multiple times, eliminating the disk I/O and query compilation time; but this will be of limited value if there are large numbers of clients making substantially different requests. Even if the cache generally holds the results, the time taken to transmit the information across the network is often the larger part of the delay.

Some applications will be able to take advantage of in-process databases, but this is the exception rather than the rule—and such databases have their own limitations.

The natural and obvious answer is to have a cache at the client end of the database connection. This is not a feature provided or supported by JDBC directly, but Hibernate provides one cache (the first-level, or L1, cache) through which all requests must pass. A second-level cache is optional and configurable.

The L1 cache ensures that within a session, requests for a given object from a database will always return the same object instance, thus preventing data from conflicting and preventing Hibernate from trying to load an object multiple times.

Items in the L1 cache can be individually discarded by invoking the `evict()` method on the session for the object that you wish to discard. To discard all items in the L1 cache, invoke the `clear()` method.

In this way, Hibernate has a major advantage over the traditional JDBC approach: with no additional effort from the developer, a Hibernate application gains the benefits of a client-side database cache.

Figure 8-3 shows the two caches available to the session: the compulsory L1 cache, through which all requests must pass, and the optional level-two (L2) cache. The L1 cache will always be consulted before any attempt is made to locate an object in the L2 cache. You will notice that the L2 cache is external to Hibernate; and although it is accessed via the session in a way that is transparent to Hibernate users, it is a pluggable interface to any one of a variety of caches that are maintained on the same JVM as your Hibernate application or on an external JVM. This allows a cache to be shared between applications on the same machine, or even between multiple applications on multiple machines.

In principle, any third-party cache can be used with Hibernate. An `org.hibernate.cache.CacheProvider` interface is provided, which must be implemented to provide Hibernate with a handle to the cache implementation. The cache provider is then specified by giving the implementation class name as the value of the `hibernate.cache.provider_class` property.

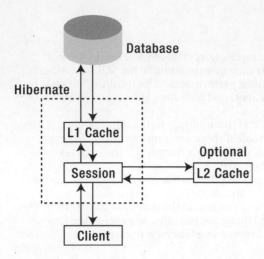

Figure 8-3. The session's relationship to the caches

In practice, the four production-ready caches, which are already supported, will be adequate for most users (see Table 8-4).

Table 8-4. L2 Cache Implementations Supported by Hibernate Out of the Box

Cache Name	Description
EHCache	An in-process cache
Infinispan	Open source successor to JBossCache that provides distributed cache support
OSCache	An alternative in-process cache
SwarmCache	A multicast distributed cache

The type of access to the L2 cache can be configured on a per-session basis by selecting a CacheMode option (see Table 8-5) and applying it with the setCacheMode() method.

Table 8-5. CacheMode Options

Mode	Description
NORMAL	Data is read from and written to the cache as necessary.
GET	Data is never added to the cache (although cache entries are invalidated when updated by the session).
PUT	Data is never read from the cache, but cache entries will be updated as they are read from the database by the session.
REFRESH	This is the same as PUT, but the use_minimal_puts Hibernate configuration option will be ignored if it has been set.
IGNORE	Data is never read from or written to the cache (except that cache entries will still be invalidated when they are updated by the session).

The CacheMode setting does not affect the way in which the L1 cache is accessed.

The decision to use an L2 cache is not clear-cut. Although it has the potential to greatly reduce access to the database, the benefits depend on the type of cache and the way in which it will be accessed.

A distributed cache will cause additional network traffic. Some types of database access may result in the contents of the cache being flushed before they are used—in which case, it will be adding unnecessary overhead to the transactions.

The L2 cache cannot account for the changes in the underlying data, which are the result of actions by an external program that is not cache-aware. This could potentially lead to problems with stale data, which is not an issue with the L1 cache.

In practice, as with most optimization problems, it is best to carry out performance testing under realistic load conditions. This will let you determine if a cache is necessary and help you select which one will offer the greatest improvement.

Threads

Having considered the caches available to a Hibernate application, you may now be concerned about the risk of a conventional Java deadlock if two threads of execution were to contend for the same object in the Hibernate session cache.

In principle, this is possible—and unlike database deadlocks, Java thread deadlocks do not time out with an error message. Fortunately, there is a very simple solution:

Patient: Doctor, it hurts when I do this.
Doctor: Don't do that then.

Do not share the Session object between threads. This will eliminate any risk of deadlocking on objects contained within the session cache.

The easiest way to ensure that you do not use the same `Session` object outside the current thread is to use an instance local to the current method. If you absolutely must maintain an instance for a longer duration, maintain the instance within a `ThreadLocal` object. For most purposes, however, the lightweight nature of the `Session` object makes it practical to construct, use, and destroy an instance, rather than to store a session.

Summary

In this chapter, we have discussed the nature of `Session` objects and how they can be used to obtain and manage transactions. We have looked at the two levels of caching that are available to applications, and how concurrent threads should manage sessions.

In the next chapter, we discuss the various ways in which you can retrieve objects from the database. We also show you how to perform more complicated queries against the database using HQL.

CHAPTER 9

■ ■ ■

Searches and Queries

In the last chapter, we discussed how the Hibernate session is used to interact with the database. Some of the session's methods take query strings in their parameter lists or return `Query` objects. These methods are used to request arbitrary information from the database. In order to fully show how they're used, we must introduce you to the Hibernate Query Language (HQL) used to phrase these requests. As well as extracting information (with `SELECT`), HQL can be used to alter the information in the database (with `INSERT`, `UPDATE`, and `DELETE`). We cover all of this basic functionality in this chapter. Hibernate's query facilities do not allow you to alter the database structure.

HQL is an object-oriented query language, similar to SQL, but instead of operating on tables and columns, HQL works with persistent objects and their properties.

HQL is a language with its own syntax and grammar. HQL is written as strings, like `from Product p`, as opposed to Hibernate's criteria queries (discussed in the next chapter), which take the form of a conventional Java API. Ultimately, your HQL queries are translated by Hibernate into conventional SQL queries, and Hibernate also provides an API that allows you to directly issue SQL queries.

Hibernate Query Language (HQL)

While most ORM tools and object databases offer an object query language, Hibernate's HQL stands out as being complete and easy to use. Although you can use SQL statements directly with Hibernate (which is covered in detail in the "Using Native SQL" section of this chapter), we recommend that you use HQL (or criteria) whenever possible to avoid database portability hassles, and to take advantage of Hibernate's SQL-generation and caching strategies. In addition to its technical advantages over traditional SQL, HQL is a more compact query language than SQL because it can make use of the relationship information defined in the Hibernate mappings.

We realize that not every developer trusts Hibernate's generated SQL to be perfectly optimized. If you do encounter a performance bottleneck in your queries, we recommend that you use SQL tracing on your database during performance testing of your critical components. If you see an area that needs optimization, we suggest trying first to optimize using HQL, and only later dropping into native SQL. Hibernate 3 provides statistics information through a JMX MBean, which you can use for analyzing Hibernate's performance. Hibernate's statistics also give you insight into how caching is performing.

■ **Note** If you would like to execute HQL statements through a GUI-based tool, the Hibernate team provides a Hibernate console for Eclipse in the Hibernate Tools subproject. This console is a plug-in for recent versions of Eclipse. This tool is described in detail in Appendix B.

Syntax Basics

HQL is inspired by SQL and is the inspiration for the Java Persistence Query Language (JPQL). The JPQL specification is included in the standard for JPA available from the Java Community Process web site (www.jcp.org/en/jsr/detail?id=220). HQL's syntax is defined as an ANTLR grammar; the grammar files are included in the grammar directory of the Hibernate core download (ANTLR is a tool for building language parsers).

As the ANTLR grammar files are somewhat cryptic, and as not every statement that is permissible according to the ANTLR grammar's rules can be used in Hibernate, we outline the syntax for the four fundamental HQL operations in this section. Note that the following descriptions of syntax are not comprehensive—there are some deprecated or more obscure usages (particularly for SELECT statements) that are not covered here.

UPDATE

UPDATE alters the details of existing objects in the database. In-memory entities will not be updated to reflect changes resulting from issuing UPDATE statements. Here's the syntax of the UPDATE statement:

```
UPDATE [VERSIONED]
    [FROM] path [[AS] alias] [, ...]
    SET property = value [, ...]
    [WHERE logicalExpression]
```

path is the fully qualified name of the entity or entities. The alias names may be used to abbreviate references to specific entities or their properties, and must be used when property names used in the query would otherwise be ambiguous.

The property names are the names of properties of entities listed in the FROM path.

The syntax of logical expressions is discussed later, in the "Using Restrictions with HQL" section.

DELETE

DELETE removes the details of existing objects from the database. In-memory entities will not be updated to reflect changes resulting from DELETE statements. This also means that Hibernate's cascade rules will not be followed for deletions carried out using HQL. However, if you have specified cascading deletes at the database level (either directly or through Hibernate using the @OnDelete annotation), the database will still remove the child rows. This approach to deletion is commonly referred to as "bulk deletion" since it is the most efficient way to remove large numbers of entities from the database. Here's the syntax of the DELETE statement:

```
DELETE
    [FROM] path [[AS] alias]
    [WHERE logicalExpression]
```

path is the fully qualified name of an entity. The **alias** names may be used to abbreviate references to specific entities or their properties, and must be used when property names used in the query would otherwise be ambiguous.

INSERT

An HQL **INSERT** cannot be used to directly insert arbitrary entities—it can only be used to insert entities constructed from information obtained from **SELECT** queries (unlike ordinary SQL, in which an **INSERT** command can be used to insert arbitrary data into a table, as well as insert values selected from other tables). Here's the syntax of the **INSERT** statement:

```
INSERT
    INTO path ( property [, ...])
    select
```

path is the name of an entity. The **property** names are the names of properties of entities listed in the **FROM** path of the incorporated **SELECT** query.

The **select** query is an HQL **SELECT** query (as described in the next section).

SELECT

An HQL **SELECT** is used to query the database for classes and their properties. As noted previously, this is very much a summary of the full expressive power of HQL **SELECT** queries—however, for more complex joins and the like, you may find that the use of the Criteria API described in the next chapter is more appropriate. Here's the syntax of the **SELECT** statement:

```
[SELECT [DISTINCT] property [, ...]]
    FROM path [[AS] alias] [, ...] [FETCH ALL PROPERTIES]
    WHERE logicalExpression
    GROUP BY property [, ...]
    HAVING logicalExpression
    ORDER BY property [ASC | DESC] [, ...]
```

path is the fully qualified name of an entity. The **alias** names may be used to abbreviate references to specific entities or their properties, and must be used when property names used in the query would otherwise be ambiguous.

The **property** names are the names of properties of entities listed in the **FROM** path.

If **FETCH ALL PROPERTIES** is used, then lazy loading semantics will be ignored, and all the immediate properties of the retrieved object(s) will be actively loaded (this does not apply recursively).

When the properties listed consist only of the names of aliases in the **FROM** clause, the **SELECT** clause can be omitted in HQL. If you are using the JPA with JPQL, one of the differences between HQL and JPQL is that the **SELECT** clause is required in JPQL.

The First Example with HQL

The simplest HQL query returns all objects for a given class in the database. In a syntax similar to that of SQL, we use the HQL clause `from`. As noted, when retrieving objects with HQL, you do not have to use the leading `select` clause for this query—instead, you can use the following simple shortcut query to select all objects from the `Product` table:

```
from Product
```

■ **Note** Like all SQL syntax, you can write `from` in lowercase or uppercase (or mixed case). However, any Java classes or properties that you reference in an HQL query have to be specified in the proper case. For example, when you query for instances of a Java class named `Product`, the HQL query `from Product` is the equivalent of `FROM Product`. However, the HQL query `from product` is not the same as the HQL query `from Product`. Because Java class names are case-sensitive, Hibernate is case-sensitive about class names as well.

Embedding the following HQL statement into our application is straightforward. The `org.hibernate.Session` object contains a method named `createQuery()`:

```
public Query createQuery(String queryString) throws HibernateException
```

The `createQuery()` method takes a valid HQL statement, and returns an `org.hibernate.Query` object. The `Query` class provides methods for returning the query results as a Java `List`, as an `Iterator`, or as a unique result. Other functionality includes named parameters, results scrolling, JDBC fetch sizes, and JDBC timeouts. You can also add a comment to the SQL that Hibernate creates, which is useful for tracing which HQL statements correspond to which SQL statements.

In order to fully illustrate our examples, we must first introduce the sample application that we are using in this chapter and the next (which discusses criteria). The sample application has three classes: `Supplier`, `Product`, and `Software`. The `Supplier` class, shown in Listing 9-1, has a `name` property and a `List` collection of `Product` objects.

Listing 9-1. The Supplier Class

```
package com.hibernatebook.queries;

import java.io.Serializable;
import java.util.ArrayList;
import java.util.List;
import javax.persistence.CascadeType;
import javax.persistence.Entity;
import javax.persistence.GeneratedValue;
import javax.persistence.GenerationType;
import javax.persistence.Id;
import javax.persistence.OneToMany;
import org.hibernate.annotations.Cascade;
```

```
@Entity
public class Supplier implements Serializable
{
    private int id;
    private String name;
    private List<Product> products = new ArrayList<Product>();

    @Id
    @GeneratedValue(strategy=GenerationType.AUTO)
    public int getId() {
        return id;
    }

    public void setId(int id) {
        this.id = id;
    }

    public String getName() {
        return name;
        }

    public void setName(String name) {
        this.name = name;
    }

    @OneToMany(cascade=CascadeType.ALL)
    @Cascade(org.hibernate.annotations.CascadeType.DELETE_ORPHAN)

    public List<Product> getProducts() {
        return products;
    }

    public void setProducts(List<Product>    products) {
        this.products = products;
    }
}
```

The **Product** class, shown in Listing 9-2, has **name**, **price**, and **description** properties, along with a reference to its parent supplier.

Listing 9-2. The Product *Class*

```
package com.hibernatebook.queries;

import java.io.Serializable;
import javax.persistence.ColumnResult;
import javax.persistence.Entity;
import javax.persistence.GeneratedValue;
import javax.persistence.GenerationType;
import javax.persistence.Id;
import javax.persistence.Inheritance;
```

```java
import javax.persistence.InheritanceType;
import javax.persistence.ManyToOne;
import javax.persistence.NamedNativeQuery;
import javax.persistence.NamedQuery;
import javax.persistence.SqlResultSetMapping;

@Entity
@NamedQuery(name="com.hibernatebook.queries.Product.HQLpricing",
query=" select product.price from Product product where product.price > 25.0")
@NamedNativeQuery(name="com.hibernatebook.queries.Product.SQLpricing",
query="select product.price from Product as product where product.price > 25.0",
        resultSetMapping="SQLPricingMapping")
@SqlResultSetMapping(name="SQLPricingMapping", columns=@ColumnResult(name="price"))
@Inheritance(
    strategy=InheritanceType.JOINED
)

public class Product implements Serializable
{
    private int id;
    private Supplier supplier;

    private String name;
    private String description;
    private double price;

    public Product() {
    }

    public Product(String name, String description, double price) {
        this.name = name;
        this.description = description;
        this.price = price;
    }

    public String getDescription() {
        return description;
    }

    public void setDescription(String description) {
        this.description = description;
    }

    @Id
    @GeneratedValue(strategy=GenerationType.AUTO)
    public int getId() {        return id;
    }

    public void setId(int id) {
        this.id = id;
    }
```

```java
    public String getName() {
        return name;
    }

    public void setName(String name) {
        this.name = name;
    }

    @ManyToOne
    public Supplier getSupplier() {
        return supplier;
    }

    public void setSupplier(Supplier supplier) {
        this.supplier = supplier;
    }

    public double getPrice() {
        return price;
    }

    public void setPrice(double price) {
        this.price = price;
    }
}
```

The **Software** class, shown in Listing 9-3, extends the **Product** class and adds a **version** property—we added this subclass so that we could demonstrate polymorphism with Hibernate's queries.

Listing 9-3. The Software Class

```java
package com.hibernatebook.queries;

import java.io.Serializable;
import javax.persistence.Entity;

@Entity
public class Software extends Product implements Serializable
{
    private String version;

    public Software() {
    }

    public Software(String name, String description,
                    double price, String version)
    {       super(name, description, price);
        this.setVersion(version);
    }
```

```
    public String getVersion() {
        return version;
    }

    public void setVersion(String version) {
        this.version = version;
    }
}
```

The Hibernate configuration XML file is in the source directory for the book, along with a test harness for populating the database and running the examples in this chapter and the next.

The first example executes our HQL statement, from Product, and then retrieves a List of Product objects.

```
Query query = session.createQuery("from Product");
List results = query.list();
```

Many of the other examples in this chapter use the same supporting Java code as this example. We are going to provide just the HQL for these examples—you can execute them the same way we did here, substituting that HQL for the from Product HQL statement. This should make each example clearer as to what you should be looking at. You could also execute these HQL statements in the Hibernate Tools scratch pad.

Logging and Commenting the Underlying SQL

Hibernate can output the underlying SQL behind your HQL queries into your application's log file. This is especially useful if the HQL query does not give the results you expect, or the query takes longer than you wanted. You can run the SQL that Hibernate generates directly against your database in the database's query analyzer at a later date to determine the causes of the problem. This is not a feature you will have to use frequently, but it is useful should you need to turn to your database administrators for help in tuning your Hibernate application.

Logging the SQL

The easiest way to see the SQL for a Hibernate HQL query is to enable SQL output in the logs with the hibernate.show_sql property. Set this property to true in your hibernate.properties or hibernate.cfg.xml configuration files, and Hibernate will output the SQL into the logs. You do not need to enable any other logging settings—although setting logging for Hibernate to debug also outputs the generated SQL statements, along with a lot of other verbiage.

After enabling SQL output in Hibernate, you should rerun the previous example. Here is the generated SQL statement for the HQL statement from Product:

```
select product0_.id as id, product0_.name as name0_, product0_.description ➥
as descript3_0_, product0_.price as price0_, product0_.supplierId ➥
as supplierId0_, product0_1_.version as version1_, ➥
case when product0_1_.productId is not null then 1 ➥
```

```
when product0_.id is not null then 0 end ➦
as clazz_ from Product product0_ left outer join Software product0_1_ ➦
on product0_.id=product0_1_.productId
```

As an aside, remember that the Software class inherits from Product, which complicates Hibernate's generated SQL for this simple query. When we select all objects from our simple Supplier class, the generated SQL for the HQL query from Supplier is much simpler:

```
select supplier0_.id as id, supplier0_.name as name2_ from Supplier supplier0_
```

When you look in your application's output for the Hibernate SQL statements, they will be prefixed with Hibernate:. The previous SQL statement would look like this:

```
Hibernate: select supplier0_.id as id, supplier0_.name as name2_ ➦
from Supplier supplier0_
```

If you turn your log4j logging up to debug for the Hibernate classes, you will see SQL statements in your log files, along with lots of information about how Hibernate parsed your HQL query and translated it into SQL.

Commenting the Generated SQL

Tracing your HQL statements through to the generated SQL can be difficult, so Hibernate provides a commenting facility on the Query object that lets you apply a comment to a specific query. The Query interface has a setComment() method that takes a String object as an argument, as follows:

```
public Query setComment(String comment)
```

Hibernate will not add comments to your SQL statements without some additional configuration, even if you use the setComment() method. You will also need to set a Hibernate property, hibernate.use_sql_comments, to true in your Hibernate configuration. If you set this property but do not set a comment on the query programmatically, Hibernate will include the HQL used to generate the SQL call in the comment. We find this to be very useful for debugging HQL.

Use commenting to identify the SQL output in your application's logs if SQL logging is enabled. For instance, if we add a comment to this example, the Java code would look like this:

```
String hql = "from Supplier";
Query query = session.createQuery(hql);
query.setComment("My HQL: " + hql);
List results = query.list();
```

The output in your application's log will have the comment in a Java-style comment before the SQL:

```
Hibernate: /*My HQL: from Supplier*/ select supplier0_.id as id, supplier0_.name ➦
as name2_ from Supplier supplier0_
```

We have found this useful for identifying SQL in our logs, especially because the generated SQL is a little difficult to follow when you are scanning large quantities of it in logs.

The from Clause and Aliases

We have already discussed the basics of the **from** clause in HQL in the earlier section, "The First Example with HQL." The most important feature to note is the *alias*. Hibernate allows you to assign aliases to the classes in your query with the **as** clause. Use the aliases to refer back to the class inside the query. For instance, our previous simple example would be the following:

```
from Product as p
```

or the following:

```
from Product as product
```

You'll see either alias-naming convention in applications. The **as** keyword is optional—you can also specify the alias directly after the class name, as follows:

```
from Product product
```

If you need to fully qualify a class name in HQL, just specify the package and class name. Hibernate will take care of most of this behind the scenes, so you only really need this if you have classes with duplicate names in your application. If you need to do this in Hibernate, use syntax such as the following:

```
from com.hibernatebook.criteria.Product
```

The **from** clause is very basic and useful for working directly with objects. However, if you want to work with the object's properties without loading the full objects into memory, you must use the **select** clause.

The select Clause and Projection

The **select** clause provides more control over the result set than the **from** clause. If you want to obtain the properties of objects in the result set, use the **select** clause. For instance, we could run a projection query on the products in the database that only returned the names, instead of loading the full object into memory, as follows:

```
select product.name from Product product
```

The result set for this query will contain a **List** of Java **String** objects. Additionally, we can retrieve the prices and the names for each product in the database, like so:

```
select product.name, product.price from Product product
```

This result set contains a **List** of **Object** arrays—each array represents one set of properties (in this case, a name and price pair).

If you're only interested in a few properties, this approach can allow you to reduce network traffic to the database server and save memory on the application's machine.

Using Restrictions with HQL

As with SQL, you use the `where` clause to select results that match your query's expressions. HQL provides many different expressions that you can use to construct a query. In the HQL language grammar, there are the following possible expressions:

- *Logic operators*: OR, AND, NOT

- *Equality operators*: =, <>, !=, ^=

- *Comparison operators*: <, >, <=, >=, like, not like, between, not between

- *Math operators*: +, -, *, /

- *Concatenation operator*: ||

- *Cases*: Case when <logical expression> then <unary expression> else _<unary expression> end

- *Collection expressions*: some, exists, all, any

In addition, you may also use the following expressions in the `where` clause:

- *HQL named parameters*: :date, :quantity

- *JDBC query parameter*: ?

- *Date and time SQL-92 functional operators*: current_time(), current_date(), current_timestamp()

- *SQL functions (supported by the database)*: length(), upper(), lower(), ltrim(), rtrim(), etc.

Using these restrictions, you can build a `where` clause in HQL that is as powerful as an SQL query. For many queries, HQL syntax is more compact and elegant than the Criteria Query API syntax (discussed in Chapter 10). For instance, here is an example of a criteria query that uses logical expressions:

```
Criteria crit = session.createCriteria(Product.class);
Criterion price = Restrictions.gt("price",new Double(25.0));
Criterion name = Restrictions.like("name","Mou%");
LogicalExpression orExp = Restrictions.or(price,name);
crit.add(orExp);
crit.add(Restrictions.ilike("description","blocks%"));
List results = crit.list();
```

The equivalent HQL would be the following:

```
from Product where price > 25.0 and name like 'Mou%'
```

We would have to wrap that HQL in a couple of lines of Java code, but even so, we find this particular example to be clearer in HQL. In the previous HQL example, you can see that we used the **where** clause with a > (greater than) comparison operator, an **and** logical operator, and a `like` comparison operator. You do have to enclose literal strings in quotes in HQL. To find names that have the literal Mou at the beginning of the string, we used % in the query.

Using Named Parameters

Hibernate supports named parameters in its HQL queries. This makes writing queries that accept input from the user easy—and you do not have to defend against SQL injection attacks.

■ **Note** SQL injection is an attack against applications that create SQL directly from user input with string concatenation. For instance, if we accept a name from the user through a web application form, then it would be very bad form to construct an SQL (or HQL) query like this:

`String sql = "select p from products where name = '" + name + "'";`

A malicious user could pass a name to the application that contained a terminating quote and semicolon, followed by another SQL command (such as `delete from products`) that would let them do whatever they wanted. They would just need to end with another command that matched the SQL statement's ending quote. This is a very common attack, especially if the malicious user can guess details of your database structure.

You could escape the user's input yourself for every query, but it is much less of a security risk if you let Hibernate manage all of your input with named parameters. Hibernate's named parameters are similar to the JDBC query parameters (?) you may already be familiar with, but Hibernate's parameters are less confusing. It is also more straightforward to use Hibernate's named parameters if you have a query that uses the same parameter in multiple places.

When you use JDBC query parameters, any time you add, change, or delete parts of the SQL statement, you need to update your Java code that sets its parameters, because the parameters are indexed based on the order they appear in the statement. Hibernate lets you provide names for the parameters in the HQL query, so you do not have to worry about accidentally moving parameters further up or back in the query.

The simplest example of named parameters uses regular SQL types for the parameters:

```
String hql = "from Product where price > :price";
Query query = session.createQuery(hql);
query.setDouble("price",25.0);
List results = query.list();
```

Normally, you do not know the values that are to be substituted for the named parameters—and if you did, you would probably encode them directly into the query string. When the value to be provided will be known only at run time, you can use some of HQL's object-oriented features to provide objects as values for named parameters. The **Query** interface has a **setEntity()** method that takes the name of a parameter and an object. Using this functionality, we could retrieve all the products that have a supplier whose object we already have:

```
String supplierHQL = "from Supplier where name='MegaInc'";
Query supplierQuery = session.createQuery(supplierHQL);
Supplier supplier = (Supplier) supplierQuery.list().get(0);

String hql = "from Product as product where product.supplier=:supplier";
Query query = session.createQuery(hql);
query.setEntity("supplier",supplier);
List results = query.list();
```

You can also use regular JDBC query parameters in your HQL queries. We do not particularly see any reason why you would want to, but they do work.

Paging Through the Result Set

Pagination through the result set of a database query is a very common application pattern. Typically, you would use pagination for a web application that returned a large set of data for a query. The web application would page through the database query result set to build the appropriate page for the user. The application would be very slow if the web application loaded all of the data into memory for each user. Instead, you can page through the result set and retrieve the results you are going to display one chunk at a time.

There are two methods on the `Query` interface for paging: `setFirstResult()` and `setMaxResults()`, just as with the `Criteria` interface. The `setFirstResult()` method takes an integer that represents the first row in your result set, starting with row 0. You can tell Hibernate to only retrieve a fixed number of objects with the `setMaxResults()` method. Your HQL is unchanged—you only need to modify the Java code that executes the query. Excuse our tiny dataset for this trivial example of pagination:

```
Query query = session.createQuery("from Product");
query.setFirstResult(1);
query.setMaxResults(2);
List results = query.list();
displayProductsList(results);
```

You can change the numbers around and play with the pagination. If you turn on SQL logging, you can see which SQL commands Hibernate uses for pagination. For the open source HSQLDB database, Hibernate uses `top` and `limit`. For other databases, Hibernate uses the appropriate commands for pagination. For instance, Microsoft SQL Server does not support the `limit` command, so Hibernate only uses the `top` command. If your application is having performance problems with pagination, this can be very useful for debugging.

If you only have one result in your HQL result set, Hibernate has a shortcut method for obtaining just that object.

Obtaining a Unique Result

HQL's query interface provides a `uniqueResult()` method for obtaining just one object from an HQL query. Although your query may only yield one object, you may also use the `uniqueResult()` method with other result sets if you limit the results to just the first result. You could use the setMaxResults() method discussed in the previous section. The uniqueResult() method on the Query object returns a single object, or null if there are zero results. If there is more than one result, the uniqueResult() method throws a NonUniqueResultException.

The following short example demonstrates having a result set that would have included more than one result, except that it was limited with the setMaxResults() method:

```
String hql = "from Product where price>25.0";
Query query = session.createQuery(hql);
query.setMaxResults(1);
Product product = (Product) query.uniqueResult();
//test for null here if needed
```

Unless your query returns one or zero results, the uniqueResult() method will throw a NonUniqueResultException exception. Do not expect Hibernate just to pick off the first result and return it—either set the maximum results of the HQL query to 1, or obtain the first object from the result list.

Sorting Results with the order by Clause

To sort your HQL query's results, you will need to use the order by clause. You can order the results by any property on the objects in the result set: either ascending (asc) or descending (desc). You can use ordering on more than one property in the query if you need to. A typical HQL query for sorting results looks like this:

```
from Product p where p.price>25.0 order by p.price desc
```

If you wanted to sort by more than one property, you would just add the additional properties to the end of the order by clause, separated by commas. For instance, you could sort by product price and the supplier's name, as follows:

```
from Product p order by p.supplier.name asc, p.price asc
```

HQL is more straightforward for ordering than the equivalent approach using the Criteria Query API.

Associations

Associations allow you to use more than one class in an HQL query, just as SQL allows you to use joins between tables in a relational database. Add an association to an HQL query with the join clause. Hibernate supports five different types of joins: inner join, cross join, left outer join, right outer join, and full outer join. If you use cross join, just specify both classes in the from clause (from Product p, Supplier s). For the other joins, use a join clause after the from clause. Specify the type of join, the object property to join on, and an alias for the other class.

You can use inner join to obtain the supplier for each product, and then retrieve the supplier name, product name, and product price, as so:

```
select s.name, p.name, p.price from Product p inner join p.supplier as s
```

You can retrieve the objects using similar syntax:

```
from Product p inner join p.supplier as s
```

We used aliases in these HQL statements to refer to the entities in our query expressions. These are particularly important in queries with associations that refer to two different entities with the same class—for instance, if we are doing a join from a table back to itself. Commonly, these types of joins are used to organize tree data structures.

Notice that Hibernate does not return `Object` objects in the result set; instead, Hibernate returns `Object` arrays in the results. You will have to access the contents of the `Object` arrays to get the `Supplier` and the `Product` objects.

If you would like to start optimizing performance, you can ask Hibernate to fetch the associated objects and collections for an object in one query. If you were using lazy loading with Hibernate, the objects in the collection would not be initialized until you accessed them. If you use `fetch` on a join in your query, you can ask Hibernate to retrieve the objects in the collection at the time the query executes. Add the `fetch` keyword after the `join` in the query, like so:

```
from Supplier s inner join fetch s.products as p
```

When you use `fetch` for a query like this, Hibernate will return only the `Supplier` objects, not the `Product` objects. This is because you are specifying the join, so Hibernate knows which objects to fetch (instead of using lazy loading). If you need to get the `Product` objects, you can access them through the associated `Supplier` object. You cannot use the properties of the `Product` objects in expressions in the `where` clause. Use of the `fetch` keyword overrides any settings you have in the mapping file for object initialization.

Aggregate Methods

HQL supports a range of aggregate methods, similar to SQL. They work the same way in HQL as in SQL, so you do not have to learn any specific Hibernate terminology. The difference is that in HQL, aggregate methods apply to the properties of persistent objects. The `count(...)` method returns the number of times the given column name appears in the result set. You may use the `count(*)` syntax to count all the objects in the result set, or `count(product.name)` to count the number of objects in the result set with a `name` property. Here is an example using the `count(*)` method to count all products:

```
select count(*) from Product product
```

The `distinct` keyword only counts the unique values in the row set—for instance, if there are 100 products, but 10 have the same price as another product in the results, then a `select count(distinct product.price) from Product` product query would return `90`. In our database, the following query will return `2`, one for each supplier:

```
select count(distinct product.supplier.name) from Product product
```

If we removed the `distinct` keyword, it would return `5`, one for each product.

All of these queries return a `Long` object in the list. You could use the `uniqueResult()` method here to obtain the result.

The aggregate functions available through HQL include the following:

- avg(*property name*): The average of a property's value

- count(*property name* or *): The number of times a property occurs in the results

- max(*property name*): The maximum value of the property values

- min(*property name*): The minimum value of the property values

- sum(*property name*): The sum total of the property values

If you have more than one aggregate method, the result set List will contain an Object array with each of the aggregates you requested. Adding another aggregate to the select clause is straightforward:

```
select min(product.price), max(product.price) from Product product
```

You can also combine these with other projection properties in the result set.

Bulk Updates and Deletes with HQL

Bulk updates are new to HQL with Hibernate 3, and deletes work differently in Hibernate 3 than they did in Hibernate 2. The Query interface now contains a method called executeUpdate() for executing HQL UPDATE or DELETE statements. The executeUpdate() method returns an int that contains the number of rows affected by the update or delete, as follows:

```
public int executeUpdate() throws HibernateException
```

HQL updates look like you would expect them to, being based on SQL UPDATE statements. Do not include an alias with the update; instead, put the set keyword right after the class name, as follows:

```
String hql = "update Supplier set name = :newName ➥
where name = :name";

Query query = session.createQuery(hql);
query.setString("name","SuperCorp");
query.setString("newName","MegaCorp");
int rowCount = query.executeUpdate();
System.out.println("Rows affected: " + rowCount);

//See the results of the update
query = session.createQuery("from Supplier");
List results = query.list();
```

After carrying out this query, any supplier previously named SuperCorp will be named MegaCorp. You may use a where clause with updates to control which rows get updated, or you may leave it off to update all rows. Notice that we printed out the number of rows affected by the query. We also used named parameters in our HQL for this bulk update.

Bulk deletes work in a similar way. Use the delete from clause with the class name you would like to delete from. Then use the where clause to narrow down which entries in the table you would like to delete. Use the executeUpdate() method to execute deletes against the database as well.

Be careful when you use bulk delete with objects that are in relationships. Hibernate will not know that you removed the underlying data in the database, and you can get foreign key integrity errors. To get around this, you could set the `not-found` attribute to `ignore` on your one-to-many and many-to-one mappings, which will make ids that are not in the database resolve to null references. The default value for the `not-found` attribute is exception. Setting the `not-found` attribute to `ignore` also has the side-effect of causing your associations to load eagerly and fetch all related records instead of using lazy loading. This can cause serious performance problems.

Our code surrounding the HQL `DELETE` statement is basically the same—we use named parameters, and we print out the number of rows affected by the delete:

```
String hql = "delete from Product where name = :name";
Query query = session.createQuery(hql);
query.setString("name","Mouse");
int rowCount = query.executeUpdate();
System.out.println("Rows affected: " + rowCount);

//See the results of the update
query = session.createQuery("from Product");
List results = query.list();
```

■ **Caution** Using bulk updates and deletes in HQL works almost the same as in SQL, so keep in mind that these are powerful and can erase the data in your tables if you make a mistake with the `where` clause.

Named Queries for HQL and SQL

One of Hibernate's best features is the named query, in which your application can store its HQL queries outside the application in the mapping file or in an annotation on the class. This has many benefits for application maintenance. The first benefit is that many objects can share queries—you could set up static final strings on classes with the HQL queries, but Hibernate already provides a nice facility for the same thing. The next benefit is that named queries could also contain native SQL queries—the application calling the named query does not need to know if the named query is SQL or HQL. This has enormous benefits for migrating SQL-based applications to Hibernate. The last benefit is that you can provide your HQL and SQL queries in a configuration file to your database administrators, who will probably find it easier to work with an XML mapping file than with HQL statements embedded in Java code.

You can add named queries in the appropriate Hibernate mapping file. HQL queries use the XML `<query>` element, and SQL queries use the XML `<sql-query>` element. Both of these XML elements require a name attribute that uniquely identifies the query in the application. With one simple HQL named query, and one simple SQL query that does the same thing, we have the Hibernate mapping file shown in Listing 9-4: `Product.hbm.xml`.

Listing 9-4. Product.hbm.xml

```xml
<?xml version='1.0' encoding='utf-8'?>
<!DOCTYPE hibernate-mapping
    PUBLIC "-//Hibernate/Hibernate Mapping DTD//EN"
    "http://hibernate.sourceforge.net/hibernate-mapping-3.0.dtd">

<hibernate-mapping package="com.hibernatebook.criteria">
    <class name="Product">
        <id name="id" type="int">
            <generator class="native"/>
        </id>

        <property name="name" type="string"/>
        <property name="description" type="string"/>
        <property name="price" type="double"/>
        <many-to-one name="supplier" class="Supplier" column="supplierId"/>

    </class>

    <query name="com.hibernatebook.criteria.Product.HQLpricing"><![CDATA[
        select product.price from Product product where product.price > 25.0]]>
    </query>
    <sql-query name="com.hibernatebook.criteria.Product.SQLpricing">
      <return-scalar column="price" type="double"/>
      <![CDATA[
      select product.price from Product as product where product.price > 25.0]]>
    </sql-query>
</hibernate-mapping>
```

Notice that we embedded the SQL and HQL queries in **CDATA** regions. This protects our SQL queries from interfering with the XML parser—we don't have to worry about special characters breaking the XML. For the native SQL query, we also had to specify a return type, so Hibernate knows what type of result data to expect from the database. When you use HQL, Hibernate handles that mapping behind the scenes, because it knows which objects went in. With SQL, you have to specify the return types yourself. In this case, we used the `<return-scalar>` XML element to define our return type as a column named `price`, with a type of **double**. Hibernate converts the JDBC result set into an array of objects, just like the previous HQL query. Functionally, they are identical. We discuss native SQL in more detail in the next section of the chapter.

You may also specify the flush mode, whether the query is cacheable, the cache region, the fetch size, and the timeout for the HQL and SQL queries. For the SQL query, you may additionally specify whether the SQL query is callable.

In addition to specifying a named HQL query in an XML mapping file, you can provide HQL named queries as annotations on classes. It doesn't matter where you specify the query – from your Java code, the way you call the query is the same. The HQL named query annotation is **@NamedQuery** and goes after the **@Entity** annotation. The equivalent annotation for the previous HQL query would go on the Product class:

```
@NamedQuery(name="com.hibernatebook.queries.Product.HQLpricing",
query=" select product.price from Product product where product.price > 25.0")
```

Notice that there is no **CDATA** region because we are not using XML. We can also use parameters in our named HQL queries. Whether the HQL is specified in Java code or in named queries doesn't make a difference. Here is the previous example, but with the price as a parameter:

```
@NamedQuery(name="com.hibernatebook.queries.Product.HQLpricing",
query=" select product.price from Product product where product.price >:price")
```

Similar to HQL named queries, we can embed the SQL query into annotations as well. For the equivalent SQL query, we used two annotations, **@NamedNativeQuery** and **@SqlResultSetMapping**:

```
@NamedNativeQuery(name="com.hibernatebook.queries.Product.SQLpricing",
query="select product.price from Product as product where product.price > 25.0",
        resultSetMapping="SQLPricingMapping")
@SqlResultSetMapping(name="SQLPricingMapping", columns=@ColumnResult(name="price"))
```

You will need to reference the result set mapping name in the **@NamedNativeQuery** annotation. Our mapping retrieved the price, which we referenced as a scalar with the **@ColumnResult** annotation. You can have more than one column in your SQL result set; however you will have to select them in your SQL query and include them in your annotation as a list:

```
@SqlResultSetMapping(name="SQLPriceAndNameMapping",
columns={@ColumnResult(name="price"),@ColumnResult(name="name")})
```

To use HQL or SQL named queries inside your application, you will need to retrieve the named query as a **Query** object from a **Session** object using the **getNamedQuery()** method. For example:

```
Query hqlPricing = session.getNamedQuery("com.hibernatebook.queries.Product.HQLpricing")
```

This example will return a Query object that you would use inside your application the same way you would as if you had specified the query in Java code.

Using Native SQL

Although you should probably use HQL whenever possible, Hibernate does provide a way to use native SQL statements directly through Hibernate. One reason to use native SQL is that your database supports some special features through its dialect of SQL that are not supported in HQL. Another reason is that you may want to call stored procedures from your Hibernate application. We discuss stored procedures and other database-specific integration solutions in Appendix A. Rather than just providing an interface to the underlying JDBC connection, like other Java ORM tools, Hibernate provides a way to define the entity (or join) that the query uses. This makes integration with the rest of your ORM-oriented application easy.

You can modify your SQL statements to make them work with Hibernate's ORM layer. You do need to modify your SQL to include Hibernate aliases that correspond to objects or object properties. You can specify all properties on an object with {**objectname.***}, or you can specify the aliases directly with {**objectname.property**}. Hibernate uses the mappings to translate your object property names into their underlying SQL columns. This may not be the exact way you expect Hibernate to work, so be aware that you do need to modify your SQL statements for full ORM support. You will especially run into problems with native SQL on classes with subclasses—be sure you understand how you mapped the inheritance across either a single table or multiple tables, in order that you select the right properties off of the table.

Underlying Hibernate's native SQL support is the `org.hibernate.SQLQuery` interface, which extends the `org.hibernate.Query` interface already discussed. Your application will create a native SQL query from the session with the `createSQLQuery()` method on the `Session` interface.

```
public SQLQuery createSQLQuery(String queryString) throws HibernateException
```

After you pass a string containing the SQL query to the `createSQLQuery()` method, you should associate the SQL result with an existing Hibernate entity, a join, or a scalar result. The `SQLQuery` interface has `addEntity()`, `addJoin()`, and `addScalar()` methods. For the entities and joins, you can specify a lock mode, which we discuss in Chapter 8. The `addEntity()` methods take an alias argument and either a class name or an entity name. The `addJoin()` methods take an alias argument and a path to join.

Using native SQL with scalar results is the simplest way to get started with native SQL. Our Java code looks like this:

```
String sql = "select avg(product.price) as avgPrice from Product product";
  SQLQuery query = session.createSQLQuery(sql);
  query.addScalar("avgPrice",Hibernate.DOUBLE);
  List results = query.list();
```

Because we did not specify any entity aliases, Hibernate executes exactly the same SQL that we passed through:

```
select avg(product.price) as avgPrice from Product product
```

The SQL is regular SQL (we did not have to do any aliasing here). We created an `SQLQuery` object, and then added a scalar mapping with the built-in **double** type (from the `org.hibernate._Hibernate` class). We needed to map the **avgPrice** SQL alias to the object type. The results are a `List` with one object—a `Double`.

A bit more complicated than the previous example is the native SQL that returns a result set of objects. In this case, we will need to map an entity to the SQL query. The entity consists of the alias we used for the object in the SQL query and its class. For this example, we used our `Supplier` class:

```
String sql = "select {supplier.*} from Supplier supplier";
SQLQuery query = session.createSQLQuery(sql);
query.addEntity("supplier", Supplier.class);
List results = query.list();
```

Hibernate modifies the SQL and executes the following command against the database:

```
select Supplier.id as id0_, Supplier.name as name2_0_ from Supplier supplier
```

The special aliases allow Hibernate to map the database columns back to the object properties.

Summary

HQL is a powerful object-oriented query language that provides the power of SQL while taking advantage of Hibernate's object-relational mapping and caching. If you are porting an existing application to Hibernate, you can use Hibernate's native SQL facilities to execute SQL against the database. The SQL functionality is also useful for executing SQL statements that are specific to a given database and have no equivalents in HQL.

You may turn on SQL logging for Hibernate, and Hibernate will log the generated SQL that it executes against the database. If you add a comment to your HQL query object, Hibernate will display a comment in the log next to the SQL statement—this helps with tracing SQL statements back to HQL in your application.

CHAPTER 10

■ ■ ■

Advanced Queries Using Criteria

Hibernate provides three different ways to retrieve data. We have already discussed HQL and the use of native SQL queries—now we add criteria.

The Criteria Query API lets you build nested, structured query expressions in Java, providing a compile-time syntax-checking that is not possible with a query language like HQL or SQL. The Criteria API also includes *query by example* (QBE) functionality—this lets you supply example objects that contain the properties you would like to retrieve instead of having to spell the components of the query out step by step. It also includes projection and aggregation methods, including counts.

In this chapter, we explore the use of the Criteria API using the sample database established in the previous chapter.

Using the Criteria API

The Criteria API allows you to build up a criteria query object programmatically—the `org.hibernate.Criteria` interface defines the available methods for one of these objects. The Hibernate `Session` interface contains several `createCriteria()` methods. Pass the persistent object's class or its entity name to the `createCriteria()` method, and Hibernate will create a `Criteria` object that returns instances of the persistence object's class when your application executes a criteria query.

The simplest example of a criteria query is one with no optional parameters or restrictions—the criteria query will simply return every object that corresponds to the class.

```
Criteria crit = session.createCriteria(Product.class);
List results = crit.list();
```

When you run this example with our sample data, you will get all objects that are instances of the `Product` class—note that this includes any instances of the `Software` class because they are derived from `Product`.

Moving on from this simple example, we will add constraints to our criteria queries so we can winnow down the result set.

Using Restrictions with Criteria

The Criteria API makes it easy to use restrictions in your queries to selectively retrieve objects; for instance, your application could retrieve only products with a price over $30. You may add these restrictions to a `Criteria` object with the `add()` method. The `add()` method takes an `org.hibernate.criterion.Criterion` object that represents an individual restriction. You can have more than one restriction for a criteria query.

Although you could create your own objects implementing the `Criterion` object, or extend an existing `Criterion` object, we recommend that you use Hibernate's built-in `Criterion` objects from your application's business logic. For instance, you could create your own factory class that returns instances of Hibernate's `Criterion` objects appropriately set up for your application's restrictions.

Use the factory methods on the `org.hibernate.criterion.Restrictions` class to obtain instances of the `Criterion` objects. To retrieve objects that have a property value that equals your restriction, use the `eq()` method on `Restrictions`, as follows:

```
public static SimpleExpression eq(String propertyName, Object value)
```

We would typically nest the `eq()` method in the `add()` method on the `Criteria` object. Here is an example of how this would look if we were searching for products with the name "Mouse":

```
Criteria crit = session.createCriteria(Product.class);
crit.add(Restrictions.eq("name","Mouse"));
List results = crit.list()
```

Next, we search for products that do *not* have the name "Mouse." For this, we would use the `ne()` method on the `Restrictions` class to obtain a not-equal restriction:

```
Criteria crit = session.createCriteria(Product.class);
crit.add(Restrictions.ne("name","Mouse"));
List results = crit.list();
```

■ **Tip** You cannot use the not-equal restriction to retrieve records with a NULL value in the database for that property (in SQL, and therefore in Hibernate, NULL represents the absence of data, and so cannot be compared with data). If you need to retrieve objects with NULL properties, you will have to use the `isNull()` restriction, which we discuss further on in the chapter. You can combine the two with an OR logical expression, which we also discuss later in the chapter.

Instead of searching for exact matches, we can also retrieve all objects that have a property matching part of a given pattern. To do this, we need to create an SQL `LIKE` clause, with either the `like()` or the `ilike()` method. The `ilike()` method is case-insensitive. In either case, we have two different ways to call the method:

```
public static SimpleExpression like(String propertyName, Object value)
```

or

```
public static SimpleExpression like(String propertyName,
                                    String value,
                                    MatchMode matchMode)
```

The first `like()` or `ilike()` method takes a pattern for matching. Use the `%` character as a wildcard to match parts of the string, like so:

```
Criteria crit = session.createCriteria(Product.class);
crit.add(Restrictions.like("name","Mou%"));
List results = crit.list();
```

The second `like()` or `ilike()` method uses an `org.hibernate.criterion.MatchMode` object to specify how to match the specified value to the stored data. The `MatchMode` object (a type-safe enumeration) has four different matches:

- `ANYWHERE`: Anyplace in the string

- `END`: The end of the string

- `EXACT`: An exact match

- `START`: The beginning of the string

Here is an example that uses the `ilike()` method to search for case-insensitive matches at the end of the string:

```
Criteria crit = session.createCriteria(Product.class);
crit.add(Restrictions.ilike("name","browser", MatchMode.END));
List results = crit.list();
```

The `isNull()` and `isNotNull()` restrictions allow you to do a search for objects that have (or do not have) null property values. This is easy to demonstrate:

```
Criteria crit = session.createCriteria(Product.class);
crit.add(Restrictions.isNull("name"));
List results = crit.list();
```

Several of the restrictions are useful for doing math comparisons. The greater-than comparison is `gt()`, the greater-than-or-equal-to comparison is `ge()`, the less-than comparison is `lt()`, and the less-than-or-equal-to comparison is `le()`. We can do a quick retrieval of all products with prices over $25 like this:

```
Criteria crit = session.createCriteria(Product.class);
crit.add(Restrictions.gt("price",new Double(25.0)));
List results = crit.list();
```

Moving on, we can start to do more complicated queries with the Criteria API. For example, we can combine `AND` and `OR` restrictions in logical expressions. When you add more than one constraint to a criteria query, it is interpreted as an `AND`, like so:

```
Criteria crit = session.createCriteria(Product.class);
crit.add(Restrictions.gt("price",new Double(25.0)));
crit.add(Restrictions.like("name","K%"));
List results = crit.list();
```

If we want to have two restrictions that return objects that satisfy either or both of the restrictions, we need to use the or() method on the **Restrictions** class, as follows:

```
Criteria crit = session.createCriteria(Product.class);
Criterion price = Restrictions.gt("price",new Double(25.0));
Criterion name = Restrictions.like("name","Mou%");
LogicalExpression orExp = Restrictions.or(price,name);
crit.add(orExp);
List results = crit.list();
```

The orExp logical expression that we have created here will be treated like any other criterion. We can therefore add another restriction to the criteria:

```
Criteria crit = session.createCriteria(Product.class);
Criterion price = Restrictions.gt("price",new Double(25.0));
Criterion name = Restrictions.like("name","Mou%");
LogicalExpression orExp = Restrictions.or(price,name);
crit.add(orExp);
crit.add(Restrictions.ilike("description","blocks%"));
List results = crit.list();
```

If we wanted to create an **OR** expression with more than two different criteria (for example, price > 25.0 OR name like Mou% OR description not like blocks%), we would use an **org.hibernate.criterion.Disjunction** object to represent a disjunction. You can obtain this object from the disjunction() factory method on the **Restrictions** class. The disjunction is more convenient than building a tree of **OR** expressions in code. To represent an **AND** expression with more than two criteria, you can use the conjunction() method—although you can easily just add those to the **Criteria** object. The conjunction is also more convenient than building a tree of **AND** expressions in code. Here is an example that uses the disjunction:

```
Criteria crit = session.createCriteria(Product.class);
Criterion price = Restrictions.gt("price",new Double(25.0));
Criterion name = Restrictions.like("name","Mou%");
Criterion desc = Restrictions.ilike("description","blocks%");
Disjunction disjunction = Restrictions.disjunction();
disjunction.add(price);
disjunction.add(name);
disjunction.add(desc);
crit.add(disjunction);
List results = crit.list();
```

The last type of restriction is the SQL restriction sqlRestriction(). This restriction allows you to directly specify SQL in the Criteria API. This is useful if you need to use SQL clauses that Hibernate does not support through the Criteria API. Your application's code does not need to know the name of the table your class uses—use {alias} to signify the class's table, as follows:

```
Criteria crit = session.createCriteria(Product.class);
crit.add(Restrictions.sqlRestriction("{alias}.name like 'Mou%'"));
List results = crit.list()
```

The other two `sqlRestriction()` methods permit you to pass JDBC parameters and values into the SQL statement. Use the standard JDBC parameter placeholder (?) in your SQL fragment.

Paging Through the Result Set

One common application pattern that criteria can address is pagination through the result set of a database query. When we say pagination, we mean an interface in which the user sees part of the result set at a time, with navigation to go forward and backward through the results. A naive pagination implementation might load the entire result set into memory for each navigation action, and would usually lead to atrocious performance. Both of us have worked on improving performance for separate projects suffering from exactly this problem. The problem appeared late in testing because the sample dataset that developers were working with was trivial, and they did not notice any performance problems until the first test data load.

If you are programming directly to the database, you will typically use proprietary database SQL or database cursors to support paging. Hibernate abstracts this away for you—behind the scenes, Hibernate uses the appropriate method for your database.

There are two methods on the **Criteria** interface for paging: `setFirstResult()` and `setMaxResults()`. The `setFirstResult()` method takes an integer that represents the first row in your result set, starting with row 0. You can tell Hibernate to retrieve a fixed number of objects with the `setMaxResults()` method. Using both of these together, we can construct a paging component in our web or Swing application. We have a very small dataset in our sample application, so here is an admittedly trivial example:

```
Criteria crit = session.createCriteria(Product.class);
crit.setFirstResult(1);
crit.setMaxResults(2);
List results = crit.list();
```

As you can see, this makes paging through the result set easy. You can increase the first result you return (for example, from 1, to 21, to 41, etc.) to page through the result set. If you only have one result in your result set, Hibernate has a shortcut method for obtaining just that object.

Obtaining a Unique Result

Sometimes you know you are only going to return zero or one objects from a given query. This could be because you are calculating an aggregate (like COUNT, which we discuss later), or because your restrictions naturally lead to a unique result—when selecting upon a property under a unique constraint, for example. You may also limit the results of any result set to just the first result, using the `setMaxResults()` method discussed earlier. In any of these circumstances, if you want obtain a single `Object` reference instead of a `List`, the `uniqueResult()` method on the `Criteria` object returns an object or null. If there is more than one result, the `uniqueResult()` method throws a `HibernateException`.

The following short example demonstrates having a result set that would have included more than one result, except that it was limited with the `setMaxResults()` method:

```
Criteria crit = session.createCriteria(Product.class);
Criterion price = Restrictions.gt("price",new Double(25.0));
crit.setMaxResults(1);
Product product = (Product) crit.uniqueResult();
```

Again, we stress that you need to make sure that your query only returns one or zero results if you use the uniqueResult() method. Otherwise, Hibernate will throw a NonUniqueResultException exception, which may not be what you would expect—Hibernate does not just pick the first result and return it.

Sorting the Query's Results

Sorting the query's results works much the same way with criteria as it would with HQL or SQL. The Criteria API provides the org.hibernate.criterion.Order class to sort your result set in either ascending or descending order, according to one of your object's properties.

Create an Order object with either of the two static factory methods on the Order class: asc() for ascending or desc() for descending. Both methods take the name of the property as their only argument. After you create an Order, use the addOrder() method on the Criteria object to add it to the query.

This example demonstrates how you would use the Order class:

```
Criteria crit = session.createCriteria(Product.class);
crit.add(Restrictions.gt("price",new Double(25.0)));
crit.addOrder(Order.desc("price"));
List results = crit.list();
```

You may add more than one Order object to the Criteria object. Hibernate will pass them through to the underlying SQL query. Your results will be sorted by the first order, then any identical matches within the first sort will be sorted by the second order, and so on. Beneath the covers, Hibernate passes this on to an SQL ORDER BY clause after substituting the proper database column name for the property.

Associations

To add a restriction on a class that is associated with your criteria's class, you will need to create another Criteria object. Pass the property name of the associated class to the createCriteria() method, and you will have another Criteria object. You can get the results from either Criteria object, although you should pick one style and be consistent for readability's sake. We find that getting the results from the top-level Criteria object (the one that takes a class as a parameter) makes it clear what type of object is expected in the results.

The association works going from one-to-many as well as from many-to-one. First, we will demonstrate how to use one-to-many associations to obtain suppliers who sell products with a price over $25. Notice that we create a new Criteria object for the products property, add restrictions to the products' criteria we just created, and then obtain the results from the supplier Criteria object:

```
Criteria crit = session.createCriteria(Supplier.class);
Criteria prdCrit = crit.createCriteria("products");
prdCrit.add(Restrictions.gt("price",new Double(25.0)));
List results = crit.list();
```

Going the other way, we obtain all the products from the supplier MegaInc using many-to-one associations:

```
Criteria crit = session.createCriteria(Product.class);
Criteria suppCrit = crit.createCriteria("supplier");
suppCrit.add(Restrictions.eq("name","MegaInc"));
List results = crit.list();
```

Although we can use either `Criteria` object to obtain the results, it makes a difference which criteria we use for ordering the results. In the following example, we are ordering the supplier results by the supplier names:

```
Criteria crit = session.createCriteria(Supplier.class);
Criteria prdCrit = crit.createCriteria("products");
prdCrit.add(Restrictions.gt("price",new Double(25.0)));
crit.addOrder(Order.desc("name"));
List results = prdCrit.list();
```

If we wanted to sort the suppliers by the descending price of their products, we would use the following line of code. This code would have to replace the previous `addOrder()` call on the supplier `Criteria` object.

```
prdCrit.addOrder(Order.desc("price"));
```

Although the products are not in the result set, SQL still allows you to order by those results. If you get mixed up with which `Criteria` object you are using and pass the wrong property name for the sort-by order, Hibernate will throw an exception.

Distinct Results

If you would like to work with distinct results from a criteria query, Hibernate provides a result transformer for distinct entities, `org.hibernate.transform.DistinctRootEntityResultTransformer`, which ensures that no duplicates will be in your query's result set. Rather than using `SELECT DISTINCT` with SQL, the distinct result transformer compares each of your results using their default `hashCode()` methods, and only adds those results with unique hash codes to your result set. This may or may not be the result you would expect from an otherwise equivalent SQL `DISTINCT` query, so be careful with this. An additional performance note: the comparison is done in Hibernate's Java code, not at the database, so non-unique results will still be transported across the network.

Projections and Aggregates

Instead of working with objects from the result set, you can treat the results from the result set as a set of rows and columns, also known as a *projection* of the data. This is similar to how you would use data from a `SELECT` query with JDBC; also, Hibernate supports properties, aggregate functions, and the `GROUP BY` clause.

To use projections, start by getting the `org.hibernate.criterion.Projection` object you need from the `org.hibernate.criterion.Projections` factory class. The `Projections` class is similar to the `Restrictions` class in that it provides several static factory methods for obtaining `Projection` instances.

After you get a `Projection` object, add it to your `Criteria` object with the `setProjection()` method. When the `Criteria` object executes, the list contains object references that you can cast to the appropriate type.

The row-counting functionality provides a simple example of applying projections. The code looks similar to the restrictions examples we were working with earlier in the chapter:

```
Criteria crit = session.createCriteria(Product.class);
crit.setProjection(Projections.rowCount());
List results = crit.list();
```

The results list will contain one object, an `Integer` that contains the results of executing the `COUNT` SQL statement. Other aggregate functions available through the `Projections` factory class include the following:

- `avg(String propertyName)`: Gives the average of a property's value

- `count(String propertyName)`: Counts the number of times a property occurs

- `countDistinct(String propertyName)`: Counts the number of unique values the - property contains

- `max(String propertyName)`: Calculates the maximum value of the property values

- `min(String propertyName)`: Calculates the minimum value of the property values

- `sum(String propertyName)`: Calculates the sum total of the property values

We can apply more than one projection to a given `Criteria` object. To add multiple projections, get a projection list from the `projectionList()` method on the `Projections` class. The `org.hibernate.criterion.ProjectionList` object has an `add()` method that takes a `Projection` object. You can pass the projections list to the `setProjection()` method on the `Criteria` object because `ProjectionList` implements the `Projection` interface. The following example demonstrates some of the aggregate functions, along with the projection list:

```
Criteria crit = session.createCriteria(Product.class);
ProjectionList projList = Projections.projectionList();
projList.add(Projections.max("price"));
projList.add(Projections.min("price"));
projList.add(Projections.avg("price"));
projList.add(Projections.countDistinct("description"));
crit.setProjection(projList);
List results = crit.list();
```

When you execute multiple aggregate projections, you get a `List` with an `Object` array as the first element. The `Object` array contains all of your values, in order.

Another use of projections is to retrieve individual properties, rather than entities. For instance, we can retrieve just the name and description from our product table, instead of faulting the classes into memory. Use the `property()` method on the `Projections` class to create a `Projection` for a property. When you execute this form of query, the `list()` method returns a `List` of `Object` arrays. Each `Object` array contains the projected properties for that row. The following example returns just the contents of the name and description columns from the `Product` data. Remember, Hibernate is polymorphic, so this also returns the name and description from the `Software` objects that inherit from `Product`.

```
Criteria crit = session.createCriteria(Product.class);
ProjectionList projList = Projections.projectionList();
projList.add(Projections.property("name"));
projList.add(Projections.property("description"));
crit.setProjection(projList);
List results = crit.list();
```

Use this query style when you want to cut down on network traffic between your application servers and your database servers. For instance, if your table has a large number of columns, this can slim down your results. In other cases, you may have a large set of joins that would return a very wide result set, but you are only interested in a few columns. Lastly, if your clients have limited memory, this can save you trouble with large datasets. But make sure you don't have to retrieve additional columns for the entire result set later, or your optimizations may actually decrease performance.

You can group your results (using SQL's GROUP BY clause) with the groupProperty projection. The following example groups the products by name and price:

```
Criteria crit = session.createCriteria(Product.class);
ProjectionList projList = Projections.projectionList();
projList.add(Projections.groupProperty("name"));
projList.add(Projections.groupProperty("price"));
crit.setProjection(projList);
List results = crit.list();
```

As you can see, projections open up aggregates to the Criteria API, which means that developers do not have to drop into HQL for aggregates. Projections offer a way to work with data that is closer to the JDBC result set style, which may be appropriate for some parts of your application.

Query By Example (QBE)

In this section, because of the confusing terminology, we will refer to excerpts from our demonstration code as "samples" rather than "examples," reserving "example" for its peculiar technical meaning in the context of QBE.

In QBE, instead of programmatically building a Criteria object with Criterion objects and logical expressions, you can partially populate an instance of the object. You use this instance as a template and have Hibernate build the criteria for you based upon its values. This keeps your code clean and makes your project easier to test. The org.hibernate.criterion.Example class contains the QBE functionality. Note that the Example class implements the Criterion interface, so you can use it like any other restriction on a criteria query.

For instance, if we have a user database, we can construct an instance of a user object, set the property values for type and creation date, and then use the Criteria API to run a QBE query. Hibernate will return a result set containing all user objects that match the property values that were set. Behind the scenes, Hibernate inspects the Example object and constructs an SQL fragment that corresponds to the properties on the Example object.

To use QBE, we need to construct an Example object first. Then we need to create an instance of the Example object, using the static create() method on the Example class. The create() method takes the Example object as its argument. You add the Example object to a Criteria object just like any other Criterion object.

The following basic example searches for suppliers that match the name on the example **Supplier** object:

```
Criteria crit = session.createCriteria(Supplier.class);
Supplier supplier = new Supplier();
supplier.setName("MegaInc");
crit.add(Example.create(supplier));
List results = crit.list();
```

When Hibernate translates our **Example** object into an SQL query, all the properties on our **Example** objects get examined. We can tell Hibernate which properties to ignore; the default is to ignore null-valued properties. To search our products or software in the sample database with QBE, we need to either specify a price or tell Hibernate to ignore properties with a value of zero, because we used a double primitive for storage instead of a **Double** object. The double primitive initializes to zero, while a **Double** would have been null; and so, left to its own devices, the QBE logic will assume that we are specifically searching for prices of zero, whereas we want it to ignore this default value.

We can make the Hibernate **Example** object exclude zero-valued properties with the **excludeZeroes()** method. We can exclude properties by name with the **excludeProperty()** method, or exclude nothing (compare for null values and zeroes exactly as they appear in the **Example** object) with the **excludeNone()** method. This sample applies the **excludeZeroes()** method to ignore the default zero prices:

```
Criteria crit = session.createCriteria(Product.class);
Product exampleProduct = new Product();
exampleProduct.setName("Mouse");
Example example = Example.create(exampleProduct);
example.excludeZeroes();
crit.add(example);
List results = crit.list();
```

Other options on the **Example** object include ignoring the case for strings with the **ignoreCase()** method, and enabling use of SQL's **LIKE** for comparing strings, instead of just using **equals()**.

We can also use associations for QBE. In the following sample, we create two examples: one for the product and one for the supplier. We use the technique explained in the "Associations" section of this chapter to retrieve objects that match both criteria.

```
Criteria prdCrit = session.createCriteria(Product.class);
Product product = new Product();
product.setName("M%");
Example prdExample = Example.create(product);
prdExample.excludeProperty("price");
prdExample.enableLike();
Criteria suppCrit = prdCrit.createCriteria("supplier");
Supplier supplier = new Supplier();
supplier.setName("SuperCorp");
suppCrit.add(Example.create(supplier));
prdCrit.add(prdExample);
List results = prdCrit.list();
```

We also ignore the price property for our product, and we use **LIKE** for object comparison, instead of equals.

The QBE API works best for searches in which you are building the search from user input. The Hibernate team recommends using QBE for advanced searches with multiple fields, because it's easier to set values on business objects than to manipulate restrictions with the Criteria API.

JPA 2 and the Type-safe Criteria API

In addition to the Hibernate Criteria API described in this chapter, Hibernate 3.5 now includes a new type-safe Criteria API based on the JPA 2 standard. The advantage of this new API is that if you use it, you will not have any errors related to typos in the Criteria restrictions – such as "prduct". Rather than relying on strings in Criteria, there is a new metamodel class for each JPA entity. You would use the references to properties in these metamodel classes in your criteria restrictions, but you would use the javax.persistence criteria classes. Hibernate can generate the metamodel classes for you from the annotations in your existing classes.

The JPA 2 type-safe criteria does not replace the Hibernate Criteria API covered in this chapter. Both criteria APIs will accomplish the same thing for building a query. In this book, we covered the Hibernate way of doing things – which you will see in existing applications, as the JPA 2 criteria API is new for Hibernate 3.5. Using the JPA 2 Criteria API is similar to the Hibernate Criteria API, but references to fields as strings are replaced with references to fields on generated metamodel classes.

In our example for this chapter, we would run the Hibernate Static Metamodel Generator against our annotated classes to generate the metamodel class files. The Metamodel Generator is a Java 6 annotation processor, so your existing build tools should automatically create the generated metamodel classes. Depending on how you have your source repository and project layout arranged, you will have to decide where to put the generated classes.

Summary

Using the Criteria API is an excellent way to get started developing with HQL. The developers of Hibernate have provided a clean API for adding restrictions to queries with Java objects. Although HQL isn't too difficult to learn, some developers prefer the Criteria Query API, as it offers compile-time syntax checking—although column names and other schema-dependent information cannot be checked until run time.

In the next chapter, we discuss the use of Hibernate filters to restrict the range of data against which queries are applied.

CHAPTER 11

■ ■ ■

Filtering the Results of Searches

Your application will often need to process only a subset of the data in the database tables. In these cases, you can create a Hibernate *filter* to eliminate the unwanted data. Filters provide a way for your application to limit the results of a query to data that passes the filter's criteria. Filters are not a new concept—you can achieve much the same effect using SQL database views—but Hibernate offers a centralized management system for them.

Unlike database views, Hibernate filters can be enabled or disabled during a Hibernate session. In addition, Hibernate filters can be parameterized, which is particularly useful when you are building applications on top of Hibernate that use security roles or personalization.

When to Use Filters

As an example, consider a web application that manages user profiles. Currently, your application presents a list of all users through a single web interface, but you receive a change request from your end user to manage active users and expired users separately. For this example, assume that the status is stored as a column on the user table.

One way to solve this problem is to rewrite every HQL SELECT query in your application, adding a WHERE clause that restricts the result by the user's status. Depending on how you built your application, this could be an easy undertaking or it could be complex, but you still end up modifying code that you have already tested thoroughly, potentially changing it in many different places.

With Hibernate 3, you can create a filter restriction for the user status. When your end user selects the user type (active or expired), your application activates the user status filter (with the proper status) for the end user's Hibernate session. Now, any SELECT queries will return the correct subset of results, and the relevant code for the user status is limited to two locations: the Hibernate session and the user status filter.

The advantage of using Hibernate filters is that you can programmatically turn filters on or off in your application code, and your filters are defined in your Hibernate mapping documents for easy maintainability. The major disadvantage of filters is that you cannot create new filters at run time. Instead, any filters your application requires need to be specified in the proper Hibernate annotations or mapping documents. Although this may sound somewhat limiting, the fact that filters can be parameterized makes them pretty flexible. For our user status filter example, only one filter would need to be defined in the mapping document (albeit in two parts). That filter would specify that the status column must match a named parameter. You would not need to define the possible values of the status column in the Hibernate annotations or mapping documents—the application can specify those parameters at run time.

Although it is certainly possible to write applications with Hibernate that do not use filters, we find them to be an excellent solution to certain types of problems—notably security and personalization.

Defining and Attaching Filters

Your first step is to define filters for your application. You can either use annotations or XML mapping documents to define filters. The basic concepts are the same no matter where you put the filter definition. You will need a filter definition, which has the name of the filter and the name and type of each of the parameters the filter uses. Filter parameters are similar to named parameters for HQL queries. Both require a : before the parameter name. Each class or collection that you want to filter needs to have a filter attached to it through an annotation or an XML element.

You may have more than one filter for each filter definition, and each class can have more than one filter. This is a little confusing—the extra level of abstraction allows you to define all the filter parameters in one place and then refer to them in the individual filter conditions. To illustrate filters, we will show examples of defining filters through annotations and through XML mapping documents.

Filters with Annotations

To use filters with annotations, you will need to use the @FilterDef, @ParamDef, and @Filter annotations. The @FilterDef annotation defines the filter and belongs to either the class or the package. To define a filter on a class, add an @FilterDef annotation after the @Entity annotation. For example:

```
@Entity
@FilterDef(name="latePaymentFilter", parameters=@ParamDef( name="dueDate", type="date" ) )
```

After you have defined your filters, you can attach them to classes or collections with the @Filter annotation. The @Filter annotation takes two parameters: name and condition. The name references a filter definition that we have previously described in an annotation. The condition parameter is an HQL WHERE clause. The parameters in the condition are denoted with colons, similar to named parameters in HQL. The parameters have to be defined on the filter definition. Here is an example of the filter annotation:

```
@Filter(name="latePaymentFilter", condition=":dueDate = paymentDate")
```

■ **Note** Defining filters on each class is simple, but if you use filters in multiple classes, you will have a lot of duplication. To define any annotation at a package level, you will need to create a Java source file named package-info.java in the package. The package-info.java class should only include the package-level annotations and then declare the package immediately afterward. It is not meant to be a Java class. You will also need to tell Hibernate to map the package when you configure Hibernate, either through the addPackage() method on AnnotationConfiguration or in your Hibernate configuration XML.

Filters with XML Mapping Documents

For the XML mapping documents, use the `<filter-def>` XML element. These filter definitions must contain the name of the filter and the names and types of any filter parameters. Specify filter parameters with the `<filter-param>` XML element. Here is an excerpt from a mapping document with a filter called latePaymentFilter defined:

```
<?xml version='1.0' encoding='utf-8'?>
<!DOCTYPE hibernate-mapping
    PUBLIC "-//Hibernate/Hibernate Mapping DTD//EN"
    "http://hibernate.sourceforge.net/hibernate-mapping-3.0.dtd">

<hibernate-mapping>
  <class ...

  </class>
  <filter-def name="latePaymentFilter">
    <filter-param name="dueDate" type="date"/>
  </filter-def>
</hibernate-mapping>
```

Once you have created the filter definitions, you need to attach the filters to class or collection mapping elements. You can attach a single filter to more than one class or collection. To do this, you add a `<filter>` XML element to each class and/or collection. The `<filter>` XML element has two attributes: name and condition. The name references a filter definition (for instance: latePaymentFilter). The condition represents a WHERE clause in HQL. Here's an example:

```
<class ...
  <filter name="latePaymentFilter" condition=":dueDate = paymentDate"/>
</class>
```

Each `<filter>` XML element must correspond to a `<filter-def>` element.

Using Filters in Your Application

Your application programmatically determines which filters to activate or deactivate for a given Hibernate session. Each session can have a different set of filters with different parameter values. By default, sessions do not have any active filters—you must explicitly enable filters programmatically for each session. The Session interface contains several methods for working with filters, as follows:

- public Filter enableFilter(String filterName)

- public Filter getEnabledFilter(String filterName)

- public void disableFilter(String filterName)

These are pretty self-explanatory—the enableFilter(String filterName) method activates the specified filter, the disableFilter(String filterName) method deactivates the method, and if you have already activated a named filter, getEnabledFilter(String filterName) retrieves that filter.

The `org.hibernate.Filter` interface has six methods. You are unlikely to use `validate()`; Hibernate uses that method when it processes the filters. The other five methods are as follows:

- `public Filter setParameter(String name, Object value)`
- `public Filter setParameterList(String name, Collection values)`
- `public Filter setParameterList(String name, Object[] values)`
- `public String getName()`
- `public FilterDefinition getFilterDefinition()`

The `setParameter()` method is the most useful. You can substitute any Java object for the parameter, although its type should match the type you specified for the parameter when you defined the filter. The two `setParameterList()` methods are useful for using `IN` clauses in your filters. If you want to use `BETWEEN` clauses, use two different filter parameters with different names. Finally, the `getFilterDefinition()` method allows you to retrieve a `FilterDefinition` object representing the filter metadata (its name, its parameters' names, and the parameter types).

Once you have enabled a particular filter on the session, you do not have to do anything else to your application to take advantage of filters, as we demonstrate in the following example.

A Basic Filtering Example

Because filters are very straightforward, a basic example allows us to demonstrate most of the filter functionality, including activating filters and defining filters in mapping documents.

In the following Hibernate XML mapping document (`User.hbm.xml`), we created a filter definition called `activatedFilter`. The parameters for the filter must be specified with `<filter-param>` XML elements (as shown in Listing 11-1), which use the `<activatedParam>` XML element. You need to specify a type for the filter parameter so that Hibernate knows how to map values to parameters. Once you have defined your filter, you need to attach the filter definition to a class. At the end of our `User` class definition, we specify that it uses a filter named `activatedFilter`. We then need to set a condition corresponding to an HQL `WHERE` clause for the attached filter. In our case, we used `:activatedParam = activated`, where `:activatedParam` is the named parameter specified on the filter definition, and `activated` is the column name from the user table. You should ensure that the named parameter goes on the left-hand side so that Hibernate's generated SQL doesn't interfere with any joins.

Listing 11-1. Hibernate XML Mapping for User

```xml
<?xml version='1.0' encoding='utf-8'?>
<!DOCTYPE hibernate-mapping
    PUBLIC "-//Hibernate/Hibernate Mapping DTD//EN"
    "http://hibernate.sourceforge.net/hibernate-mapping-3.0.dtd">

<hibernate-mapping>
  <class name="com.hibernatebook.filters.User">
    <id name="id" type="int">
      <generator class="native"/>
    </id>
```

```
      <property name="username" type="string" length="32"/>
      <property name="activated" type="boolean"/>
      <filter name="activatedFilter" condition=":activatedParam = activated"/>
    </class>
    <filter-def name="activatedFilter">
      <filter-param name="activatedParam" type="boolean"/>
    </filter-def>
</hibernate-mapping>
```

With the filter definition created and attached to a class with a suitable condition, we need to activate the filter. The next class, `SimpleFilterExample`, inserts several user records into the database, and then immediately displays them to the screen. The class uses a very simple HQL query (`from User`) to obtain the result set from Hibernate. The `displayUsers()` method writes the usernames and activation status out to the console. Before you have enabled any filters on the database, this method will return the full list of users. Once you have enabled the first filter (`activatedFilter`) to show only activated users, call the same `displayUsers()` method—the results of the query are the same as if you had added a WHERE clause containing an `"activated=true"` clause. You can just as easily change the filter's parameter value to show inactive users, as shown in Listing 11-2.

Listing 11-2. Invoking Filters from Code

```
package com.hibernatebook.filters;

import java.util.Iterator;

import org.hibernate.Filter;
import org.hibernate.Query;
import org.hibernate.Session;
import org.hibernate.SessionFactory;
import org.hibernate.Transaction;

import org.hibernate.cfg.Configuration;

public class SimpleFilterExample {
    public static void main (String args[]) {
        SessionFactory factory =
            new Configuration().configure().buildSessionFactory();
        Session session = factory.openSession();

        //insert the users
        insertUser("ray",true,session);
        insertUser("jason",true,session);
        insertUser("beth",false,session);
        insertUser("judy",false,session);
        insertUser("rob",false,session);

        //Show all users
        System.out.println("===ALL USERS===");
        displayUsers(session);
```

```java
        //Show activated users
        Filter filter = session.enableFilter("activatedFilter");
        filter.setParameter("activatedParam",new Boolean(true));
        System.out.println("===ACTIVATED USERS===");
        displayUsers(session);

        //Show nonactivated users
        filter.setParameter("activatedParam",new Boolean(false));
        System.out.println("===NON-ACTIVATED USERS===");
        displayUsers(session);

        session.close();
    }

    public static void displayUsers(Session session) {
        session.beginTransaction();
        Query query = session.createQuery("from User");
        Iterator results = query.iterate();
        while (results.hasNext())
        {
            User user = (User) results.next();
            System.out.print(user.getUsername() + " is ");
            if (user.isActivated())
            {
                System.out.println("activated.");
            }
            else
            {
                System.out.println("not activated.");
            }
        }

        session.getTransaction().commit();
    }

    public static void insertUser(String name, boolean activated, Session session) {
        session.beginTransaction();

        User user = new User();
        user.setUsername(name);
        user.setActivated(activated);
        session.save(user);

        session.getTransaction().commit();
    }
}
```

The output of SimpleFilterExample is as follows:

```
===ALL USERS===
ray is activated.
jason is activated.
beth is not activated.
judy is not activated.
rob is not activated.
===ACTIVATED USERS===
ray is activated.
jason is activated.
===NON-ACTIVATED USERS===
beth is not activated.
judy is not activated.
rob is not activated.
```

Listing 11-3 gives the User class used for this chapter's examples. The only fields it contains are id, username, and activated.

Listing 11-3. The Source Code for the User Class

```
package com.hibernatebook.filters;

public class User {
    private int id;
    private String username;
    private boolean activated;

    public boolean isActivated() {
        return activated;
    }

    public void setActivated(boolean activated) {
        this.activated = activated;
    }

    public int getId() {
        return id;
    }

    public void setId(int id) {
        this.id = id;
    }

    public String getUsername() {
        return username;
    }

    public void setUsername(String username) {
        this.username = username;
    }
}
```

Because filters do not use any database-specific functionality beyond the Hibernate configuration, you should not encounter any difficulty running this example on databases other than HSQLDB. The Hibernate configuration file defines the database configuration and connection information, along with the XML mapping document for the User class (see Listing 11-4).

Listing 11-4. The Hibernate XML Configuration File for the Example

```xml
<?xml version='1.0' encoding='utf-8'?>
<!DOCTYPE hibernate-configuration PUBLIC
    "-//Hibernate/Hibernate Configuration DTD//EN"
    "http://hibernate.sourceforge.net/hibernate-configuration-3.0.dtd">
<hibernate-configuration>
    <session-factory>
        <property name="hibernate.connection.driver_class">
            org.hsqldb.jdbcDriver
        </property>
        <property name="hibernate.connection.url">
            jdbc:hsqldb:file:filterdb;SHUTDOWN=true
        </property>
        <property name="hibernate.connection.username">sa</property>
        <property name="hibernate.connection.password"></property>
        <property name="hibernate.connection.pool_size">0</property>
        <property name="dialect">
            org.hibernate.dialect.HSQLDialect
        </property>

        <!-- Mapping files -->
        <mapping resource="com/hibernatebook/filters/User.hbm.xml"/>
    </session-factory>
</hibernate-configuration>
```

The source code for this chapter includes the schema we used for the HSQL database to create the table for the filterdb database.

Summary

Filters are a useful way to separate some database concerns from the rest of your code. A set of filters can cut back on the complexity of the HQL queries used in the rest of your application, at the expense of some runtime flexibility. Instead of using views (which must be created at the database level), your applications can take advantage of dynamic filters that can be activated as and when they are required.

## CHAPTER 12

Case Study – Using Hibernate with an Existing Database

Many projects you work on with Hibernate will be with existing databases. In contrast to some of the examples we have shown so far where we have created our database from the Java object model, this example project starts with a database that already has a schema. In our example in this chapter, we are going to create a new Java object model for the database, using annotations for our Hibernate mappings, and then run some queries that use the Hibernate Query Language.

Our example application will find the highest point (in meters) of every state in the United States, and then list them out. To do this, we will need to have a set of data that contains the elevation of various geographic points. The GeoNames group at `http://www.geonames.org` provides a freely available data set of geographic places for download. The data is licensed under a Creative Commons Attribution 3.0 License.

We are not going to create a web application or another user interface for this case study to avoid bringing more technologies into the example than we have to, so the example is somewhat limited. At the end of the chapter, we will discuss ways to improve the case study example if you want to learn more about Hibernate.

Setting up the Database

The first step for our example is setting up a database. For the example, we are going to use MySQL, although you can certainly use another database. We will need to download the data from the GeoNames web site, create the database schema, and then load the data into the database. After creating the database, we can start to explore the data and determine what we will need to do to create a Java object model that maps to the database.

Downloading the Data

The GeoNames data download page is at http://download.geonames.org/export/dump/. The bulk of the data is organized by country, by the International Standards Organization (ISO) code. The ISO code for the United States is US. At the time of this writing, the US.zip file at http://download.geonames.org/export/dump/US.zip was 53 megabytes. Data for other countries is also available at the same download page, or you can download data for all countries in the allCountries.zip file, which was 176 megabytes at the time of writing.

In addition to the US.zip main data file, you will also need the following auxiliary data files, all much smaller, also available from the same download page:

- admin1Codes.txt

- admin2Codes.txt

- featureCodes_en.txt

Unzip the US.zip file to get a text file that you will import into the database. But first, take some time to review and understand the data.

Understanding the Data

Before we can create an application that uses the GeoNames data, we have to understand what data we have and how it is organized. The following subsections describe each of the four files that you have downloaded.

■ **Note** The GeoNames web site has a README file available at http://download.geonames.org/export/dump/readme.txt. The README explains what data is available from GeoNames and how it is organized if you want to read in more detail than this chapter provides about the data formats and the other available data on the web site.

Geographic Names

For our example, the most important information is the list of geographic names, latitudes, longitudes, elevations, and other information in the geonames table. In order, the columns in the geonames table are as shown in Table 12-1. You can review the data by looking at the contents of US.zip, which contains a README file named readme.txt and a data file named US.txt.

Table 12-1. The Columns in the geonames Database Table

Name	Type	Description
geonameid	integer	Primary key for geonames database
name	varchar(200)	Name of this location in UTF-8
asciiname	varchar(200)	Name of this location in ASCII
alternatenames	varchar(5000)	Other names this location has, as a comma separated list. This information also exists in another table called alternatenames in denormalized form.

Name	Type	Description
latitude	double	In decimal degrees
longitude	double	In decimal degrees
feature_class	char(1)	General type of place this location is. Refer to http://www.geonames.org/export/codes.html
feature_code	varchar(10)	Description of what specific type of place this location is. Refer to http://www.geonames.org/export/codes.html
country_code	char(2)	Two-letter ISO country codes, such as US for United States or GB for United Kingdom
cc2	varchar(60)	Other country codes that may correspond to place – comma separated
admin1_code	varchar(20)	Code corresponding to first administrative division within a country (State for the USA). Can be looked up in admin1Codes table.
admin2_code	varchar(80)	Code corresponding to second administrative division within a country (County for the USA). Can be looked up in admin2Codes table.
admin3_code	varchar(20)	Code corresponding to third administrative division within a country.
admin4_code	varchar(20)	Code corresponding to fourth administrative division within a country.
population	bigint (equivalent of Java long)	Human population of the location
elevation	integer	The height of the place (in meters)
gtopo30	integer	Average elevation of a 1 kilometer by 1 kilometer area (in meters)
timezone	varchar(40)	The timezone id, which can be looked up in the timezone table
modification_date	date	The last time the record was modified in yyyy-MM-dd format

For our purposes, the most important fields in the table are geonameid, name, elevation, admin1_code, and admin2_code. The geonameid field is the primary key, and it will satisfy Hibernate's requirements for a primary key for each record. We will use the name field for display, and the elevation field is how we will determine heights. The `admin1_code` and `admin2_code` fields correspond to states and counties (for the United States), and we will need these to determine what the names of these geographic units are.

Country Subdivision Codes

The next data file we will examine is the `admin1Codes.txt` data file. It only has two columns – one contains the country code and the first level administrative subdivision code, and the other column contains the name of the subdivision. For instance:

```
US.AK Alaska
```

If we imported this directly into a table with two columns, using the first column as a primary key, we would have to create a new column that concatenated the `country_code` and the `admin1_code` on the `geonames` table to use as the foreign key for the many-to-one relationship between `geonames` and `admin1Codes`.

It would be much better if we could split the data up into three columns, and then use the first two columns as a composite primary key. For instance:

```
US AK Alaska
```

We can take advantage of the fact that the data is delimited with both the tab character (the whitespace between US.AK and Alaska in our first example) and a period character. When we load the data into MySQL, we will split the first field up as we load the data. This approach is very MySQL specific, but is the sort of problem that can be common when you work with sources of data you don't control. The result will be the three-column database table described in Table 12-2.

Table 12-2. The Columns in the admin1Codes Database Table

Name	Type	Description
country_code	char(2)	Two-letter ISO country codes, such as US for United States or GB for United Kingdom. Forms composite primary key with admin1_code.
admin1_code	varchar(20)	Code corresponding to first administrative division within a country (State for the USA). Forms composite primary key with country_code.
name	varchar(200)	Name of this location in UTF-8

Second-Level Subdivisions

The admin2Codes.txt file contains similar information to admin1Codes, but it is more complicated. The data in this file contains second level political subdivision names. For instance, in the United States our states are subdivided into counties, so the admin2Codes.txt file contains county names. Here is an example line for Travis County in the state of Texas in the United States:

```
US.TX.453     Travis County     Travis County     4737316
```

The first field in this file is the identifier, <country code>.<admin 1 code>.<admin 2 code>. Similar to what we did for the previous file, we will have to split this first field apart during the data loading process. The next field is the name in UTF-8, followed by the name in ASCII. After both names is a number signifying the geonameId. We are going to keep this number in the database but not use it as an identifier, as we don't have that information in the geonames table to use as a foreign key. Table 12-3 shows the resulting database columns.

Table 12-3. The Columns in the admin2Codes Database Table

Name	Type	Description
country_code	char(2)	Two-letter ISO country codes, such as US for United States or GB for United Kingdom. Forms composite primary key with admin1_code and admin2_code
admin1_code	varchar(20)	Code corresponding to first administrative division within a country (State for the USA). Forms composite primary key with country_code and admin2_code
admin2_code	varchar(20)	Code corresponding to second administrative division within a country (County for the USA). Forms composite primary key with country_code and admin1_code
name	varchar(200)	Name of this location in UTF-8
asciiname	varchar(200)	Name of this location in ASCII
geonameid	int	Identifier as a unique place

Feature Codes

The last file we will load is the feature codes. The feature codes describe the type of location each place is. The descriptions are somewhat generic, but could be useful for determining whether a highpoint is an actual mountain. The feature codes are located in featurecodes_en.txt. Other versions of this file are available for other languages. Here is a sample line from the feature codes download:

```
T.MESA  mesa(s) a flat-topped, isolated elevation with steep slopes on all sides, less
extensive than a plateau
```

Similar to the last two files we discussed, the unique id for each feature code is identified with a concatenation of the feature class with the feature code, using a period as the separator. The next field is the name, and the last field is the description. Table 12-4 describes these fields as columns in a database table.

Table 12-4. The Columns in the featurecodes Database Table

Name	Type	Description
feature_class	char(1)	One letter Feature code. Forms composite primary key with feature_code
feature_code	varchar(10)	Code corresponding to a type of geographic feature. Forms composite primary key with feature_class
name	varchar(200)	Name of this feature in UTF-8

Creating the Database Schema

From the names and data types, we can construct a table definition for the MySQL database for the geonames table. Most of the work is already done for us – the GeoNames README includes the data types for each column, saving us the trouble of inspecting the tab-delimited file for maximum field lengths and whether a column is nullable.

In addition to the README, we used information provided in the Frequently Asked Questions (FAQ) section of the GeoNames forum to create a script to create the database and tables. We also placed indexes on the elevation, admin1_code and admin2_code fields on the geonames table to speed up our searches. In our experiments with MySQL, we found that adding the indexes before loading the data took about the same amount of total time as loading the data and then adding the indexes. Depending on the database, your experience will vary.

Listing 12-1 shows our script for creating the database, the tables, and indexes.

Listing 12-1. MySQL Script for Creating the Geonames Database

```
# set character-set to utf8
SET NAMES 'utf8';

# create the database
CREATE DATABASE IF NOT EXISTS `geonames` ;

# use the database
USE `geonames`;

# drop the geonames table
DROP TABLE IF EXISTS `geonames`.`geonames`;

# create the geonames table
CREATE TABLE `geonames`.`geonames` (
`geonameId` int(10) unsigned NOT NULL default '0',
`name` varchar(200) NOT NULL default '',
`asciiname` varchar(200) NOT NULL default '',
`alternatenames` varchar(5000) NOT NULL default '',
`latitude` double NOT NULL default '0',
`longitude` double NOT NULL default '0',
```

```
`feature_class` char(1) ,
`feature_code` varchar(10) ,
`country_code` char(2),
`cc2` varchar(60),
`admin1_code` varchar(20),
`admin2_code` varchar(80),
`admin3_code` varchar(20),
`admin4_code` varchar(20),
`population` bigint(11),
`elevation` int(11),
`gtopo30` int(11),
`timezone` varchar(40),
`modification_date` date,
PRIMARY KEY (`geonameid`)
) CHARACTER SET utf8 ;

# create the geonames indexes
CREATE INDEX elevation_index ON geonames (elevation);
CREATE INDEX admin1_code_index ON geonames (admin1_code);
CREATE INDEX admin2_code ON geonames (admin2_code);


# drop the admin1codes table
DROP TABLE IF EXISTS `geonames`.`admin1codes`;

#create the admin1codes table
CREATE TABLE `geonames`.`admin1codes` (
`country_code` char(2) NOT NULL,
`admin1_code` varchar(20),
`name` varchar(200) NOT NULL default '',
PRIMARY KEY (`country_code`,`admin1_code`)
) CHARACTER SET utf8 ;

# drop the admin2codes table
DROP TABLE IF EXISTS `geonames`.`admin2codes`;

#create the admin2codes table
CREATE TABLE `geonames`.`admin2codes` (
`country_code` char(2) NOT NULL,
`admin1_code` varchar(20),
`admin2_code` varchar(20),
`name` varchar(200) NOT NULL default '',
`asciiname` varchar(200) NOT NULL default '',
`geonameid` int,
PRIMARY KEY (`country_code`,`admin1_code`,`admin2_code`)
) CHARACTER SET utf8 ;

# drop the featurecodes table
DROP TABLE IF EXISTS `geonames`.`featurecodes`;
```

```
#create the featurecodes table
CREATE TABLE `geonames`.`featurecodes` (
`feature_class` char(1) NOT NULL,
`feature_code` varchar(10) NOT NULL,
`name` varchar(200) NOT NULL default '',
`description` varchar(200) NOT NULL default '',
PRIMARY KEY (`feature_class`,`feature_code`)
) CHARACTER SET utf8 ;
```

From the database script, you can see that we have set up composite primary keys on the admin1codes, admin2codes and featurecodes tables.

Loading the Data

Loading the data directly into the database using a native import tool is usually the best way to bulk load very large data sets. You will need to have created the table in the database first, then run the import tool against the tab-delimited file. Unfortunately, the details of this process differ greatly from database to database. Some have a nice graphical user interface to the database management. Others only offer command line tools.

For the MySQL database, we can use a simple command named LOAD DATA INFILE to do a bulk import. You will need to tell MySQL the name of the file to be imported, the table to import it into, the character set of the import, and the names of the columns within the file. We also used information from the FAQ section of the GeoNames forum to develop this script.

The geonames table import is straightforward, although it can take a while on a slower computer. The concatenated ids for the other three tables have to be split up, however, so we could join the geonames table to the other tables with many-to-one relationships. To do this requires some MySQL string manipulation of the values in the tab-delimited import files before they are inserted into the database. The two MySQL functions we use are SET and SUBSTRING_INDEX . The SET function assigns the right-hand side of an expression to the variable on the left-hand side (signified with an @ sign). The SUBSTRING_INDEX function is a clever piece of functionality that can split any string that has regular field delimiters such as "." or "|" into subsections. We use it to split the concatenated ids apart by the ".". Tell the SUBSTRING_INDEX function which string you want to split, which delimiter you want to split it with, and which piece you want as an integer (counting from the left if positive, from the right if negative).

From the below Listing 12-2, here is a piece of code that illustrates what we did:

```
SET country_code=SUBSTRING_INDEX(@concatid,'.',1),
admin1_code=SUBSTRING_INDEX(SUBSTRING_INDEX(@concatid,'.',2),'.',-1),
admin2_code=SUBSTRING_INDEX(@concatid,'.',-1);
```

The @concatid variable would be something similar to

US.DE.003

The result would be that the country_code would be US, the admin1_code would be DE, and the admin2_code would be 003.

Listing 12-2. MySQL Script for Loading the Geonames Database

```
# set character-set to utf8
SET NAMES 'utf8';

# use the database
USE `geonames`;

#load data into the admin1codes table
LOAD DATA LOCAL INFILE '../admin1Codes.txt' INTO TABLE `geonames`.`admin1Codes` CHARACTER
SET utf8 (@concatid,name)
SET country_code=SUBSTRING_INDEX(@concatid,'.',1),
admin1_code=SUBSTRING_INDEX(@concatid,'.',-1);


#load data into the admin2codes table
LOAD DATA LOCAL INFILE '../admin2Codes.txt' INTO TABLE `geonames`.`admin2Codes` CHARACTER
SET utf8 (@concatid,name,asciiname,geonameid)
SET country_code=SUBSTRING_INDEX(@concatid,'.',1),
admin1_code=SUBSTRING_INDEX(SUBSTRING_INDEX(@concatid,'.',2),'.',-1),
admin2_code=SUBSTRING_INDEX(@concatid,'.',-1);


#load data into the featurecodes table
LOAD DATA LOCAL INFILE '../featureCodes_en.txt' INTO TABLE `geonames`.`featurecodes`
CHARACTER SET utf8 (@concatid,name,description)
SET feature_class=SUBSTRING_INDEX(@concatid,'.',1),
feature_code=SUBSTRING_INDEX(@concatid,'.',-1);

LOAD DATA LOCAL INFILE '../US/US.txt' INTO TABLE `geonames`.`geonames` CHARACTER SET utf8
(geonameId,name,asciiname,alternatenames,latitude,longitude,feature_class,feature_code,count
ry_code,cc2,admin1_code,admin2_code,admin3_code,admin4_code,population,elevation,gtopo30,tim
ezone,modification_date);
```

Creating a Java Object Model

Now that we have a populated database, we can create a Java object model that corresponds to our tables. In some cases, we will not want to have a direct correspondence between Java objects and database tables, but because we are building a new application, it will make our code easier to understand and easier to develop if we map Java objects directly to database tables.

That said, we do not need and do not necessarily want to have a Java class that has every field in the database table as it is stored in the database. For instance, a very basic translation of the geonames table to a class might look like (without getters and setters or Hibernate mappings) that shown in Listing 12-3.

Listing 12-3. Very Basic Java Object for the Geonames Table

```java
package com.hibernatebook.highpoint.entity;

import java.util.Date;

public class BasicGeoName {

    private int geonameId;
    private String name;
    private String asciiName;
    private String alternateNames;
    private double latitude;
    private double longitude;
    private String featureClass;
    private String featureCode;
    private String countryCode;
    private String cc2;
    private String admin1Code;
    private String admin2Code;
    private String admin3Code;
    private String admin4Code;
    private long population;
    private int elevation;
    private int gtopo30;
    private String timezone;
    private Date modificationDate;
}
```

The class in Listing 12-3 would be alright, but we can do much better with Hibernate. For instance, rather than have a String `admin1Code` field, we should have an object reference. The same goes for the `admin2Code` field and the `featureCode` field. We will keep the door open for future expansion to other countries, where the names of the political subdivisions aren't necessarily state and county.

We will come back to mapping the `geonames` table to a Java class (which we will name `Place` instead of `BasicGeoName`). Our `Place` class has many-to-one relationships with the other three classes (from the other three tables), so we create those first.

Creating the Admin1Code Class

The three auxiliary classes all share common traits – composite primary keys and only string or integers for fields. Modeling composite primary keys with Hibernate annotations is discussed in Chapter 6, where we describe three different approaches. For each of these auxiliary classes, we chose to use the `@IdClass` annotation. In some cases, the composite primary keys for a database table actually have some coherent structure. For instance, some legacy databases use a first name and last name with a birth date. A case like this calls for creating a new business object with the primary key fields and marking it as an `@Embeddable` annotation.

For these three tables, the structure of the composite primary key is basically the structure we are trying to model – a hierarchy. Moving the data to an embedded object wouldn't make a lot of sense when we go to use the class.

Before we can use the `@IdClass` annotation on the entity class, we need to create a primary key class that is not part of the structure of our `Admin1Code` class. The primary key class has to follow several rules. The class must

- be a public class

- have a default constructor

- be serializable

- allow public access to fields or getter/setter methods for setting each field in the composite primary key

- implement equals() and hashCode() properly (Most IDEs, including NetBeans and Eclipse will generate those methods for you)

The two fields we use for the primary key are `countryCode` and `admin1_code`. We create a new class called `@com.hibernatebook.highpoint.entity.Admin1CodePK` and add those two fields to it along with getters and setters. We mark the class as Serializable and generate equals() and hashCode() methods from NetBeans. Listing 12-4 shows the class. Notice that there are no Hibernate or JPA imports.

Listing 12-4. Primary Key Class for the Admin1Code Class

```
package com.hibernatebook.highpoint.entity;

import java.io.Serializable;

public class Admin1CodePK implements Serializable {

    public Admin1CodePK() {
    }
    private String countryCode;
    private String admin1Code;

    public String getCountryCode() {
        return countryCode;
    }

    public void setCountryCode(String countryCode) {
        this.countryCode = countryCode;
    }

    public String getAdmin1Code() {
        return admin1Code;
    }

    public void setAdmin1Code(String admin1Code) {
        this.admin1Code = admin1Code;
    }
```

```
    @Override
    public boolean equals(Object obj) {
        if (obj == null) {
            return false;
        }
        if (getClass() != obj.getClass()) {
            return false;
        }
        final Admin1CodePK other = (Admin1CodePK) obj;
        if ((this.countryCode == null) ? (other.countryCode != null) :
!this.countryCode.equals(other.countryCode)) {
            return false;
        }
        if ((this.admin1Code == null) ? (other.admin1Code != null) :
!this.admin1Code.equals(other.admin1Code)) {
            return false;
        }
        return true;
    }

    @Override
    public int hashCode() {
        int hash = 7;
        hash = 71 * hash + (this.countryCode != null ? this.countryCode.hashCode() : 0);
        return hash;
    }
}
```

After creating the primary key class, we can create the `Admin1Code` class shown in Listing 12-5. We model the fields like any other Java class we use for Hibernate. The name of our class is a little different from the name of the database table, so we used the `@Table` annotation We also changed some of the property names to have a camel case style, so to map those to the database field names, we use the `@Column` annotation. More interesting is the way we set up the class to use a composite primary key. On the class, we put the `@IdClass` annotation with the name of our primary key class, and on the two composite primary key getter methods, we put the `@Id` annotation.

Listing 12-5. *The Admin1Code Class*

```
package com.hibernatebook.highpoint.entity;

import javax.persistence.Column;
import javax.persistence.Entity;
import javax.persistence.Id;
import javax.persistence.IdClass;
import javax.persistence.Table;

@IdClass(com.hibernatebook.highpoint.entity.Admin1CodePK.class)
@Entity
@Table(name = "Admin1Codes")
public class Admin1Code {
```

```
    @Id
    @Column(name = "country_code")
    private String countryCode;
    @Id
    @Column(name = "admin1_code")
    private String admin1Code;
    private String name;

    public String getCountryCode() {
        return countryCode;
    }

    public void setCountryCode(String countryCode) {
        this.countryCode = countryCode;
    }

    public String getAdmin1Code() {
        return admin1Code;
    }

    public void setAdmin1Code(String admin1Code) {
        this.admin1Code = admin1Code;
    }

    public String getName() {
        return name;
    }

    public void setName(String name) {
        this.name = name;
    }
}
```

Creating the Admin2Code Class

The Admin2Code class is very similar to the Admin1Code class. The major difference is that the composite primary key has three fields instead of two. We develop the class in a similar manner. For the primary key class, Admin2CodePK, we choose not to use inheritance from the Admin1CodePK class because that would imply a relationship that does not really exist between the two composite primary keys – they are related but not interdependent. Listing 12-6 shows the Admin2CodePK class. Listing 12-7 shows the Admin2Code class.

Listing 12-6. Primary Key Class for the Admin2Code Class

```java
package com.hibernatebook.highpoint.entity;

import java.io.Serializable;

public class Admin2CodePK implements Serializable {

    public Admin2CodePK() {
    }
    private String countryCode;
    private String admin1Code;
    private String admin2Code;

    public String getCountryCode() {
        return countryCode;
    }

    public void setCountryCode(String countryCode) {
        this.countryCode = countryCode;
    }

    public String getAdmin1Code() {
        return admin1Code;
    }

    public void setAdmin1Code(String admin1Code) {
        this.admin1Code = admin1Code;
    }

    public String getAdmin2Code() {
        return admin2Code;
    }

    public void setAdmin2Code(String admin2Code) {
        this.admin2Code = admin2Code;
    }

    @Override
    public boolean equals(Object obj) {
        if (obj == null) {
            return false;
        }
        if (getClass() != obj.getClass()) {
            return false;
        }
        final Admin2CodePK other = (Admin2CodePK) obj;
        if ((this.countryCode == null) ? (other.countryCode != null) :
!this.countryCode.equals(other.countryCode)) {
            return false;
        }
```

```
        if ((this.admin1Code == null) ? (other.admin1Code != null) :
!this.admin1Code.equals(other.admin1Code)) {
            return false;
        }
        if ((this.admin2Code == null) ? (other.admin2Code != null) :
!this.admin2Code.equals(other.admin2Code)) {
            return false;
        }
        return true;
    }

    @Override
    public int hashCode() {
        int hash = 7;
        hash = 67 * hash + (this.countryCode != null ? this.countryCode.hashCode() : 0);
        hash = 67 * hash + (this.admin1Code != null ? this.admin1Code.hashCode() : 0);
        hash = 67 * hash + (this.admin2Code != null ? this.admin2Code.hashCode() : 0);
        return hash;
    }
}
```

Listing 12-7. The Admin2Code Class

```
package com.hibernatebook.highpoint.entity;

import javax.persistence.Column;
import javax.persistence.Entity;
import javax.persistence.Id;
import javax.persistence.IdClass;
import javax.persistence.Table;

@IdClass(com.hibernatebook.highpoint.entity.Admin2CodePK.class)
@Entity
@Table(name = "Admin2Codes")
public class Admin2Code {

    @Id
    @Column(name = "country_code")
    public String getCountryCode() {
        return countryCode;
    }

    public void setCountryCode(String countryCode) {
        this.countryCode = countryCode;
    }

    @Id
    @Column(name = "admin1_code")
    public String getAdmin1Code() {
        return admin1Code;
    }
```

```
    public void setAdmin1Code(String admin1Code) {
        this.admin1Code = admin1Code;
    }

    @Id
    @Column(name = "admin2_code")
    public String getAdmin2Code() {
        return admin2Code;
    }

    public void setAdmin2Code(String admin2Code) {
        this.admin2Code = admin2Code;
    }

    public String getAsciiName() {
        return asciiName;
    }

    public void setAsciiName(String asciiName) {
        this.asciiName = asciiName;
    }

    public int getGeonameid() {
        return geonameid;
    }

    public void setGeonameid(int geonameid) {
        this.geonameid = geonameid;
    }

    public String getName() {
        return name;
    }

    public void setName(String name) {
        this.name = name;
    }
    private String countryCode;
    private String admin1Code;
    private String admin2Code;
    private String name;
    private String asciiName;
    private int geonameid;
}
```

Creating the Feature Codes Class

The feature codes classes are similar to the classes just shown in the preceding section. You must create a composite primary key and a name and description. Listing 12-8 shows the primary key class, while

Listing 12-9 shows the main class. After these two classes, we discuss the `Place` class that maps to the main `geonames` table, which is the most interesting part of the mapping.

Listing 12-8. Primary Key Class for the FeatureCode Class

```java
package com.hibernatebook.highpoint.entity;

import java.io.Serializable;

public class FeatureCodePK implements Serializable {

    public String getFeatureClass() {
        return featureClass;
    }

    public void setFeatureClass(String featureClass) {
        this.featureClass = featureClass;
    }

    public String getFeatureCode() {
        return featureCode;
    }

    public void setFeatureCode(String featureCode) {
        this.featureCode = featureCode;
    }
    private String featureClass;
    private String featureCode;

    @Override
    public boolean equals(Object obj) {
        if (obj == null) {
            return false;
        }
        if (getClass() != obj.getClass()) {
            return false;
        }
        final FeatureCodePK other = (FeatureCodePK) obj;
        if ((this.featureClass == null) ? (other.featureClass != null) :
!this.featureClass.equals(other.featureClass)) {
            return false;
        }
        if ((this.featureCode == null) ? (other.featureCode != null) :
!this.featureCode.equals(other.featureCode)) {
            return false;
        }
        return true;
    }
```

```
    @Override
    public int hashCode() {
        int hash = 5;
        hash = 53 * hash + (this.featureClass != null ? this.featureClass.hashCode() : 0);
        hash = 53 * hash + (this.featureCode != null ? this.featureCode.hashCode() : 0);
        return hash;
    }
}
```

Listing 12-9. The FeatureCode Class

```
package com.hibernatebook.highpoint.entity;

import javax.persistence.Column;
import javax.persistence.Entity;
import javax.persistence.Id;
import javax.persistence.IdClass;
import javax.persistence.Table;

@IdClass(com.hibernatebook.highpoint.entity.FeatureCodePK.class)
@Entity
@Table(name = "featurecodes")
public class FeatureCode {

    @Id
    @Column(name = "feature_class")
    public String getFeatureClass() {
        return featureClass;
    }

    public void setFeatureClass(String featureClass) {
        this.featureClass = featureClass;
    }

    @Id
    @Column(name = "feature_code")
    public String getFeatureCode() {
        return featureCode;
    }

    public void setFeatureCode(String featureCode) {
        this.featureCode = featureCode;
    }

    public String getName() {
        return name;
    }

    public void setName(String name) {
        this.name = name;
    }
```

```
    public String getDescription() {
        return description;
    }

    public void setDescription(String description) {
        this.description = description;
    }
    private String featureClass;
    private String featureCode;
    private String name;
    private String description;
}
```

Creating the Place Class

Rather than naming our main Java class `GeoName`, like our database table, we name it `Place`, to make it more generic. This way we could add data from other sources in the future and not mislead ourselves into thinking that all of the data came from the GeoNames database. We also choose not to build on our `BasicGeoName` class from earlier in the chapter, which we used to illustrate a naïve mapping of the database table to a Java class.

We'll start by creating a Java class named `Place` in the `com.hibernatebook.highpoint.entity` package. Because we named our Java class something other than the name of the database table, we need to use the `@Table` annotation as well as the `@Entity` annotation. Listing 12-10 shows the final code for the class.

Unlike the three previous classes, the `Place` class has a simple primary key, the `geonameid` that we mark with the `@Id` annotation. We don't put a `@GeneratedValue` annotation on the id because it is assigned. If we add more data to the table, we will need to assign our own ids – as these could clash with ids that GeoNames uses later, it would be better to create a new table. This will also make it easy to drop the data in the table and get a fresh import of data from the GeoNames web site.

More interesting is the way we create many-to-one relationships with the state, county, and feature code tables. In each case, we add a `@ManyToOne` annotation to our getter method for each of the three objects. Because they use composite primary keys, we have to tell Hibernate to specifically use more than one column when Hibernate does a join between the two tables using the `@JoinColumns` annotation and `@JoinColumn` annotation. Each `@JoinColumn` annotation has to contain a reference to the column on the `geonames` table and to a column on the other table. We also have to tell Hibernate not to allow inserts or updates to those columns because we are using `admin1_code` and `country_code` for two relationships.

Finally, our data is not perfect. Some places are missing `admin1_code`, `admin2_code` or `feature_code` values. This data isn't critical for our project, so we don't want our application to crash if it can't find an object on the other side of the relationship. By default, Hibernate will throw an exception if you load a value that doesn't exist in a many-to-one relationship and then try and use it. Hibernate will create a proxy object to represent that value, and if it doesn't exist, it will throw an exception.

You can override this default behavior with the `@NotFound` annotation on the many-to-one relationship, on the same getter method as the `@ManyToOne` annotation. It has two possible values – exception (the default) and ignore. The downside of telling Hibernate to ignore values that aren't found is that Hibernate now has to query the database to determine if the other end of the many-to-one relationship should be a null value (instead of a proxy object that will throw an exception if you create it with nothing on the other end of a many-to-one relationship). We decided to use the `@NotFound` annotation, but we need to check for null values before using the `Admin1Code`, `Admin2Code` or `FeatureCode` objects. If you use this annotation, and your application is experiencing performance problems, turn SQL debugging on (in your Hibernate configuration, hibernate.show_sql=true) and trace the SQL statements Hibernate uses. You may need to clean up your data or rethink the usage of a many-to-one relationship.

We also mapped the modification date using the @Temporal annotation to tell Hibernate to use java.sql.Date to represent the modification date, as we are interested in the year, month, and day, not the time. See Chapter 6 for more information about the @Temporal annotation.

One last note – we did not include the alternatenames column in the Place class. The reason for this is that the field is a comma-delimited list of alternative place names that can also be downloaded as a text file and placed in its own table.

Listing 12-10. The Place Class for the Geonames Table

```java
package com.hibernatebook.highpoint.entity;

import java.util.Date;
import javax.persistence.Column;
import javax.persistence.Entity;
import javax.persistence.Id;
import javax.persistence.JoinColumn;
import javax.persistence.JoinColumns;
import javax.persistence.ManyToOne;
import javax.persistence.Table;
import javax.persistence.Temporal;
import org.hibernate.annotations.NotFound;
import org.hibernate.annotations.NotFoundAction;

@Entity
@Table(name = "geonames")
public class Place {

    @Id
    public int getGeonameId() {
        return geonameId;
    }

    public void setGeonameId(int geonameId) {
        this.geonameId = geonameId;
    }

    @ManyToOne
    @NotFound(action = NotFoundAction.IGNORE)
    @JoinColumns({
        @JoinColumn(name = "country_code", referencedColumnName = "country_code", insertable
= false, updatable = false),
        @JoinColumn(name = "admin1_code", referencedColumnName = "admin1_code", insertable =
false, updatable = false)
    })
    public Admin1Code getAdmin1Code() {
        return admin1Code;
    }
```

```java
    public void setAdmin1Code(Admin1Code admin1Code) {
        this.admin1Code = admin1Code;
    }

    @ManyToOne
    @NotFound(action = NotFoundAction.IGNORE)
    @JoinColumns({
        @JoinColumn(name = "country_code", referencedColumnName = "country_code", insertable
= false, updatable = false),
        @JoinColumn(name = "admin1_code", referencedColumnName = "admin1_code", insertable =
false, updatable = false),
        @JoinColumn(name = "admin2_code", referencedColumnName = "admin2_code", insertable =
false, updatable = false)
    })
    public Admin2Code getAdmin2Code() {
        return admin2Code;
    }

    public void setAdmin2Code(Admin2Code admin2Code) {
        this.admin2Code = admin2Code;
    }

    @ManyToOne
    @NotFound(action = NotFoundAction.IGNORE)
    @JoinColumns({
        @JoinColumn(name = "feature_code", referencedColumnName = "feature_code"),
        @JoinColumn(name = "feature_class", referencedColumnName = "feature_class")
    })
    public FeatureCode getFeatureCode() {
        return featureCode;
    }

    public void setFeatureCode(FeatureCode featureCode) {
        this.featureCode = featureCode;
    }

    public String getName() {
        return name;
    }

    public void setName(String name) {
        this.name = name;
    }

    public String getAsciiName() {
        return asciiName;
    }

    public void setAsciiName(String asciiName) {
        this.asciiName = asciiName;
    }
```

```java
public double getLatitude() {
    return latitude;
}

public void setLatitude(double latitude) {
    this.latitude = latitude;
}

public double getLongitude() {
    return longitude;
}

public void setLongitude(double longitude) {
    this.longitude = longitude;
}

public long getPopulation() {
    return population;
}

public void setPopulation(long population) {
    this.population = population;
}

public int getElevation() {
    return elevation;
}

public void setElevation(int elevation) {
    this.elevation = elevation;
}

public int getGtopo30() {
    return gtopo30;
}

public void setGtopo30(int gtopo30) {
    this.gtopo30 = gtopo30;
}

public String getTimezone() {
    return timezone;
}

public void setTimezone(String timezone) {
    this.timezone = timezone;
}
```

```
@Column(name = "modification_date")
@Temporal(javax.persistence.TemporalType.DATE)
public Date getModificationDate() {
    return modificationDate;
}

public void setModificationDate(Date modificationDate) {
    this.modificationDate = modificationDate;
}
private int geonameId;
private String name;
private String asciiName;
private double latitude;
private double longitude;
private long population;
private int elevation;
private int gtopo30;
private String timezone;
private Date modificationDate;
private Admin1Code admin1Code;
private Admin2Code admin2Code;
private FeatureCode featureCode;
}
```

Configuring Hibernate

To get our application to run, we re-used some of the Ant harness from Chapter 3. You will need a copy of the hibernate.cfg.xml file (shown in Listing 12-11) that points to the MySQL database with your GeoNames data. It also needs to map our four entity classes.

Listing 12-11. The Hibernate.cfg.xml configuration file

```
<!DOCTYPE hibernate-configuration PUBLIC
    "-//Hibernate/Hibernate Configuration DTD 3.0//EN"
    "http://hibernate.sourceforge.net/hibernate-configuration-3.0.dtd">

<hibernate-configuration>
  <session-factory>
    <property name="hibernate.connection.url">
      jdbc:mysql://localhost/geonames?characterEncoding=utf-8
    </property>
    <property name="hibernate.connection.driver_class">
      com.mysql.jdbc.Driver
    </property>
    <property name="hibernate.connection.username">root</property>
    <property name="hibernate.connection.password"></property>
    <property name="hibernate.connection.pool_size">0</property>
```

```
    <property name="hibernate.dialect">
        org.hibernate.dialect.MySQLDialect
    </property>
    <property name="hibernate.show_sql">false</property>

    <!-- "Import" the mapping resources here -->
    <mapping class="com.hibernatebook.highpoint.entity.Place"/>
    <mapping class="com.hibernatebook.highpoint.entity.Admin1Code"/>
    <mapping class="com.hibernatebook.highpoint.entity.Admin2Code"/>
    <mapping class="com.hibernatebook.highpoint.entity.FeatureCode"/>

  </session-factory>
</hibernate-configuration>
```

The Ant harness just runs a class that lists the highpoints. We don't do anything with the Hibernate tools for this chapter, as we started with a database. Listing 12-12 shows the code for the harness.

Listing 12-12. The build.xml Ant Harness

```
<project name="highpoint">

    <property file="build.properties"/>

    <property name="src" location="src"/>
    <property name="bin" location="bin"/>
    <property name="sql" location="sql"/>
    <property name="hibernate.tools"
      value="${hibernate.tools.home}${hibernate.tools.path}"/>
    <property name="hibernate.tools.lib"
      value="${hibernate.tools.home}${hibernate.tools.lib.path}"/>

    <path id="classpath.base">
        <pathelement location="${src}"/>
        <pathelement location="${bin}"/>
        <pathelement location="${slf4j.implementation.jar}"/>
        <pathelement location="${hibernate.home}/hibernate3.jar"/>
        <fileset dir="${hibernate.home}/lib" includes="**/*.jar"/>
        <pathelement location="${mysql.jdbc.jar}"/>
    </path>

    <target name="compile">
        <mkdir dir="${bin}"/>
        <javac srcdir="${src}" destdir="${bin}" classpathref="classpath.base"/>
    </target>

    <target name="showHighpoints" depends="compile">
        <java classname="com.hibernatebook.highpoint.ShowHighpoints"
classpathref="classpath.base"/>
    </target>
</project>
```

We will also need a build.properties file that points to the location of our MySQL JDBC Driver jar (downloadable from www.mysql.com). Listing 12-13 shows this file. Edit this file to point to the correct directories for your development environment.

Listing 12-13 The build.properties file for Ant

```
# Path to the hibernate install directory
hibernate.home=/hibernate/hibernate-3.5.0

# Path to the SLF4J implementation JAR for the logging framework to use
slf4j.implementation.jar=/slf4j/slf4j-1.5.11/slf4j-simple-1.5.11.jar

# Path to the MySQL JDBC Driver JAR
mysql.jdbc.jar=../mysql-connector-java-5.1.12-bin.jar
```

Building the List of High Points

After doing all the data importing and object mapping, actually creating a list of high points will be straightforward. Our basic algorithm will be to ask the database what the highest elevation is for each state, and then ask the database for all of the locations in that state with that elevation. Because the data isn't perfectly sanitized, and because there could certainly be more than one point in a geographic area with the same elevation as another, we ask for a list of locations. We will then print them nicely to standard output.

Developing the HQL Query

HQL supports standard SQL aggregate methods – in particular the `Max()` method. The `Max()` method will return the maximum value from a numerical column in a results set. For instance, you could ask for the highest population of a city in the dataset with a query like:

```
select max(population) from Place
```

For our example, we are going to ask for the maximum elevation by state (admin1Code). There are several ways to go about this – we could use a GROUP BY clause, for instance to limit database traffic. In this case, we want to get more than one highpoint if they exist, so we should break up our queries.
    The first query we will use just asks for the highest elevation in the state:

```
select max(elevation) from Place where admin1_code = :state
```

After that runs, we can use the elevation to get a list of **Place** objects from Hibernate. This saves us the trouble of loading them ourselves. We may be trading off a little performance, with one extra query per state.

```
from Place where admin1_code = :state and elevation = :highpointElevation
```

Using these **Place** objects, we can perform any standard operations we want to.

Running the Query

Our code is very simple – it asks for a list of states, then it executes the two HQL queries for each state. After retrieving the list of highpoints for each state, it creates nicely formatted output for the list. Listing 12-14 shows our solution.

Listing 12-14. The Application that Finds and Shows the Highpoints.

```java
package com.hibernatebook.highpoint;

import com.hibernatebook.highpoint.entity.Admin1Code;
import com.hibernatebook.highpoint.entity.Place;
import java.util.List;
import org.hibernate.Query;
import org.hibernate.Session;
import org.hibernate.SessionFactory;
import org.hibernate.cfg.AnnotationConfiguration;

public class ShowHighpoints {
public static void main(String[] args) {
        SessionFactory factory =
                new AnnotationConfiguration().configure().buildSessionFactory();
        Session session = factory.openSession();


        Query statesQuery = session.createQuery("from Admin1Code where country_code =
'US'");
        List<Admin1Code> states = statesQuery.list();
        for (Admin1Code state : states) {
            Query elevationQuery = session.createQuery(
                    "select max(elevation) from Place where admin1_code = :state");
            elevationQuery.setString("state", state.getAdmin1Code());
            Integer highpointElevation = (Integer) elevationQuery.uniqueResult();


            Query stateHighpointsQuery = session.createQuery(
                    "from Place where admin1_code = :state and elevation =
:highpointElevation");
            stateHighpointsQuery.setString("state", state.getAdmin1Code());
            stateHighpointsQuery.setInteger("highpointElevation", highpointElevation);

            List<Place> highpoints = stateHighpointsQuery.list();
            for (Place highpoint : highpoints)
            {
                highpointElevation = highpoint.getElevation();
                String output = state.getName() + ":" + highpoint.getName() + ":" +
highpointElevation + ":";
```

```java
            if (highpoint.getFeatureCode() != null)
            {
                output = output + highpoint.getFeatureCode().getName() + ":";
            }
            else
            {
                output = output + "N/A:";
            }

            if (highpoint.getAdmin2Code() != null)
            {
                output = output + highpoint.getAdmin2Code().getName();
            }
            else
            {
                output = output + "N/A";
            }

            System.out.println(output);

        }
    }

    session.close();
    }
}
```

We can run this basic example with:

```
ant showHighpoints
```

Just a heads-up: the elevations are in meters, not feet.. You can easily enough add the math to the solution in Listing 12-14 if you want to show feet in your output. Listing 12-15 shows some partial results from running the application.

Listing 12-15. Partial Results from running ant showHighpoints

```
[java] Alaska:Churchill Peaks:6105:mountain:Denali Borough
[java] Alaska:Mount McKinley:6105:mountain:Denali Borough
[java] Alaska:South Peak:6105:mountain:Denali Borough
[java] Alabama:WCIQ-TV (Mount Cheaha):731:tower:Cleburne County
[java] Arkansas:Magazine Mountain:837:mountain:Logan County
[java] Arkansas:Magazine Mountain:837:ridge(s):Logan County
[java] Arkansas:Signal Hill:837:mountain:Logan County
[java] Arizona:Humphreys Peak:3829:mountain:Coconino County
[java] California:Mount Whitney:4405:mountain:Tulare County
[java] Colorado:Mount Elbert:4397:mountain:Lake County
```

Moving Forward with the Example

There are several things you could do to get more out of this example. The first would be to port it to whatever database you usually use – SQL Server, Oracle, PostgreSQL, or anything else supported by Hibernate. Another idea would be to add support for alternative names using the downloadable text file from GeoNames. This example was not interactive – if you are a web or Swing programmer, build a simple front end to the GeoNames database that lets users search for high points. You could also try writing a bulk importer using Hibernate that would load the large US.txt data import file.

Summary

This example started with a real world existing database with a number of issues that made it interesting to adapt to Hibernate – composite primary keys and missing data on one side of a relationship. We also created a database schema and loaded our data into MySQL after extracting the primary keys for some of the tables. We built a small client that used our Java classes and some HQL to find the highest point in every state. There is certainly plenty of room to expand on our very simple example and do some interesting projects!

■ ■ ■

More Advanced Features

In this appendix, we discuss some of the features that, strictly speaking, lie outside the scope of this book, but that you should be aware of if you go on to use Hibernate in more depth.

Managed Versioning and Optimistic Locking

While we have saved versioning for this appendix's discussion of advanced features, it is actually quite straightforward to understand and apply. Consider the following scenario:

- Client A loads and edits a record.

- Client B loads and edits the same record.

- Client A commits its edited record data.

- Client B commits its differently edited record data.

While the scenario is simple, the problems it presents are not. If Client A establishes a transaction, then Client B may not be able to load and edit the same record. Yet in a web environment, it is not unlikely that Client A will close a browser window on the open record, never committing or canceling the transaction, so that the record remains locked until the session times out. Clearly this is not a satisfactory solution. Usually, you will not want to permit the alternative scenario, in which no locking is used, and the last person to save a record wins!

The solution, versioning, is essentially a type of optimistic locking (see Chapter 8). When any changes to an entity are stored, a version column is updated to reflect the fact that the entity has changed. When a subsequent user tries to commit changes to the same entity, the original version number will be compared against the current value if they differ, the commit will be rejected.

The Hibernate/JPA 2 annotation mappings and the Hibernate XML-based mappings both provide a simple syntax for indicating which field should be used for storing the managed version information. The annotation for this field is shown in Listing A-1.

Listing A-1. Marking the Version Attribute Using Annotations

```
@Version
protected int getVersionNum() {
    return versionNum;
}
```

The default optimistic locking strategy for Hibernate is versioning, so if you provide a `<version>` element in your XML configuration, this will be used as long as you have enabled dynamic updates (as shown in Listing A-2).

Listing A-2. Marking the Version Attribute Using XML Mappings

```
<class dynamic-update="version" optimistic-lock="version" ... >
    ...
    <version name="versionNum"/>
</class>
```

The version attribute is defined in a very similar way to the normal property attribute configuration. The version can be of type `long`, `integer`, `short`, `timestamp`, or `calendar` (note that using the `<timestamp ... />` element is an equivalent alternative to the use of the `<version type="timestamp" ... />` element syntax).

The `<class>` element's `optimistic-lock` attribute can be used to override the default versioning-based optimistic locking strategy. You can disable it entirely (despite the presence of a version field) using a value of `none`. You can explicitly state that versioning should be used with a value of `version`. You can elect to use dirty checking, with the `dirty` and `all` options.

If you elect not to use versioning, dirty checking offers an alternative form of optimistic locking. Here, the values of the entities are themselves checked to see if they have changed since the entity was originally obtained. As with versioning-based optimistic locking, the check against the database is carried out when the changes are committed. If an optimistic lock type of `dirty` is selected, then only those fields that have changed since the persistent entity was obtained will be checked (the `Session` keeps track of the appropriate state information). If an optimistic lock type of `all` is selected, then all the fields comprising the entity will be checked for changes. If the fields being checked have changed prior to the commit, then the commit will fail.

Versioning is generally a simpler and more reliable approach, so we suggest that you use this whenever you need optimistic locking features.

Maps

In addition to the default mode (POJO) and the XML mode (Dom4J) described previously, the Hibernate session can be accessed in one more way: as a map of name/value pairs. This mode is accessed by calling the `getSession()` method with a parameter of `EntityMode.MAP` (see Listing A-3).

Listing A-3. Accessing a Hibernate Session in Map Mode

```
package sample.map;

import java.util.*;
import org.hibernate.EntityMode;
import org.hibernate.*;
import org.hibernate.cfg.Configuration;

public class AccessAsMap {
    private static final SessionFactory sessionFactory = new Configuration()
        .configure().buildSessionFactory();
```

```
public static void main(String[] args) throws Exception {

    System.out.println("Preparing the Session objects");
    Session session = sessionFactory.openSession();
    Session mapSession = session.getSession(EntityMode.MAP);

    System.out.println("Reading the map entries for XXX");
    session.beginTransaction();

    Map entity = (Map)mapSession.get("sample.entity.Category",new Long(2));
    System.out.println("Category Title: " + entity.get("title"));

    System.out.println("Contains Adverts:");
    Set adverts = (Set)entity.get("adverts");
    Iterator adIt = adverts.iterator();
    while(adIt.hasNext()) {
        Map advert = (Map)adIt.next();
        System.out.println(advert.get("title"));
    }

    session.getTransaction().commit();
    session.close();

    System.out.println("Done.");
    }
}
```

Changes written to the Map objects will be persisted exactly as if a normal persistent POJO object had been updated. Note that only the entities themselves will be represented as Maps—not any of their attributes having a value type, or associations using Collection types. For example, in Listing A-3, the Category entity is represented as a Map, but its title attribute is represented as a String and its adverts attribute is represented as a Set—however, the Set itself contains Advert entities represented as Maps.

■ **Note** You may find problems in edge cases where Hibernate expects certain objects to be POJOs and not hashmaps, such as composite primary key id classes.

Limitations of Hibernate

First and foremost, Hibernate wants every entity to be identifiable with a primary key. Ideally, it would like this to be a *surrogate key* (a single column distinct from the fields of the table). Hibernate will accept a primary key that is not a surrogate key. For example, the username column might be used to uniquely identify an entry in the user table. Hibernate will also accept a composite key as its primary key, so that the username and hostname might be used to form the primary key if the username alone does not serve to identify the row.

In the real world, things do not really work like that. Any database that has been around the block a few times is likely to have at least one table for which the primary key has been omitted. For instance, the contents of the table may not have needed to be involved in any relations with other tables. While this is still bad database design, the error is only exposed when Hibernate tries to map objects to data. It may be that adding a suitable surrogate key column is an option—when this is the case, we urge you to do so. In practice, however, the fundamental schema may not be under the developer's control, or other applications may break if the schema is radically changed.

In most scenarios, a developer will be able to arrange the creation of views or stored procedures. It may be possible to create the appearance of a suitable primary key using these if no other options present themselves, but you should consult with your database administrators, since a table for which no true primary key can be obtained is likely to cause long-term corruption of your data.

Finally, if you can neither change a broken schema nor add views or stored procedures to ameliorate its effects, you have the option of obtaining a pure JDBC connection (see Listing A-4) from the session to the database, and carrying out traditional connected database access. This is the option of last resort, and is only truly of value when you anticipate being able to correct the faulty schema at some future time.

Listing A-4. *Obtaining a JDBC Connection from Hibernate*

```
SessionFactory factory =
    new Configuration().configure().buildSessionFactory();
Session session = factory.openSession();
Connection connection = session.getConnection();
```

Hand-Rolled SQL

While Hibernate cannot operate upon entities that lack primary keys, it is also extremely awkward to use Hibernate when there is a poor correspondence between the tables and the classes of your object model.

Using a Direct Mapping

Figure A-1 presents a fairly typical example of a valid database model that may be painful to represent in our mapping files.

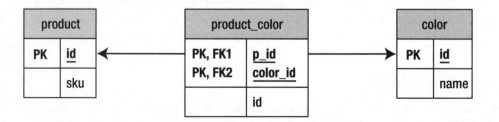

Figure A-1. *A problematic but legal schema*

Here, the `product` table represents a product (for example, a flashlight). The `color` table represents the colors in which it is sold. The link table named `product_color` then allows us to identify a product by stock keeping unit (SKU), and identify the colors in which it is available.

If we do not mind the **Product** object retaining a set of colors (representing the colors in which it can be sold), then we have no problem; but if we want to distinguish between a red flashlight and a green one, things become more difficult (see Listing A-5).

Listing A-5. A Fairly Direct Representation of the Product as an XML mapping

```
<class name="com.hibernatebook.legacy.Product" table="product_color">

    <composite-id
        class="com.hibernatebook.legacy.ProductKey"
        name="key">

        <key-property type="int" name="id" column="product_id"/>
        <key-property type="int" name="colorId" column="color_id"/>

    </composite-id>


    <many-to-one
        name="color"
        class="com.hibernatebook.legacy.Color"
        column="color_id"
        insert="false"
        update="false"/>

    <many-to-one
        name="data"
        class="com.hibernatebook.legacy.ProductData"
        column="product_id"
        insert="false"
        update="false"/>

</class>
```

There are several dissatisfying aspects to the mapping in Listing A-5. First, rather than mapping our product table, we have mapped the link table. This makes sense when you consider that the primary key formed from the two columns of this table uniquely identifies a "colored product," which the **product** table alone cannot do.

Second, we are obliged to create a number of distinct objects to represent the class: the **Product** class itself, a class to represent the primary key (inevitable where a composite **id** occurs), a class to represent the other attributes of the product, and the **Color** class.

Last, the use of the columns more than once within the mapping requires us to flag them so that they cannot be written—this is a *read-only mapping*.

Using a View

Fortunately, most databases provide a simple mechanism for manipulating a schema so that it better matches the business requirements. A database view will allow you to put together a join that appears to be a table. By a suitable choice of columns from the existing tables, you can construct a view that is much easier to map (see Listing A-6).

Listing A-6. A View on the Product Tables

```
create view vwProduct (ProductKey,ColorKey,Id,SKU,ColorId)
AS
    select
        p.id as ProductKey,
        c.id as ColorKey,
        p.id as Id,
        p.sku as SKU,
        c.id as ColorId
    from
        product p,
        product_color pc,
        color c
    where
        p.id = pc.product_id
    and
        pc.color_id = c.id;
```

This view effectively reformats our table so that it has a correct (composite) primary key formed from the link table's two columns. It makes the SKU data available directly, and it retains the foreign key into the color table.

Listing A-7 is a much more natural mapping.

Listing A-7. The Revised Mapping

```
<class name="com.hibernatebook.legacy.Product" table="vwProduct">
  <composite-id
      class="com.hibernatebook.legacy.ProductKey"
      name="key">
      <key-property
          type="int"
          name="id"
          column="ProductKey"/>
      <key-property
          type="int"
          name="colorId"
          column="ColorKey" />
  </composite-id>

  <property
      name="id"
      type="int"
      column="id"
      insert="false"
      update="false"
      unique="true"/>
```

```
<property
    name="SKU"
    type="int"
    column="sku"
    insert="false"/>

<many-to-one
    name="color"
    class="com.hibernatebook.legacy.Color"
    column="ColorId"/>
</class>
```

The behavior of the composite primary key is unchanged, but the SKU now becomes a simple property. The color entity is mapped as before.

The caveat for this approach is the problem of writing data to the mapping. Some databases (for example, versions 4 and lower of MySQL) do not support writable views, and others may have only limited support for them. To avoid views in these circumstances, we must abandon complete portability in favor of database-specific SQL inserted directly into the mapping file.

Putting SQL into an Annotation or Mapping

Hibernate provides three annotations and several XML tags that can be used to override the default behavior when writing to the database. Instead of accepting the SQL generated by Hibernate from the information in the mapping file, you can dictate exactly how changes to an entity should be enforced. The disadvantage is that you will lose Hibernate's guarantee of cross-database platform portability. The advantage is that you can carry out operations that are not explicitly described in the mapping, such as calculating and inserting values in the process of carrying out an insert.

The annotations are @SQLInsert, @SQLUpdate, and @SQLDelete; while the XML mapping elements are <sql-insert>, <sql-update>, and <sql-delete>. All of these work in the same way.

If you take a look at the DDL script for this example, you will see that our client table includes seven fields, the last of which is the country field, as shown in Listing A-8.

Listing A-8. The DDL Script to Create the Client Table

```
create table client (
    id int not null primary key,
    name varchar(32) not null,
    number varchar(10),
    streetname varchar(128),
    town varchar(32),
    city varchar(32),
    country varchar(32)
);
```

We will, however, ignore the country field in our mapping file. We would like this to be automatically set to UK whenever a client entity is persisted.

Depending on the database, this could be implemented as part of the view's support for writing operations, or as a trigger invoked when the other fields are written—but we use the @SQLInsert annotation or <sql-insert> tag to specify the operation to perform.

The necessary ordering of the parameters can be determined by running Hibernate with logging enabled for the `org.hibernate.persister.entity` level. You must do this before you add the mapping. Listing A-9 shows a suitably formatted `<sql-insert>` element with the parameters suitably ordered. Note that the identifier field `id` is in the last position—not the first, as you might have expected.

Listing A-9. The Mapping File Using Explicit SQL to Update the Tables

```
<class name="com.hibernatebook.legacy.Client" table="Client">
    <id type="int" name="id" column="id">
       <generator class="native"/>
    </id>
    <property type="text" name="name" column="name"/>
    <property type="text" name="number" column="number"/>
    <property type="text" name="streetname" column="streetname"/>
    <property type="text" name="town" column="town"/>
    <property type="text" name="city" column="city"/>

    <sql-insert>
    insert into client(name,number,streetname,town,city,id,country)
    values (?,?,?,?,?,?,'UK');
    </sql-insert>
</class>
```

In addition to the three SQL terms for writing to the database, you can specify hand-rolled SQL for reading. This is appended as `<sql-query>` tags outside the `class` tag (see Listing A-10). They are not intrinsically a part of the mapping. However, you *can* specify that one of them should be used as the default loader for your class.

Listing A-10. An Alternative Mapping File Defining a Default Loader

```
...
<hibernate-mapping>
    <class name="com.hibernatebook.legacy.Client"
           table="Client">
       <id type="int" name="id" column="id">
          <generator class="native"/>
       </id>
       <property name="name"/>
       <property name="number"/>
       <property name="streetname"/>
       <property name="town"/>
       <property name="city"/>

       <loader query-ref="DefaultQuery"/>
    </class>
```

```
<sql-query name="DefaultQuery">
   <return alias="c"
           class="com.hibernatebook.legacy.Client"/>
   SELECT
      id as {c.id},
      'NOT SPECIFIED' as {c.name},
      number as {c.number},
      streetname as {c.streetname},
      town as {c.town},
      city as {c.city}
   FROM
      Client
   WHERE
      id = ?
</sql-query>

</hibernate-mapping>
```

■ **Tip** Unfortunately, this technique is not quite as sophisticated as you might hope—the custom SQL will not be invoked in general terms. Only if the `id` is explicitly supplied, as is the case when calling the `Session` class's `get()` method, will the default handling be overridden in favor of the loader query.

Invoking Stored Procedures

Data outlives application logic. This is a general rule of thumb, and as we can attest, it holds true in practice. The natural lifespan of a database will tend to see multiple applications. The lifespan of some of these applications will, in turn, tend to overlap, so that at any one time we expect substantially different code bases to be accessing the same data.

To resolve such issues, databases usually provide their own programming language to allow complex business rules to be expressed and enforced within the boundary of the database itself. These languages are expressed in stored procedures—essentially an API to the database. Often, free-form SQL access to such a database is denied, and only access through stored procedures is permitted. Barring errors in the code of the stored procedures themselves, this removes any risk of corruption.

One final advantage of using stored procedures is that when a substantial calculation is required, the use of a stored procedure can reduce the network traffic involved. For example, if you invoke a stored procedure to calculate the grand total of a table of accounts, only the request and the result figure would need to traverse the network. The equivalent client-side implementation would need to acquire the value to be totaled from every row!

Taking the client example from the "Putting SQL into a Mapping" section, we could replace the SQL logic in the `<sql-insert>` tag with a call to a suitable stored procedure. The callable attribute is set to `true` to indicate that Hibernate needs to issue a call to a stored procedure instead of a standard query (see Listing A-11).

Listing A-11. Mapping a Call to the Stored Procedure

```
<sql-insert callable="true">
   {call insertClient(?,?,?,?,?,?)}
</sql-insert>
```

In the stored procedure definition (see Listing A-12), you will note that the order of the parameters to be passed in has been tailored to match the order in which they will be provided by Hibernate.

Listing A-12. The Logic of the Stored Procedure

```
CREATE PROCEDURE
    insertClient( p_name varchar(32),
                  p_number varchar(10),
                  p_streetname varchar(128),
                  p_town varchar(32),
                  p_city varchar(32),
                  p_id int)
AS
BEGIN
   INSERT INTO client
       (id,name,number,streetname,town,city,country)
   VALUES
       (:p_id,:p_name,:p_number,:p_streetname,:p_town,:p_city,'UK');
END
```

By obtaining a JDBC connection from the session, it is of course possible to invoke stored procedures directly; however, you must be aware that the Hibernate session cache cannot track these updates.

Events

Hibernate 3 actually implements most of its functionality as event listeners. When you register a listener with Hibernate, the listener entirely supplants the default functionality.

If you look at the methods of the `SessionImpl` class, which is the internal Hibernate implementation of the `Session` interface, you'll see why this is the case. Most of the methods have a form very similar to that shown in Listing A-13.

Listing A-13. The Implementation of a Typical Method in `SessionImpl`

```
        private void fireSaveOrUpdate(SaveOrUpdateEvent event) {
                errorIfClosed();
                checkTransactionSynchStatus();
                SaveOrUpdateEventListener[] saveOrUpdateEventListener =
```

```
listeners.getSaveOrUpdateEventListeners();
                for ( int i = 0; i < saveOrUpdateEventListener.length; i++ ) {
                    saveOrUpdateEventListener[i].onSaveOrUpdate(event);
                }
        }
```

The `listeners` field is an instance of `SessionEventListenerConfig`, which provides the requested event listener, or the default if none is specified. So, if your event listener is provided and doesn't call the default one, nothing else can.

Event listeners are always registered globally for the event that they handle. You can register them in the configuration file or programmatically. Either way, you will need to map your implementation of one of the interfaces to the associated types, which you can look up in Table A-1. (The names are almost—but not quite—standardized.)

Table A-1. *The Listener Names and Their Corresponding Interfaces*

Type Name	Listener
auto-flush	AutoFlushEventListener
delete	DeleteEventListener
dirty-check	DirtyCheckEventListener
evict	EvictEventListener
flush	FlushEventListener
flush-entity	FlushEntityEventListener
load	LoadEventListener
load-collection	InitializeCollectionEventListener
lock	LockEventListener
merge	MergeEventListener
persist	PersistEventListener
post-delete	PostDeleteEventListener
post-insert	PostInsertEventListener
post-load	PostLoadEventListener
post-update	PostUpdateEventListener

273

Continued

Type Name	Listener
pre-delete	PreDeleteEventListener
pre-insert	PreInsertEventListener
pre-load	PreLoadEventListener
pre-update	PreUpdateEventListener
refresh	RefreshEventListener
replicate	ReplicateEventListener
save-update	SaveOrUpdateEventListener

So, for example, your listener for the SaveOrUpdateEvent is mapped to the type name save-update, must implement the SaveOrUpdateEventListener interface, and would normally have been implemented by the DefaultSaveOrUpdateEventListener class. It is wise to follow a similar convention with your own naming, so your mapping file listener entry might read like this:

```
<listener type="save-or-update"
        class="com.hibernatebook.advanced.BookingSaveOrUpdateEventListener"/>
```

Alternatively, a programmatic registration of the same event would be given thus:

```
Configuration config = new Configuration();
config.setListener("save-update", new BookingSaveOrUpdateEventListener());
```

Because they override the default behavior, events are suitable for situations in which you want to fundamentally change the Session's behavior—particularly if you want to prevent a certain event from being processed. Probably the best example of this requirement is in authorizing access to the database, and, in fact, Hibernate provides a set of event listeners for just this purpose. The four events listeners in question override the PreDelete, PreUpdate, PreInsert, and PreLoad listeners. The logic in each case (in pseudocode) runs something like this:

```
if( user does not have permission ) throw RuntimeException
Invoke default listener…
```

Because events are invoked in the same thread as the user's call to the session, the result of an exception in the first step will be an exception (actually a security exception) as the unprivileged user carries out the relevant operation.

To enable policy configuration of security, you would add the following:

```
<listener type="pre-delete"
          class="org.hibernate.secure.JACCPreDeleteEventListener"/>
<listener type="pre-update"
          class="org.hibernate.secure.JACCPreUpdateEventListener"/>
<listener type="pre-insert"
          class="org.hibernate.secure.JACCPreInsertEventListener"/>
<listener type="pre-load"
          class="org.hibernate.secure.JACCPreLoadEventListener"/>
```

An Example Event Listener

Before we get stuck in a simple example, a word of caution: events are very much an exposed part of the inner workings of the Session. While this is ideal for something requiring the level of interference of a security tool, you will not need this for most purposes. Listing A-14 is more in the nature of an illustrative "hack" than a real solution. In a real application, you would probably solve this particular problem either within the body of the application, by using interceptors, or by using triggers.

Listing A-14 shows how an event listener could be used to prevent the booking of certain seats from being persisted to the database in a concert hall ticket booking application (we revisit this example application in a little more detail with a slightly more realistic scenario in the later section, "Interceptors").

Listing A-14. Programmatically Installing an Event Listener

```
public class EventExample {
    public static void main(String[] args) {
        Configuration config = new Configuration();

        // Apply this event listener (programmatically)
        config.setListener("save-update", new BookingSaveOrUpdateEventListener());

        SessionFactory factory = config.configure().buildSessionFactory();
        Session session = factory.openSession();

        Transaction tx = session.beginTransaction();

        // Make our bookings... seat R1 is NOT to be saved.
        session.saveOrUpdate(new Booking("charles","R1"));
        session.saveOrUpdate(new Booking("camilla","R2"));

        // The confirmation letters should not be sent
        // out until AFTER the commit completes.
        tx.commit();
    }
}
```

Our example is only going to implement the SaveOrUpdateEventListener interface. You will notice that in Listing A-14, the original calls to save() have been replaced with calls to saveOrUpdate(). There is a close correspondence between the methods on the Session interface and the event listeners with similar names. A call to **save()** will not invoke **saveOrUpdate()**, and vice versa. Try using the **save()** method in the **EventExample**, and you will see that the **BookingSaveOrUpdateListener** is not invoked. In Listing A-15, we present the logic of the listener registered in Listing A-14.

Listing A-15. The Implementation of an Event Listener

```
package com.hibernatebook.advanced.events;

import java.io.Serializable;

import org.hibernate.HibernateException;
import org.hibernate.event.SaveOrUpdateEvent;
import org.hibernate.event.def.DefaultSaveOrUpdateEventListener;

public class BookingSaveOrUpdateEventListener
    extends DefaultSaveOrUpdateEventListener
{
    public Serializable onSaveOrUpdate(SaveOrUpdateEvent event)
            throws HibernateException {
        if( event.getObject() instanceof Booking ) {
            Booking booking = (Booking)event.getObject();
            System.out.println("Preparing to book seat " + booking.getSeat());

            if( booking.getSeat().equalsIgnoreCase("R1")) {
                System.out.println("Royal box booked");
                System.out.println("Conventional booking not recorded.");

                // By returning null instead of invoking the
                // default behavior, we prevent the invocation
                // of saveOrUpdate on the Session from having
                // any effect on the database!
                return null;
            }
        }

        // The default behavior:
        return super.onSaveOrUpdate(event);
    }
}
```

Interceptors

Interceptors are privy to a blow-by-blow account of what is going on as Hibernate carries out its duties. While you can listen in, you can only make limited changes to the way in which Hibernate actually behaves. This is the common requirement; unless you are making substantial changes to the persistence behavior, you will usually want only to track what is going on.

Financial packages often require considerable auditing information to be maintained to prevent fraud and aid accountability. Auditing is a natural candidate for implementation as an interceptor, as it would normally require that no changes be made to the persistence process at all.

The question that usually arises when discussing interceptors is "why not use triggers?" Triggers should never embody application logic, only business logic. If any application is going to have audit-free access to the database, you cannot implement the auditing in triggers. Worse, the triggers may not have access to the user information that's needed. In most multi-tier situations, the need to pool the database connections precludes establishing individual user logins to the database. So, for example, the trigger would only know that a user with the login "MonolithicApplication" carried out an update of last year's sales figures—not that it was carried out by, say, Jim from accounts, which is who the auditors are likely to be interested in! Table A-2 summarizes the points in the application life cycle at which the various methods will be invoked.

Table A-2. The Interceptor Methods

Name	When Invoked	Comments
afterTransactionBegin()	Invoked immediately after a call to begin() on a Transaction object retrieved from the Session object.	This method can change the state of the transaction—for example, it can call rollback().
afterTransactionCompletion()	Invoked immediately after the completion of a transaction.	
beforeTransactionCompletion()	Invoked immediately prior to the completion of a transaction. This method can change the state of the transaction—for example, it can call rollback().	
findDirty()	Invoked during calls to flush().	This allows the saving of changes to attributes to be prevented or forced.
getEntity()	Invoked when an entity not in the Session object's own cache is requested by its identifier.	
getEntityName()	Invoked when the Session object needs to determine the name of a given entity.	

Continued

Name	When Invoked	Comments
instantiate()	Invoked when the Session object needs to create an entity instance. Because the "empty" object can be created here, this allows Hibernate (in legacy applications, for example) to use entities that do not have a default constructor.	
isTransient()	Invoked when the Session object needs to determine whether an entity it has been asked to persist is transient—for example, during calls to saveOrUpdate().	
onDelete()	Invoked before an object is deleted.	The object's state should not be tampered with at this point.
onFlushDirty()	Invoked during a call to flush() after entities have been determined to be dirty. (If the entities are not dirty, then there are no changes to be persisted and Hibernate has no actions to perform—therefore, there is no general case interceptor, and this interceptor will *not* be invoked if the entities are clean.)	
onLoad()	Invoked immediately before an entity object is populated from the database.	The loading can be overridden (by returning false), and the instantiated but uninitialized object is available if supplementary initialization from the listener is needed.
onSave()	Invoked before an object is saved.	This permits the state of the object to be changed immediately before it is saved.
postFlush()	Invoked after the Session object is flushed, if and only if the Session object had to carry out SQL opera-tions to synchronize state with the database.	
preFlush()	Invoked immediately before the Session object is flushed.	

An Example Interceptor

To illustrate how all this works in practice, we will create a simple interceptor from scratch. While the auditing example is a good one, it is rather too involved for our demonstration. Instead, we will consider a concert hall seat-booking system (the entity to represent an entity is shown in Listing A-16) for which the details of bookings will be sent out to customers as they are pushed into the database.

Listing A-16. The Booking POJO

```java
package com.hibernatebook.advanced.events;

public class Booking {
    public Booking(String name, String seat) {
        this.name = name;
        this.seat = seat;
    }

    Booking() {
    }

    protected String getName() {
        return name;
    }

    protected void setName(String name) {
        this.name = name;
    }

    protected String getSeat() {
        return seat;
    }

    protected void setSeat(String seat) {
        this.seat = seat;
    }

    private String seat;
    private String name;
}
```

Interceptors have to override the **org.hibernate.Interceptor** interface. You can set a global interceptor for the configuration (see Listing A-17), or you can apply interceptors on a per-session basis. You have to install the interceptor programmatically—there is no syntax for specifying this in the Hibernate configuration file.

Listing A-17. Installing a Global Interceptor

```java
package com.hibernatebook.advanced.events;

import org.hibernate.Session;
import org.hibernate.SessionFactory;
import org.hibernate.Transaction;
import org.hibernate.cfg.Configuration;

public class MailingExample {
    public static void main(String[] argv) {
        Configuration config = new Configuration();

        // Apply this interceptor at a global level...
        config.setInterceptor(new BookingInterceptor());

        SessionFactory factory = config.configure().buildSessionFactory();
        Session session = factory.openSession();

        // A local interceptor could alternatively
        // be applied here:
        // session.setInterceptor(new BookingInterceptor());

        Transaction tx = session.beginTransaction();

        // Make our bookings...
        session.save(new Booking("dave","F1"));
        session.save(new Booking("jeff","C3"));

        // The confirmation letters should not be sent
        // out until AFTER the commit completes.
        tx.commit();
    }
}
```

The interceptor that we are applying is going to capture the information from the Booking objects that we are storing in the database. Listing A-18 demonstrates the basic mechanism, but it is only a toy example. We will discuss some of its deficiencies in a moment.

Listing A-18. An Interceptor Implementation

```java
package com.hibernatebook.advanced.events;

import java.io.Serializable;
import java.util.Collection;
import java.util.HashSet;
import java.util.Iterator;

import org.hibernate.CallbackException;
import org.hibernate.EntityMode;
```

```java
import org.hibernate.Interceptor;
import org.hibernate.Transaction;
import org.hibernate.type.Type;

public class BookingInterceptor implements Interceptor {

    public BookingInterceptor() {
    }

    private ThreadLocal stored = new ThreadLocal();

    public void afterTransactionBegin(Transaction tx) {
        stored.set(new HashSet());
    }

    public void afterTransactionCompletion(Transaction tx) {
        if (tx.wasCommitted()) {
            Iterator i = ((Collection) stored.get()).iterator();
            while (i.hasNext()) {
                Booking b = (Booking) i.next();
                sendMail(b);
            }
        }
        stored.set(null);
    }

    public boolean onSave(Object entity, Serializable id,
            Object[] state, String[] propertyNames, Type[] types)
            throws CallbackException {
        ((Collection) stored.get()).add(entity);
        return false;
    }

    private void sendMail(Booking b) {
        // Here we would actually send out the e-mail
        System.out.print("Name: " + b.getName());
        System.out.println(", Seat: " + b.getSeat());
    }

    public void beforeTransactionCompletion(Transaction tx) {
    }

    public int[] findDirty(Object entity, Serializable id,
            Object[] currentState, Object[] previousState,
            String[] propertyNames, Type[] types) {
        return null;
    }

    public Object getEntity(String entityName, Serializable id)
            throws CallbackException {
        return null;
    }
```

```
    public String getEntityName(Object object) throws CallbackException {
        return null;
    }

    public Object instantiate(String entityName, EntityMode entityMode,
            Serializable id) throws CallbackException {
        return null;
    }

    public Boolean isTransient(Object object) {
        return null;
    }

    public void onDelete(Object entity, Serializable id, Object[] state,
            String[] propertyNames, Type[] types) throws CallbackException {
    }

    public boolean onFlushDirty(Object entity, Serializable id,
            Object[] currentState, Object[] previousState,
            String[] propertyNames, Type[] types) throws CallbackException {
        return false;
    }

    public boolean onLoad(Object entity, Serializable id,
            Object[] state, String[] propertyNames, Type[] types)
            throws CallbackException {
        return false;
    }

    public void postFlush(Iterator entities) throws CallbackException {
    }

    public void preFlush(Iterator entities) throws CallbackException {
    }
}
```

Our interceptor makes use of the `afterTransactionBegin()` method to prepare to collect booking details, the `onSave()` method to collect them, and the `afterTransactionCompletion()` method to report the successful bookings. This sequence guarantees that bookings will not be reported to the users until after we are confident that they have been retained in the database.

A minor deficiency of this implementation is that the e-mail is sent outside the transaction—a system failure immediately after the commit completes could cause the e-mail not to be sent. In our scenario, this is unimportant, because e-mail is already an unreliable transport mechanism; but there are other situations, such as the auditing example discussed earlier, in which this may be unacceptable. In these cases, interception may not be appropriate, and an integrated solution tied into a two-phase commit transaction may be required.

More importantly, our example assumes that the `Booking` object will not be altered between its addition to the set of e-mails to be sent and their transmission. This is an extremely dangerous assumption! A safer approach would be to create copies of the `Booking` objects or, better yet, to copy their data into a more appropriate object, as shown in Listing A-19.

Listing A-19. A Better Approach to Preparing the Mailshot

```
public boolean onSave(Object entity, Serializable id,
     Object[] state, String[] propertyNames, Type[] types)
     throws CallbackException
{
   if( entity instanceof Booking ) {
      Booking booking = (Booking)entity.
      Mailshot mailshot = new Mailshot(booking.getName(), booking.getSeat() );
      ((Collection) stored.get()).add(mailshot);
   }
   return false;
}
```

Finally, we don't necessarily have enough information to prepare our mailshot—the e-mail address may be missing. If the `name` field actually represents the e-mail address, then we are fine; but if it represents a key into other objects, and hence tables in the database, then we have to be careful. It is possible to write database logic from within an interceptor, but the risk of accidentally recursing back into your interceptor logic is high, so we don't recommend it. It's slightly less tricky if you are only using a session-scoped interceptor, but there are probably safer ways to achieve the same end result.

In this example, the methods that we are not using have been given a default implementation. You will note that some of these methods return `null` or `false`. These methods are permitted to change the data that is preserved or returned by the session. Returning to the `onSave()` method, we will consider another possible implementation, shown in Listing A-20.

Listing A-20. Changing the Data from Within an Interceptor

```
public boolean onSave(Object entity, Serializable id,
     Object[] state, String[] propertyNames, Type[] types)
     throws CallbackException
{
   if( entity instanceof Booking ) {
      state[1] = "unknown";
   }
   return true;
}
```

Here we are altering the `state` array. This contains the values of each of the objects' fields that are to be stored (in the order defined in the mapping file). In our `Booking` class, field `0` is the `id`, field `1` is the name, and field `2` is the `seat`—so here we have changed the `name` value to be preserved in the database. Returning `true` causes Hibernate to reflect this change when it saves the data. If we left the `return` flag as `false`, nothing would happen when the method was called.

The temptation is to assume that returning `false` guarantees the safety of the data to be preserved, but, in fact, this is not the case. The `state` array represents copies of the data to be preserved—but we have also been given access to the actual object (entity) that contains the original values. If you amend the fields of the entity before returning, the flag will not prevent your changes from being made. Listing A-21 illustrates how this might occur.

Listing A-21. Changing the Data in an Unorthodox Way

```
public boolean onSave(Object entity, Serializable id,
        Object[] state, String[] propertyNames, Type[] types)
        throws CallbackException
{
    if( entity instanceof Booking ) {
        Booking booking = (Booking)entity;
        booking.setName("unknown");
    }
    // The flag can't save us from ourselves here!
    return false;
}
```

Again, this is probably not the best way to make the changes, but it can be useful when you already have a considerable body of logic prepared to process the entity type.

Overriding the Default Constructor

Occasionally, you will find that it is necessary to persist a POJO that has no default constructor. Usually you will have access to the source code, and should just make the change directly. Occasionally, however, you may find that you are working with classes for which the source code is not available—or that you are working with large bodies of generated objects for which it is extremely inconvenient to manage changes made to the source code. In these circumstances, it is possible to use an interceptor to replace the default object-creation logic.

This technique can be used as long as you have some way of obtaining or applying default values for the parameters of the POJO's non-default constructor. Listing A-22 shows an example of the use of this technique to instantiate a POJO whose only constructor demands a **String** parameter.

Listing A-22. Invoking a non-Default Constructor

```
private static class OverrideCtor implements Interceptor {

    public Object instantiate(
        String entityName,
        EntityMode entityMode,
        Serializable id)
            throws CallbackException
    {
        if( entityName.equals(MissingDefaultCtorClass.class.getName())) {
            // My call to CTor
            return new MissingDefaultCtorClass("NOT SET");
        } else {
```

```
        // Some other class - continue to default handling
        return null;
    }
}

// ... the remaining default method declarations...
}
```

Hibernate Search

Hibernate Search allows you to easily use the Apache Lucene search engine with your Hibernate object model. Lucene is a freely available open source search engine that was built for the text world; it analyzes large quantities of text and creates a search index. Lucene itself is a component that provides core search functionality, including analyzing, indexing, and querying. Your application integrates with Lucene to provide content to index and queries to run against the index. This could be frustrating when working with Hibernate because there is a mismatch between Lucene and Java objects that use Hibernate, similar to the object/relational mismatch.

The Hibernate Search project attempts to bridge that gap by working with your Java object model directly. You can add Hibernate Search annotations to your POJOs to tell Lucene which object fields should be indexed. As you update the database through Hibernate transactions, Lucene will receive events telling it to update its search index.

Although you could use your database's native full-text search functionality to provide a small fraction of what Lucene does, Lucene excels in its query parsing and field weighting—features that can't be easily built on top of full-text search.

If you want to get started with Hibernate Search, take the time to read Lucene's excellent documentation first; this will help you understand the concepts behind Lucene, such as the query parser, analyzers, and indexing. After you configure your application to use Hibernate Search and add search-specific annotations to your entities, the API for querying your data with Hibernate Search is straightforward:

1. Get a `FullTextSession` from the `Search` class, which is similar to retrieving a `Session` object from the `SessionFactory`.

2. Issue Lucene-syntax query string to create a Lucene query object.

3. Use Hibernate Search's `FullTextSession` object to create a Hibernate query object from the Lucene query.

You end up with the same Hibernate query object that you can create with HQL or Criteria; in essence, Lucene is now on the same level as HQL or Criteria for search and retrieval. The major difference is that Lucene maintains an index, and you have to tell Lucene which entities to index. You do that with the `@Indexed` annotation on a class. Similarly, you indicate which fields to index with the `@Field` annotation.

Listing A-23 shows how simple search can be once the database is properly indexed; this listing presents some example code that searches our `geonames` database from Chapter 12 for places where the names contain either "McKinley" or "Denali".

Listing A-23. A Lucene Search Example

```
SessionFactory factory =
            new AnnotationConfiguration().configure(
            "hibernate.search.cfg.xml").buildSessionFactory();
      Session session = factory.openSession();

      FullTextSession fullTextSession =
            Search.getFullTextSession(session);
      Transaction tx = fullTextSession.beginTransaction();

      QueryParser queryParser = new QueryParser("name",
            new StandardAnalyzer());
      org.apache.lucene.search.Query luceneQuery =
            queryParser.parse("name:Denali OR McKinley");
      org.hibernate.Query hibernateQuery =
            fullTextSession.createFullTextQuery(luceneQuery, Place.class);

      List<Place> results = (List<Place>) hibernateQuery.list();
      for (Place place : results)
      {
          System.out.println(place.getName());
      }

      tx.commit();
      session.close();
```

Summary

In this appendix, we have looked at alternative mechanisms for accessing Hibernate entities. We have shown how SQL and stored procedures can be integrated into the Hibernate environment, and we have discussed how events and listeners provide internal access to Hibernate's persistence mechanism.

■■■

Hibernate Tools

The Hibernate Tools toolset really consists of two quite distinct tools: a set of plug-ins to enhance the Eclipse integrated development environment (IDE), and a set of tasks for the Ant build tool. They are packaged together because they share significant chunks of implementation despite their very different façades. We have already used one of the Ant tasks from Hibernate Tools in earlier chapters to generate our database schemas. In this appendix, we will discuss the other available tasks. First, however, we will discuss the use of the toolset as a plug-in for Eclipse.

It is beyond the scope of this book to attempt to teach you how to use Ant or Eclipse (although we do walk you through some of the less common configuration details). To get the most from this appendix, you should be familiar with both Ant and Eclipse—although it is possible to use both parts of the plug-in independently.

General information on the latest versions of Hibernate Tools, any changes or new features, the online documentation, and the locations of the various downloads are available from the Hibernate web site under the Hibernate Tools heading (www.hibernate.org).

The Eclipse Plug-In

Eclipse is one of the best-known and liked Java development environments to emerge in recent years. Eclipse evolved originally as a proprietary component of IBM's WebSphere Application Developer (WSAD) environment. IBM chose to release Eclipse, the IDE, as an open source application. Thus, the open source Eclipse IDE emerged as a mature product virtually overnight.

Eclipse is designed as a core application, the Eclipse platform, extended by various plug-ins, typically including Java Development Tools (JDT). For our purposes, we assume that you will start out with this combination (known rather confusingly as the Software Development Kit, or SDK) as the basis for installing Hibernate Tools. At the time of writing, the latest version of the SDK is 3.5.2.

■ **Note** Eclipse can be downloaded from the Eclipse Foundation web site (www.eclipse.org).

The Hibernate team is now employed by JBoss, which provides a branded version of Eclipse that includes the Hibernate plug-ins, including several JBoss-specific ones. This can be purchased and downloaded from the JBoss web site (www.jboss.com). If you choose to use this version of Eclipse, then you can omit the installation steps described in the next section. You have two choices for installing the

Eclipse plug-in: you can either download the Hibernate Tools plug-in and install it manually into Eclipse; or you can use Eclipse's software installer to have Eclipse download the plug-in and install it.

Downloading the Hibernate Tools Plug-in

At the time of writing, Hibernate Tools is at version 3.3.0. However, the version of Hibernate Tools for download at www.hibernate.org is 3.2.4. We had to download the latest version of Hibernate Tools from the JBoss Tools 3.1 Download Page (www.jboss.org/tools/download/stable/3_1_GA.html). These tools target version 3.5 of the Eclipse IDE.

Installing the Plug-In

We will now walk you through the process of installing the plug-in using Eclipse's standard updates feature. Here are the steps to follow:

1. Select the Install New Software... menu option from the Help menu, and you will see the Available Software dialog.

2. Click the Add... button shown in the upper right of the Available Software dialog (see Figure B-1) to add the site from which you will obtain the Hibernate Tools plug-in.

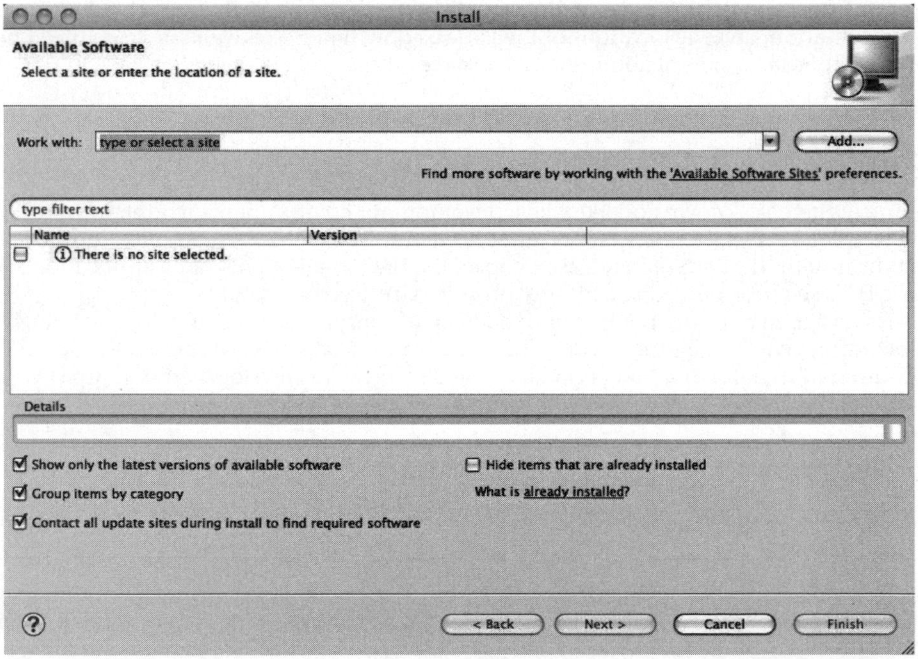

Figure B-1. Adding a plug-in update site to Eclipse

3. You will now need to enter the URL for the site from which Eclipse will obtain the plug-in and an informal name for the site into the dialog shown in Figure B-2. You will use the JBoss Tools site (`http://download.jboss.org/jbosstools/updates/JBossTools-3.1.0.GA`); note that this URL is subject to change as new versions are released.

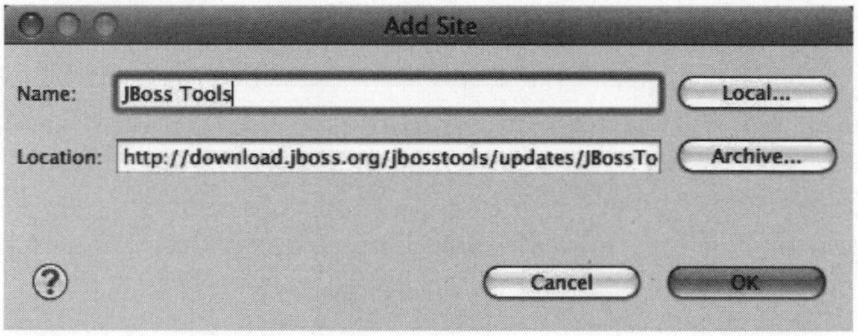

Figure B-2. Specifying the new download site

4. You will then be returned to the Available Software dialog shown in Figure B-3, where you can see which plug-ins are available from the JBoss Tools web site.

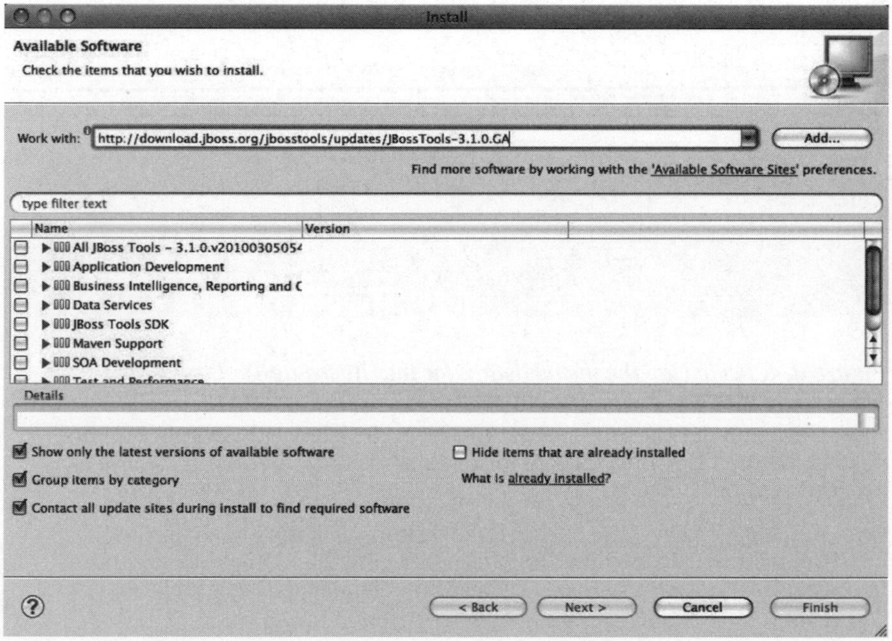

Figure B-3. The available plug-ins for the JBoss Tools 3.1

5. The Hibernate Tools plug-in is available in several different categories. Expand the "All JBoss Tools" option and select the check box next to Hibernate Tools. You can also take a shortcut and type Hibernate into the box that says "type filter text"; and the Hibernate Tools plug-in will show up under several categories. You only need to select the Hibernate Tools check box once.

6. Click Next. Eclipse will calculate dependencies and requirements. You will see a list of features similar to that in Figure B-4 showing what is to be installed.

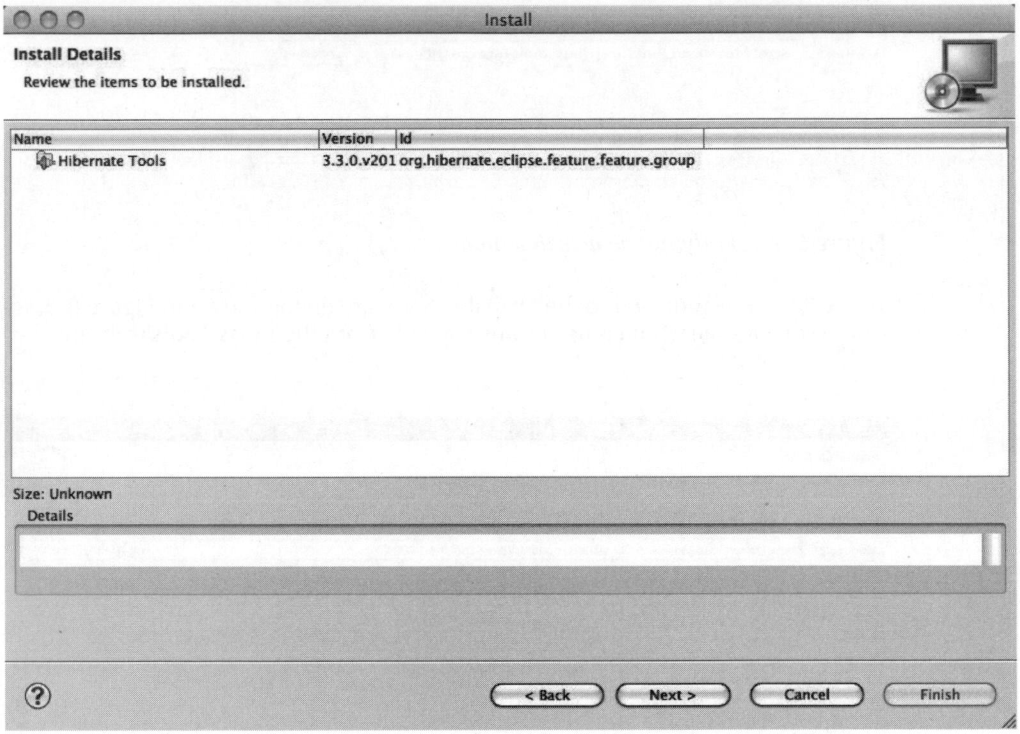

Figure B-4. Reviewing the install details for the Hibernate Tools plug-in

7. Click Next, and Eclipse prompts you to accept the license that applies to the plug-in features. You must accept the terms and conditions of the license to proceed beyond this step.

8. Once you have checked the Accept radio button, click the Finish button to proceed. Eclipse will download and install the plug-ins. This process can run in the background while you use Eclipse; note that it can take a while on a slow connection.

■ **Note** Currently, the Hibernate Tools plug-in is not digitally signed. Eclipse warns you of this. In principle, it is possible that a malicious third party with access to servers between you and the Eclipse download site could substitute their own code for the Eclipse tools. In practice this is unlikely, but it is to be hoped that the Hibernate or JBoss teams will start code signing their final releases. To proceed with the plug-in installation, you must accept the verification prompt.

9. Finally, Eclipse prompts you to restart or apply the changes directly. Generally when installing Eclipse plug-ins, it is safest to select the restart option. Though we know of no specific problems with the Hibernate Tools, we recommend choosing restart here anyway—it won't be necessary to reboot the PC, though!

At this point, you will have successfully completed the installation of the Hibernate Tools plug-in. There will be no immediate visible change to the layout of the workbench—however, as you will see in the next step, there should be some new options for you, accessible via the various menus—including a new Eclipse perspective onto some of the Hibernate workbench views.

The Eclipse plug-in installation process is now quite streamlined, so it is unlikely that you will encounter any serious problems. However, if you do have problems, first check that you have the correct versions of the downloads described here, and check that you have followed the installation steps as given previously. If you are still encountering problems, you should search the Tools forum on the Hibernate Forums page (`www.hibernate.org`) to see if other users have encountered the same problems. You should also check the Hibernate bug database (`www.hibernate.org/`) to see if there are known problems that match yours.

The Boilerplate Project Configuration

Now that the tools plug-in has been installed, you are ready to set up a project that will take advantage of it. As a first step, we recommend configuring a user library to make adding the appropriate JAR files to new projects more straightforward and to make the resulting project view less cluttered.

You should be aware that Eclipse user libraries are not a Java standard, and do not exist as independent entities. They are merely a grouping of paths to JAR files to make configuring Eclipse projects more convenient. The user library will not reflect changes made to the underlying JAR files themselves (moving or deleting them, for instance).

Because user libraries belong to the Eclipse workspace, rather than to the individual projects, you can create a library from the Preferences menu before you have created any projects.

You should then drill down through the tree view to select the Java Build Path User Libraries node.

Initially there are no user libraries configured. You will need to click the New button to create your own.

You will be prompted for a name for the library. The first library will contain the JAR files for the Hibernate core. We recommend including the full version number in the library name so that you will be able to readily distinguish between versions if you are managing more than one Eclipse project in the same workspace over an extended period of time. (Hibernate updates come thick and fast!)

The library name will be added to the list of libraries, but it does not yet contain any JAR files. You should select the library name in the list, and then click the Add JARs button.

You now want to add all the core Hibernate JAR files to the library. You can add multiple files, but not directories, so this must be carried out in a few steps.

You will be presented with a normal file-selection dialog. You should navigate to your core Hibernate install directory and select the `hibernate3.jar` file.

You should select the library name and again click Add Jars, but now navigate to each subdirectory under the `lib` subdirectory beneath the core Hibernate install directory. Select all the JAR files in each directory and add them to the library.

Figure B-5 shows part of an exploded view of the resulting user library.

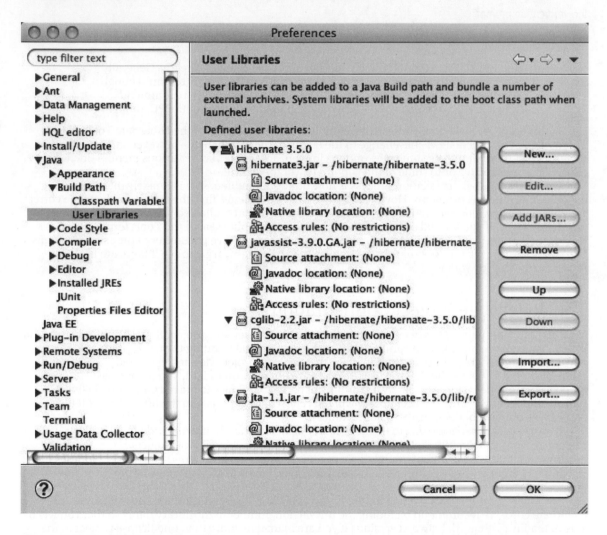

Figure B-5. The Hibernate user library

Having created it initially, Hibernate allows you to export your user library configuration so that it does not need to be created afresh on each machine that you work on, or when creating a new Eclipse workspace.

You should now create a new Java project called **ToolsExample**. The source code for the example is available from the Apress web site (**www.apress.com**). Copy the files into the **ToolsExample** folder in the workspace directory, and refresh the project.

You now need to add your Hibernate user library to the project. Select the Build Path ➤ Add Libraries context menu option on the project. You will be presented with a list of library types. Select the User Library option from the list, and click Next.

This will in turn present you with a list of the available user libraries. Check the box next to the Hibernate library that you configured previously, and click Finish.

The libraries will be added to the list in the Libraries tab of the Java Build Path dialog; you should click OK to accept the changes to the path.

You will also need to add your JDBC driver and the Simple Logging Facade for Java (SLF4J) implementation to your Java project; do this using the Add External Archives... command under the Build Path item on the project's context menu.

So far in this section, we have configured a Java project in a conventional way. None of the steps we have taken so far would be unusual in preparing to use a third-party library such as the Spring Framework. The next few steps open a Hibernate Console perspective that will allow you to manage the Hibernate-specific aspects of your project.

To open a new Eclipse perspective, you can either select the Window ➤ Open Perspective menu option or click the Open Perspective icon.

Select the Other option from the resulting menu. This will present you with the list of available perspectives. Select the Hibernate option from the resulting dialog.

Much as when entering the Eclipse debugging perspective, the layout of Eclipse will change, with various Hibernate-specific views being opened (although you will still have access to the Package Explorer as one of the tabbed options behind the new Hibernate configuration view).

To switch between the perspectives, you can select the Java or Hibernate perspective icons on the top right of the main Eclipse window (you may need to adjust the menu layout slightly if these are obscured). Figure B-6 shows the icons for the Hibernate, Java, and Java EE perspectives, with the Hibernate perspective selected.

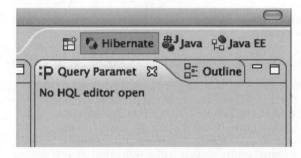

Figure B-6. The Eclipse perspective icons

Using the Hibernate Console

With the project set up and the Hibernate perspective added to Eclipse, you can now start using some of the Hibernate Tools plug-in features more directly.

Creating a Hibernate Console Configuration

The Hibernate Console represents a view onto the Hibernate object store. It therefore needs the same basic configuration information as any other client of Hibernate. You will need a Hibernate XML configuration file and/or a properties file (see Listing B-1).

Listing B-1. The Configuration File Used in Our Example: `hibernate.cfg.xml`

```xml
<?xml version="1.0" encoding="UTF-8"?>
<!DOCTYPE hibernate-configuration PUBLIC
    "-//Hibernate/Hibernate Configuration DTD 3.0//EN"
    "http://hibernate.sourceforge.net/hibernate-configuration-3.0.dtd">
<hibernate-configuration>
    <session-factory>
        <!-- The database settings -->
        <property name="hibernate.connection.driver_class">
            org.hsqldb.jdbcDriver
        </property>
        <property name="hibernate.connection.url">
jdbc:hsqldb:file:/workspace/ToolsExample/db/annotationsdb;shutdown=true
        </property>
        <property name="hibernate.dialect">
            org.hibernate.dialect.HSQLDialect
        </property>
        <property name="hibernate.connection.username">sa</property>
        <property name="hibernate.connection.password"/>
        <property name="hibernate.connection.pool_size">0</property>
        <property name="show_sql">false</property>

        <!-- The class mappings for our example -->
        <mapping class="com.hibernatebook.tools.Note"/>
        <mapping class="com.hibernatebook.tools.Notepad"/>
    </session-factory>
</hibernate-configuration>
```

If you are using the HSQLDB database in conjunction with Hibernate Tools, we recommend that you use fully qualified path names (shown in bold in the preceding code) to avoid possible clashes between the working directories and classpaths used by Ant, the Eclipse IDE, and the Hibernate Console. In our example, we will be working with the annotations-based mappings, so we use the `mapping` element with a `class` attribute to determine the mapped classes. However, the console configuration will automatically find any correctly annotated entity classes using reflection, so it is possible to omit these entries.

If you choose to use XML-based mappings, you can use the `file` attribute to specify the mapping file instead, or specify the paths to the mapping files in the Hibernate configuration entry used by the Hibernate Console.

Hibernate Tools provides a wizard to create the Hibernate configuration entry. To use the wizard, select the File ➤ New ➤ Hibernate Console Configuration menu option.

This will bring up the Create Hibernate Console Configuration dialog page. In the first part of the form shown in Figure B-7, set a suitable name for this configuration, choose the ToolsExample project as the project, and also set the path to the Hibernate configuration file. You should also choose Annotations as the type, as you will be using annotations for your mappings.

After filling in the form, you should see the error message about the classpath disappear.

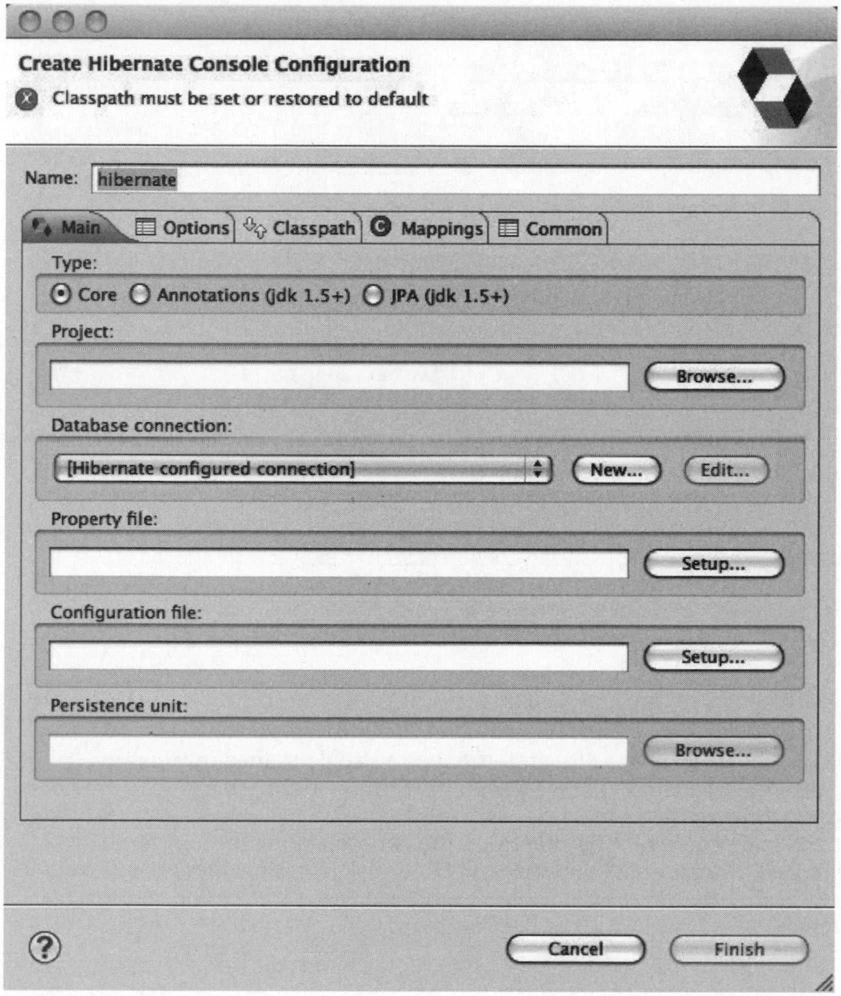

Figure B-7. The Main Hibernate Console Configuration settings

The middle section of the form shown in Figure B-8 allows you to specify mapping files for inclusion in the console configuration that are not explicitly included in the configuration file. You would add entries here if your application added these options to the configuration at run time instead of drawing the information from the configuration file (for example, if it only used the properties file for its other configuration settings).

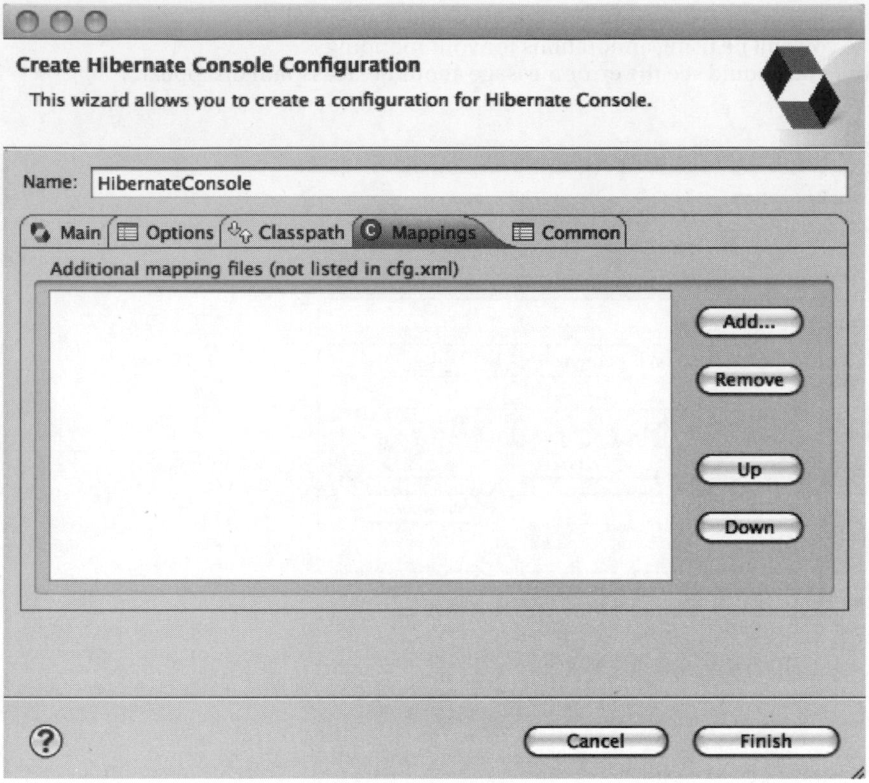

Figure B-8. The additional mapping file settings

The other pieces of the form allow you to specify settings that are also contained in your `hibernate.cfg.xml` file, so you do not need to set them through the form. For example, you do not need to set the database dialect to use through the form.

Click the Finish button, and you should now be able to see the console configuration Name (we used ToolsExample). You will need to ensure that the Note and Notebook Java class files exist in your source directory before using the Hibernate Console. They are included in the source code for this book, which you can download from the Apress web site (www.apress.com).

■ **Warning** You may run into problems with Eclipse/Hibernate Tools not being able to find classes in your classpath that are in your project. The most likely problem is that the compiler is set up to use a more recent version of Java (such as Java 6), while the Eclipse IDE is running on an older version of Java (such as Java 5). To fix the problem, you can either change the Java version to compile to in your Eclipse Project settings, or you can tell Eclipse to run on a more recent version of Java (consult the Eclipse Documentation for your platform).

Generating the Schema

Expand the ToolsExample entry that you created in the console configuration window. There will be three nodes beneath it: Configuration, Session Factory, and Database (see Figure B-9).

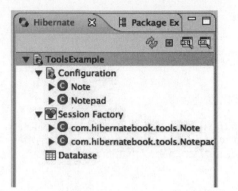

Figure B-9. The three nodes beneath ToolsExample

The third of these is a view of the tables in the database that correspond to the entities mapped in your console configuration (either explicitly or via the `hibernate.cfg.xml` file). Unless your database contains preexisting tables, the database view will be empty when you attempt to drill down into it, as shown previously in Figure B-9.

The Hibernate Console now has all of the entity mapping and database connection information. It therefore offers a Run SchemaExport context menu option (accessed from the ToolsExample node) to generate the appropriate tables.

■ **Caution** There are currently no safeguards built in here. If the configured database user has table deletion privileges, running SchemaExport in this way will drop and re-create all of your tables with no further warning!

If you select Run SchemaExport from this menu, the database view will be updated to reflect the changes, and you will be able to drill down to view the individual table column names and data types, as shown in Figure B-10.

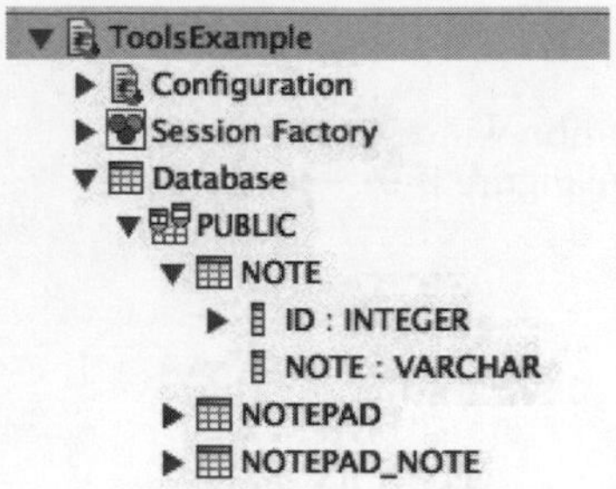

Figure B-10. *A column-level view of the newly generated database*

This view does not offer the sort of comprehensive access to the database metadata that is available from some tools, and it does not permit you to directly change any of the features. It does, however, offer a useful visual confirmation that the appropriate tables and columns have been created.

Running the Test Program

For the purpose of generating some test data for manipulation in the remainder of this section, we have created a test application (available with the other source code for this book on the Apress web site) to populate the database with some suitable records. Now that you have created an appropriate database schema, it is possible to run this application.

Switch back to the Java perspective and add a new Java Application run configuration for the `PopulateNotes` class.

Now run the application. You should see the following output, which confirms that a `Notepad` entity and 100 associated `Note` entities have been persisted to the database:

```
Creating test notepad...
Test notepad created.
```

You can now switch back to the Hibernate Console perspective in order to browse this data.

Browsing the Model

Back in the Hibernate Console perspective, you can access the contents of the object model using the Session Factory node of the console configuration view. This node is named after the `SessionFactory` object created and maintained internally by the Hibernate Eclipse plug-in tools when you drill down into the console configuration view.

■ **Tip** If you manage to put the internal `SessionFactory` object into a bad state, it is possible to close and re-create it from the configuration view's context menu when the configuration view is collapsed to a single node.

Opening the Session factory node, you will see nodes representing each of the mapped classes. Drilling down further, you can see a representation of the mapped fields and attributes (along with a graphical representation of the association rules, primary keys, and so on, where appropriate).

If you double-click the mapped class, and then click the Run button in the resulting query window, all the instances of the class in the database will be retrieved, and a `toString` representation will be displayed in the Hibernate Query Result view.

As you can see from Figure B-11, the generated HQL query to produce this information is shown in a second tabbed pane (further queries will be added as new tabs within this window). The column is numbered, as no column name can be specified. Note that we have overridden the `Note` class's `toString()` method to ensure that a human-readable representation of the class contents is displayed in this view.

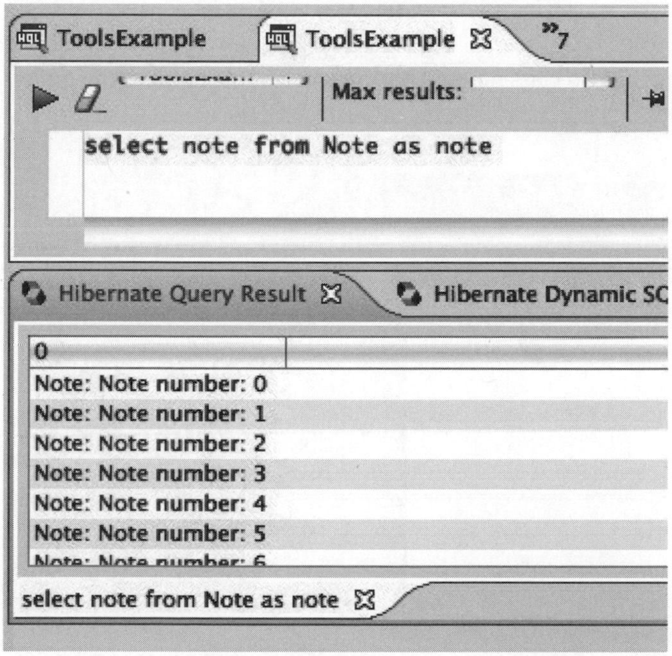

Figure B-11. The Hibernate Query Result view of the mapped Noteclass

All results of queries generated manually or automatically through the Hibernate Console perspective will be displayed in the Hibernate Query Result view.

Testing HQL Queries

HQL is a powerful way to interact with the database; but traditionally, debugging errors in these queries has been a long-winded process. Typically, a developer would end up creating a unit test for the query and then spending considerable time tweaking it into working correctly. Hibernate Tools now provides a query editor that allows you to prototype your HQL queries and run them against the database without needing to write any code.

To run an HQL query, select HQL Editor from the context menu for the project in the configuration view (by default, this is to the left of the main window in the Hibernate Console perspective).

A new HQL editor window will be created. This is an HQL editor with some context sensitivity. Context sensitivity is activated with the Ctrl+Space key combination, as is usual for Eclipse editors. For example, enter the following query in the scratch pad editor and press Ctrl+Space:

```
from Note
```

This will display a context menu offering the two class names that are legal at this point in the query. Figure B-12 shows an example of this menu.

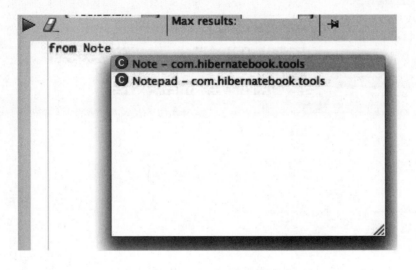

Figure B-12. *The context-sensitive scratch pad*

As you create the query, the corresponding SQL query against the underlying relational database is updated in the Hibernate Dynamic SQL Preview window shown in Figure B-13.

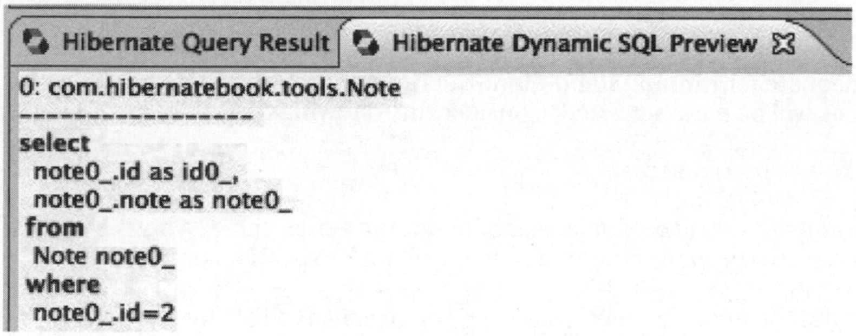

```
Hibernate Query Result   Hibernate Dynamic SQL Preview  ⊠

0: com.hibernatebook.tools.Note
------------------
select
 note0_.id as id0_,
 note0_.note as note0_
from
 Note note0_
where
 note0_.id=2
```

Figure B-13. The Hibernate Dynamic SQL Preview window

The generated SQL will be visible whenever the HQL query is syntactically valid, allowing you to confirm the basic correctness of the HQL and confirm the sanity of the underlying query at the same time.

Once you have a satisfactory HQL query, it can be executed against the database to validate the returned results. Enter the following query in the scratch pad window, and then click the green Run button above the editor window:

```
select note as Note_Entry
from Note
where id > 10 and id < 20
```

The view shown in Figure B-14 will list the results of the query. Note that the results have been given the correct column heading.

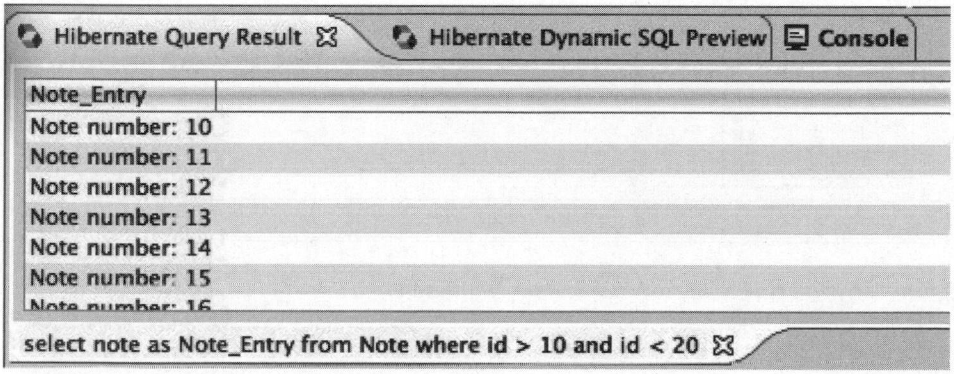

```
Hibernate Query Result ⊠   Hibernate Dynamic SQL Preview   Console

Note_Entry
Note number: 10
Note number: 11
Note number: 12
Note number: 13
Note number: 14
Note number: 15
Note number: 16

select note as Note_Entry from Note where id > 10 and id < 20  ⊠
```

Figure B-14. The output from the query

Query Parameters

While the scratch pad alone is adequate for running stand-alone queries, much of the HQL that you will use in practice in your applications will be parameterized. Consider the following typical query:

```
select owner from Notepad where owner = :username
```

This query uses a named parameter, `username`, as a placeholder for the actual value. When converted to SQL, this will become a parameter in a prepared statement, and will not be specified until the application is actually running.

The Hibernate Console provides the novel feature of allowing you to specify the values of parameters in Hibernate queries of this type.[1] This means that you can cut and paste an HQL query from your code into the scratch pad, and test it there without having to edit any of the parameters themselves.

If you paste the preceding query into a scratch pad window and try to run it as is, the console will log an appropriate error, warning you that the query parameters have not all been set (currently this appears in the Hibernate Query Result view). On the right-hand side of the perspective's default layout, there is a view called Query Parameters. Adjust the layout so that you can see the three columns within this view, labeled Name, Type, and Value.

With the query still in the scratch pad, click the icon shaped like the letter *P* (shown in Figure B-15, just to the right of the Outline tab). A new row will be added to the view, representing the parameter in the query. By editing the values in this row, you can change the details of the parameter (both the value assigned to it and the type of that value).

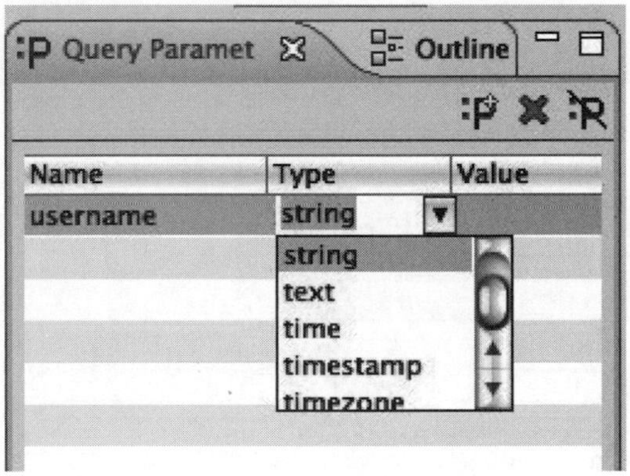

Figure B-15. *Assigning a typed value to the username query parameter*

---

[1] If you've ever encountered problems debugging complex SQL queries, in which the process of manually substituting in parameters disguised the cause of the problem during testing, you will understand why we are extremely enthusiastic about this ingenious feature!

Now assume that you edit the query parameter row so that it contains the value "Dave Minter"; running the query will return results equivalent to those produced by the following code fragment:

```
Query query = session.createQuery(
    "select owner from Notepad where owner = :username");
query.setString("username","Dave Minter");
List results = query.list();
```

All the standard Hibernate types are available to you, and the console will log appropriate errors when you try to execute queries that combine types in inappropriate ways for the object model.

Creating a Mapping Diagram

You can create professional-looking mapping diagrams of your classes and database tables from within Hibernate Tools. These diagrams are much improved over previous versions of the Hibernate Tools. To create a mapping diagram, select Mapping Diagram from the context menu of the ToolsExample console configuration. The mapping diagram may appear a little jumbled at first, but you can drag the boxes in the diagram around. There are a few options under the View menu to help you create a more presentable diagram, including a ruler and a grid. There is also an option to use straight lines instead of routed lines; however, the lines will quickly become confusing in any kind of diagram with more than a few entities.

After creating a Mapping Diagram from our ToolsExample project and rearranging the boxes, you have a graphical representation of the classes and database tables in the model (see Figure B-16).

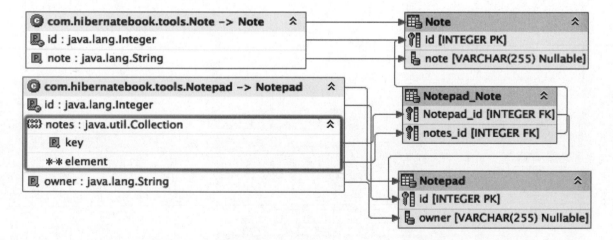

Figure B-16. The Mapping Diagram view of our model

Generating a Configuration File

Hibernate Tools provides a wizard to aid in the creation of a Hibernate configuration XML file. This wizard is accessed from the File ➤ New ➤ Hibernate Configuration File menu option from within the Hibernate Console perspective.

This wizard prompts you to specify a path and file name for the generated configuration file. You don't want to overwrite the configuration file used by our sample application, so for this exercise, specify a file name of `hibernate-wizard.cfg.xml` in the root of the project directory, as shown in Figure B-17.

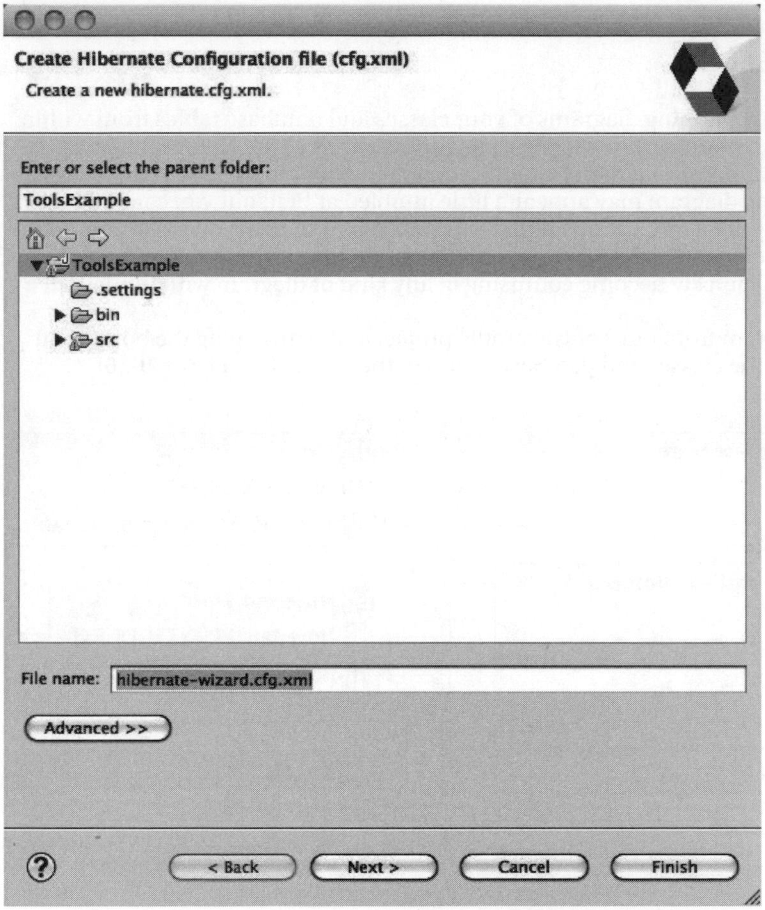

Figure B-17. The Create Hibernate Configuration file wizard

Clicking the Next button will then take you to the dialog shown in Figure B-18, in which all the basic configuration properties can be specified. When possible, a set of default options are provided as combo box lists. The "Database dialect" field presents the dialects in a more human-readable format, and also filters the Driver class and Connection URL fields to the likely options.

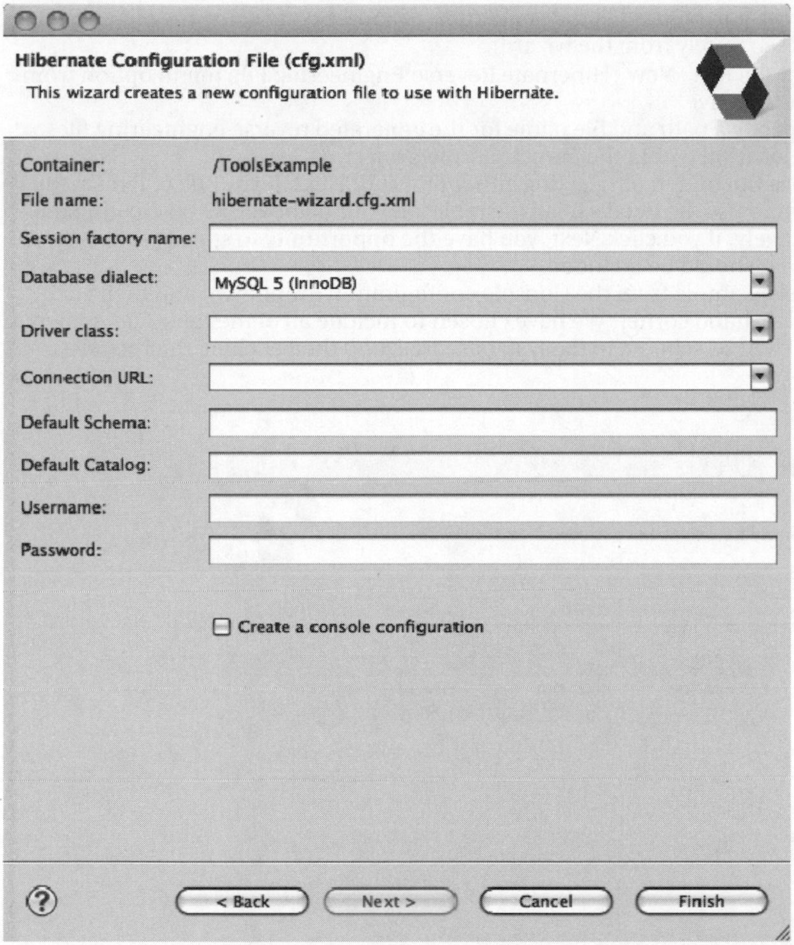

Hibernate Configuration File (cfg.xml)

This wizard creates a new configuration file to use with Hibernate.

Container:	/ToolsExample
File name:	hibernate-wizard.cfg.xml
Session factory name:	
Database dialect:	MySQL 5 (InnoDB)
Driver class:	
Connection URL:	
Default Schema:	
Default Catalog:	
Username:	
Password:	

☐ Create a console configuration

(< Back)   (Next >)   (Cancel)   (Finish)

Figure B-18. Selecting default values for the configuration file

All the values selected in the drop-down menus can be overtyped if the option you need is not listed. You can also type in the fully qualified dialect class name instead of choosing from the short names available from the drop-down list.

At this point, you also have the option of selecting the Create a console configuration check box. If you do so, the Hibernate Configuration File wizard will pass you to the Hibernate Console Configuration wizard (and will automatically populate the configuration file field). However, since we've already discussed this earlier in the chapter, leave the check box empty and click Finish.

The Reverse Engineering and Code Generation Tools

The last Hibernate Tools wizard is for the reverse engineering tool. This allows you to extract the schema information from the database into an XML file. Additional information can be added to this file using a tabbed control panel, which allows it to be used in the generation of source code using the Hibernate Code Generation tool (accessed separately from the wizard).

This wizard is accessed from the File New Hibernate Reverse Engineering File menu option from within the Hibernate Console perspective.

This then prompts you to specify a path and file name for the generated reverse engineering file. Select the default file name and location within the ToolsExample project.

When you are done, you have the option of selecting either Finish or Next. If you select Finish, the wizard will assume that you want to use the details of all the tables in your database when creating the reverse engineering file. Alternatively, if you click Next, you have the opportunity to specify the individual tables and columns that should be included.

To choose tables, select ToolsExample from the Console configuration dropdown, and then click the Refresh button in the lower left-hand corner. We have chosen to include all of the tables (as shown in Figure B-19) by selecting the PUBLIC schema in the Database tree, and then clicking the Include... button.

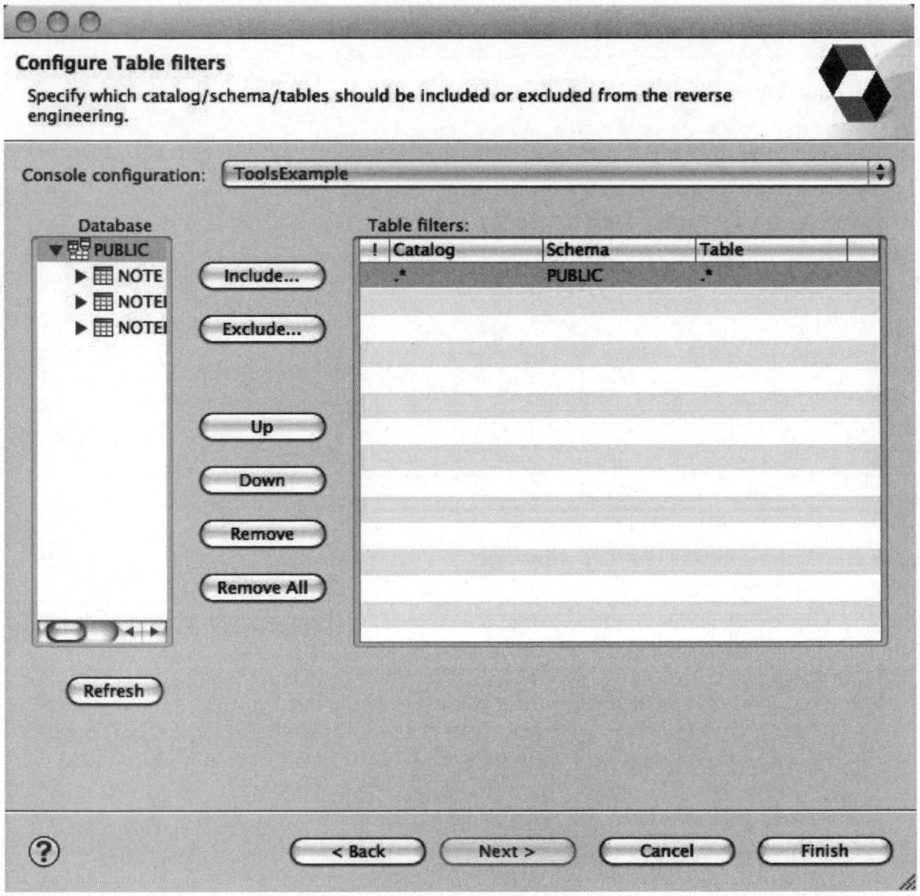

Figure B-19. Selecting the tables to reverse engineer

Once you click Finish, the reverse engineering file will be generated, and an editor will be opened for it. This is a tabbed view of the XML file (the last tab shows the XML source code). This allows you to change the default mappings between the database and Hibernate types, to alter the table and column details, and to apply additional filters to the file itself that dictate which details will be ignored when generating output from the reverse engineering file.

We would not recommend trying to get to grips too closely with the reverse engineering tool until you have some experience in creating mappings manually—the various settings will seem quite opaque when taken out of context. Once you have created a few simple entity models from scratch, however, the need for the various options should become clearer.

In order to actually generate output from the tool, you will need to first select a Hibernate Console Configuration, as shown in Figure B-20.

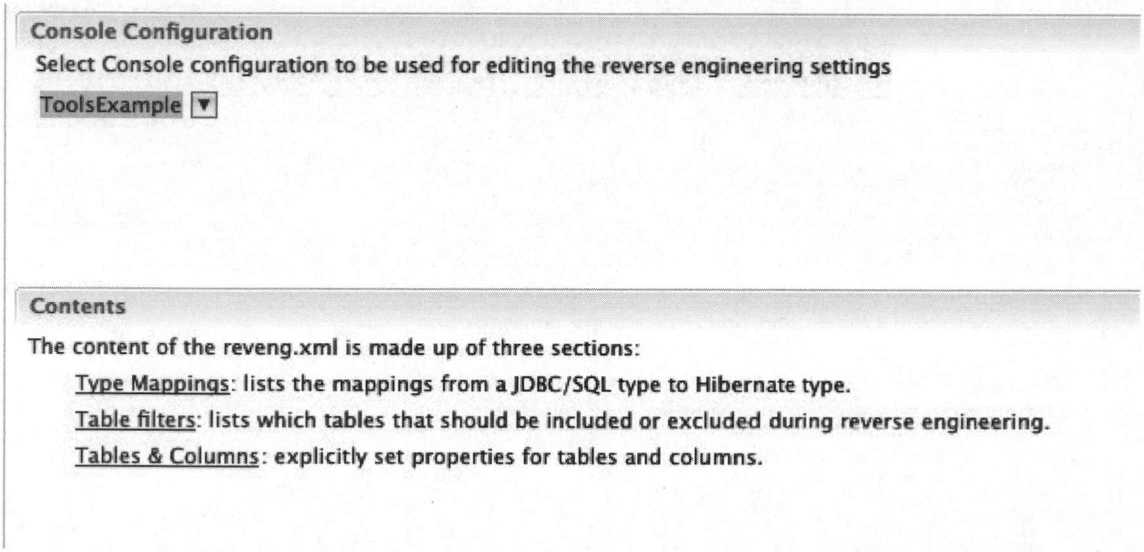

Console Configuration

Select Console configuration to be used for editing the reverse engineering settings

ToolsExample ▼

Contents

The content of the reveng.xml is made up of three sections:

Type Mappings: lists the mappings from a JDBC/SQL type to Hibernate type.

Table filters: lists which tables that should be included or excluded during reverse engineering.

Tables & Columns: explicitly set properties for tables and columns.

Figure B-20. Selecting a Hibernate Console configuration

The next step is to create a Hibernate code generation configuration by selecting the Hibernate Code Generation... submenu from the Run menu, and then selecting a Hibernate Code Generation... configuration, as shown in Figure B-21.

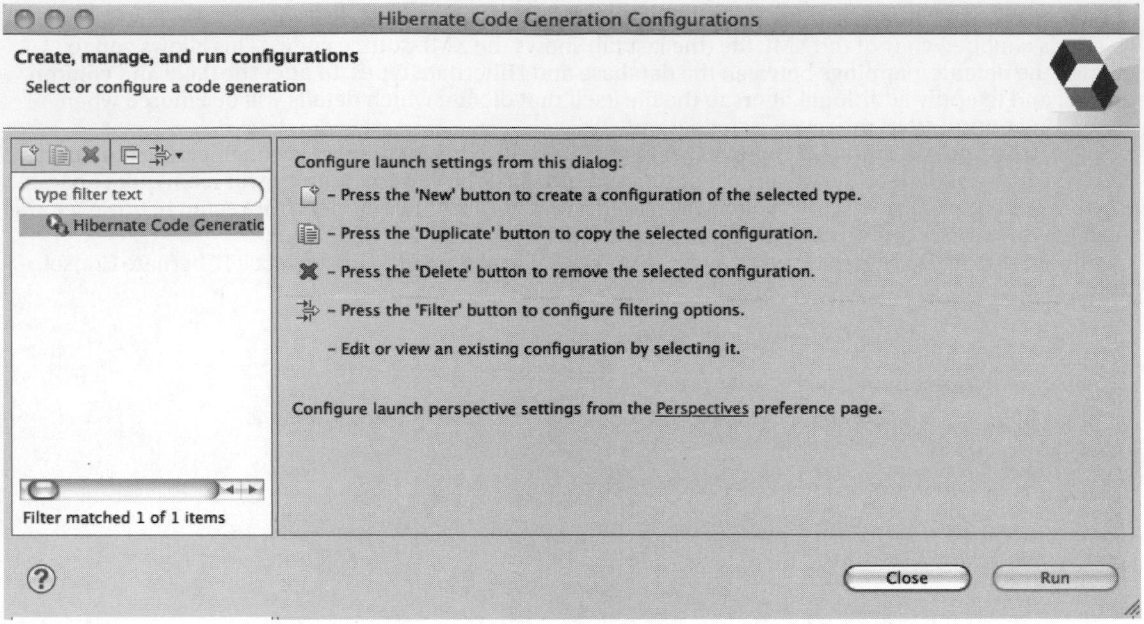

Figure B-21. Selecting a HibernateCode Generation... configuration

Press the New button on the toolbar and a new configuration will be created. We will need to make some changes to the defaults for our code-generation process.

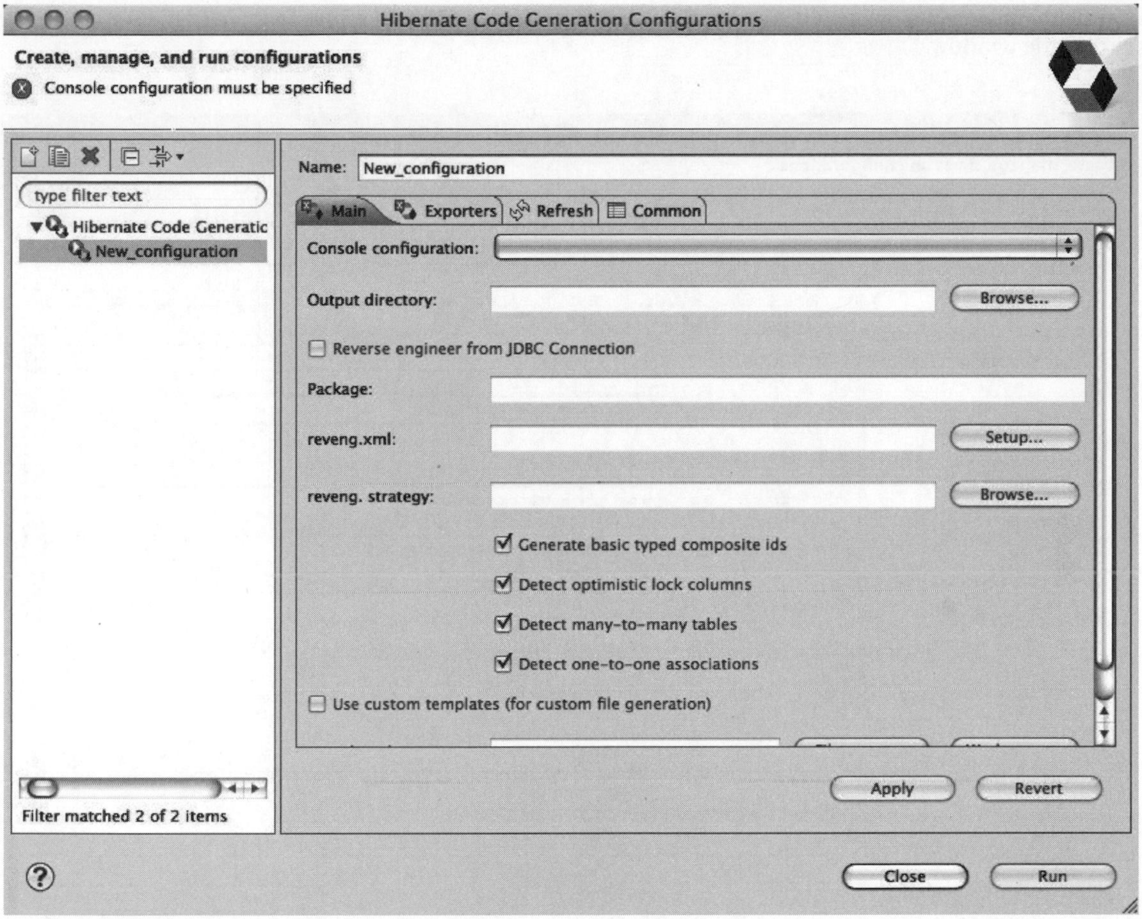

Figure B-22. The Hibernate Code Generation... configuration defaults

We need to enter a lot of information into this window:

- Change the name to ToolsExampleGenerator.

- Choose ToolsExample for the Console configuration.

- Choose the output directory. Earlier, you created a new directory under the project root called generated-src.

- Check Reverse engineer the code from JDBC connection.

- Use com.hibernatebook.generated for the Package name.

- Choose the reveng.xml reverse engineering configuration file you just created. You will add exporters on the next screen.

The tool does help you out; if it is not ready to run, there will be an error message in the upper-most part of the window.

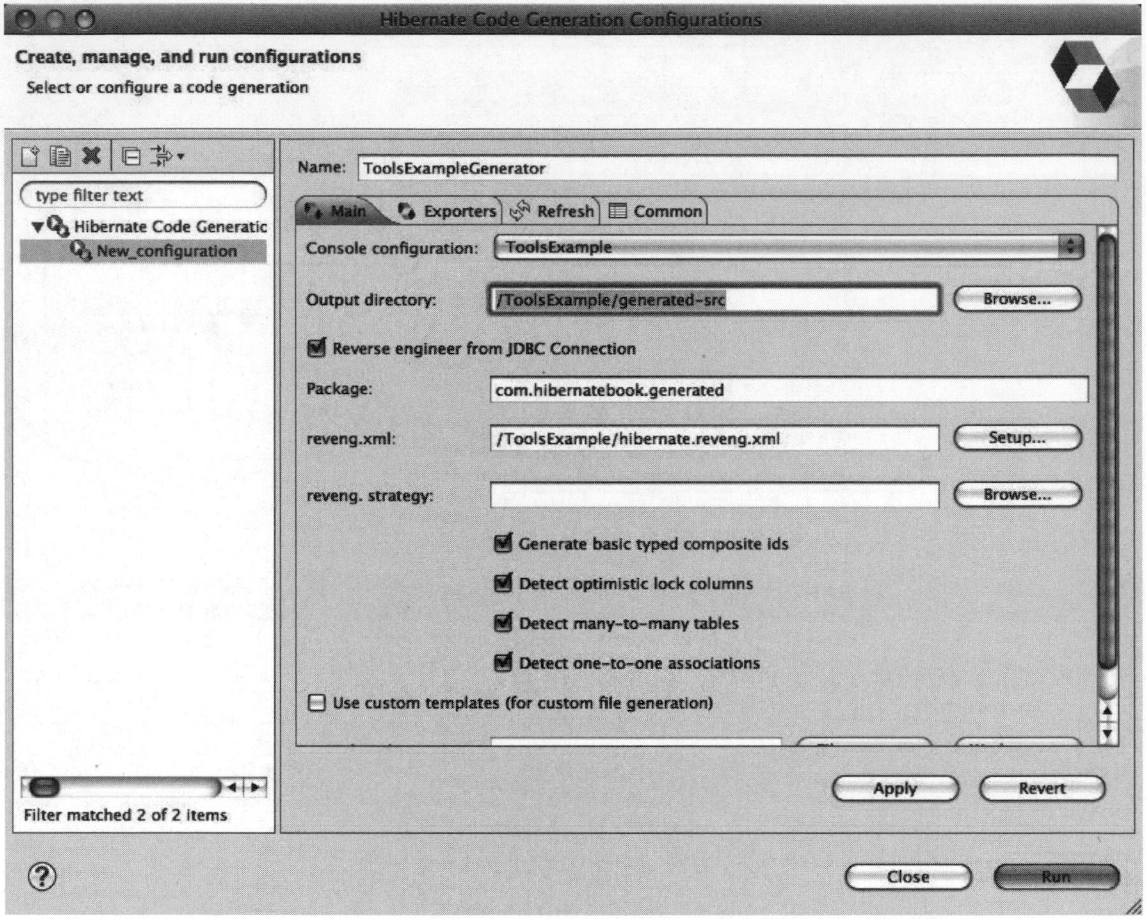

Figure B-23. The Hibernate Code Generation... configuration with our entries

Select the Exporters tab. The code generation tool offers several exporting options (for more information about Hibernate reverse engineering and code generation, see the "Reverse Engineering" section later in this chapter). The tool can output the following:

- Ordinary POJOs

- POJOs using generics

- POJOs using JPA 2/Hibernate annotations (with or without generics)

- DAO objects

- XML mapping files

- Generic export using user-defined template files

- Hibernate configuration files

- Database Schema export files

- HTML documentation of the database schema

You will then need to select the types of output to be generated, as shown in Figure B-24. After you select Run, you will be able to switch to the Java perspective in Eclipse and view the generated source in the `generated-src` directory.

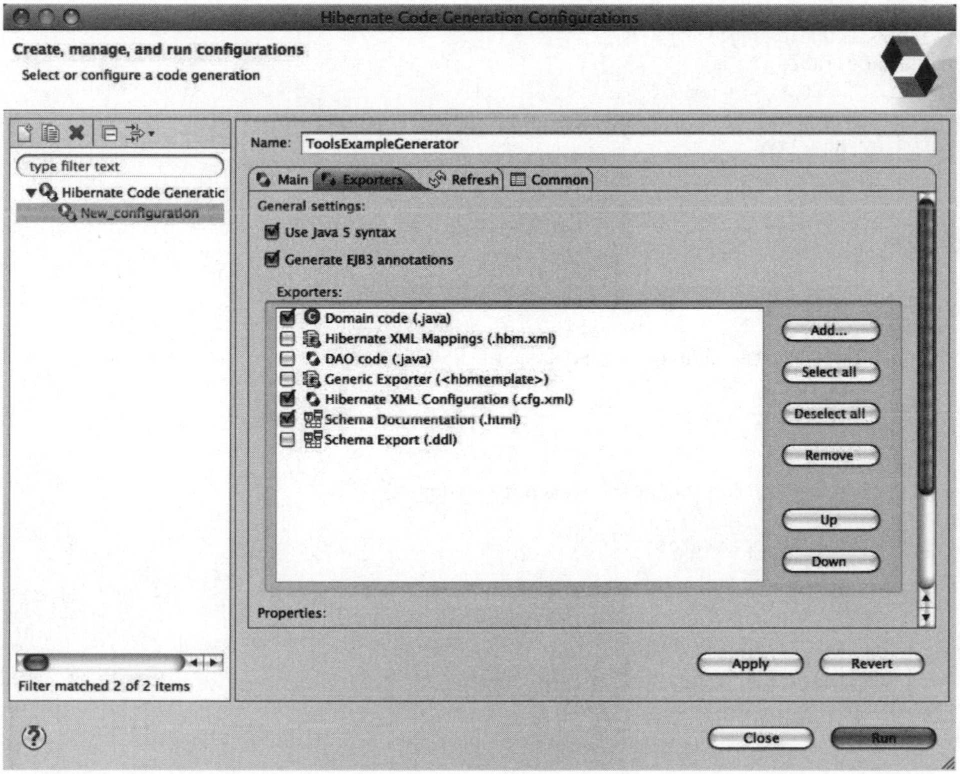

Figure B-24. Selecting the types of output to be generated

Listing B-2. The Generated Notepad. java class file from the Reverse Engineering Tool

```java
package com.hibernatebook.generated;

// Generated Apr 5, 2010 2:01:23 PM by Hibernate Tools 3.3.0.GA

import java.util.HashSet;
import java.util.Set;
import javax.persistence.Column;
import javax.persistence.Entity;
import javax.persistence.FetchType;
import javax.persistence.GeneratedValue;
import static javax.persistence.GenerationType.IDENTITY;
import javax.persistence.Id;
import javax.persistence.OneToMany;
import javax.persistence.Table;

/**
 * Notepad generated by hbm2java
 */
@Entity
@Table(name = "NOTEPAD", schema = "PUBLIC")
public class Notepad implements java.io.Serializable {

    private Integer id;
    private String owner;
    private Set<NotepadNote> notepadNotes = new HashSet<NotepadNote>(0);

    public Notepad() {
    }

    public Notepad(String owner, Set<NotepadNote> notepadNotes) {
        this.owner = owner;
        this.notepadNotes = notepadNotes;
    }

    @Id
    @GeneratedValue(strategy = IDENTITY)
    @Column(name = "ID", unique = true, nullable = false)
    public Integer getId() {
        return this.id;
    }

    public void setId(Integer id) {
        this.id = id;
    }

    @Column(name = "OWNER")
    public String getOwner() {
        return this.owner;
    }
}
```

```java
public void setOwner(String owner) {
    this.owner = owner;
}

@OneToMany(fetch = FetchType.LAZY, mappedBy = "notepad")
public Set<NotepadNote> getNotepadNotes() {
    return this.notepadNotes;
}

public void setNotepadNotes(Set<NotepadNote> notepadNotes) {
    this.notepadNotes = notepadNotes;
}

}
```

After using the Eclipse-based Hibernate tools, such as the Reverse Engineering tool, you may want to use some of these tools from a build file. Hibernate Tools provides a set of Ant tasks that share common functionality with the Eclipse tasks.

The Ant Tasks

As you will have noticed if you followed through the Eclipse discussion, our example project for this appendix includes build.xml and build.properties files. These are not strictly necessary when working with Eclipse, but it is often desirable to be able to build all the components of a project outside the IDE. This can be useful in maintaining automated builds for regression testing—and of course, not all Java IDEs offer integrated support for Hibernate anyway, while most of them do offer support for the Ant build tool. And besides, you might not be using an IDE in the first place!

The Ant tasks are part of the Hibernate Tools download, which is largely oriented toward use as an Eclipse plug-in. The Ant tools themselves rely upon a set of four JAR files: hibernate-tools.jar, bsh-2.0b1.jar, freemarker.jar, and jtidy-r8-20060801.jar. The hibernate-tools.jar file is currently only available as a download with the rest of the plug-in files. You will find the JAR file within the ZIP file in a directory called plugins\org.hibernate.eclipse_X.x.x.x\lib\tools, where the Xs are substituted for the Hibernate Tools version number. The bsh, freemarker, and jtidy JAR files will also be available from this directory. Since these JAR files have no dependencies upon the other parts of the plug-in, you can copy them to a directory with a less unwieldy name without further consequences.

How the Ant Tasks Work

Despite their diverse set of outputs, the Hibernate tasks actually all work in the same way. The task is imported into Ant using the standard TaskDef element. This makes the Hibernate tools libraries available to Ant itself, and allows you to select an appropriate element representing the Hibernate tools to use in your script.

```xml
<taskdef
   name="htools"
   classname="org.hibernate.tool.ant.HibernateToolTask"
   classpathref="classpath.tools"/>
```

The Hibernate Tools JAR file must be made available to Ant on the classpath—our example uses a preexisting classpath declaration (referenced through its id of `classpath.tools`—see the "Configuring the Classpath" subsection later in this section).

A standard Ant target is declared to contain the set of operations that you want to perform.

```
<target name="exportDDL" depends="compile">
...
</target>
```

Within the target with any other standard (or imported) Ant tasks, you can then include the element that you declared using the `<taskdef>` element. The other Hibernate task elements are only applicable within this task element.

```
<target name="exportDDL" depends="compile">
   <htools destdir="${sql}">
   ...
   </htools>
</target>
```

This outermost task element accepts three attributes, as listed in Table B-1.

Table B-1. *The Daughter Elements of the Hibernate Tools Task*

Attribute	Description
classpath	The path to use when locating libraries and configuration files.
destDir	The base directory (relative to the build script's own base directory) into which any generated output will be written.
templatePath	The path containing user-created template files (see the further discussion of templates in the "Templates" section later in the chapter.)

Within the declared Hibernate task, a number of additional standard elements can be created, consisting of a classpath declaration (an alternative to using the `classpath` attribute), a set of configuration elements, and a set of exporter elements.

The `classpath` element and attribute are standard Ant features that allow you to bring in any necessary resources used by the Hibernate tasks.

The clever bit of the Hibernate Ant task lies in the configuration elements. Declaring a configuration task causes an appropriate configuration object to be built in memory. These in-memory configuration objects all extend the standard `org.hibernate.cfg.Configuration` class. The `Configuration` class represents the mapping relationships between entities (combined with information from any configuration, properties, or reverse engineering files), and it is this information, the metamodel, that is then used to generate the various output files. The provided configuration elements can conjure up a `Configuration` object from the standard mapping files, from the metadata information gathered over a JDBC connection, and from the annotations discussed in Chapter 6.

```
<target name="exportDDL" depends="compile">
    <htools destdir="${sql}">
        <annotationconfiguration
            configurationfile="${src}/hibernate.cfg.xml"/>
        ...
    </htools>
</target>
```

Within any given Hibernate Tools task, you can only have one configuration element configured—normally, you would not want to generate output from two distinct representations of the mapping information, so the single declaration is shared between the generation tasks enclosed within the toolset task elements. The following list describes the configuration tasks and the attributes of each:

- <configuration>: Mapping relationships are generated from conventional XML-based mapping files and information in a *.cfg.xml or *.properties file.

  - configurationfile: The name of the XML configuration file being used.

  - propertyfile: The name of the properties file being used.

  - entityresolver: The name of the SAX EntityResolver to use when resolving "external" XML entities (rarely used).

  - namingstrategy: A naming strategy to use (see Chapter 3) to establish table names from entity names.

- <annotationconfiguration>: Mapping relationships are generated from the Hibernate 3 annotations in conjunction with a *.cfg.xml or *.properties file.

  - Identical to <configuration>.

- <jdbcconfiguration>: Mapping relationships are generated from the schema metadata obtained over a JDBC connection. The connection details are configured from a properties file.

  - All those from <configuration>, plus the following:

  - packagename: The name of the package that entities should belong to.

  - reversestrategy: The fully qualified name of a class implementing the -org.hibernate.cfg.reveng.ReverseEngineeringStrategy interface. This is the programmatic equivalent of the reveng.xml file approach.

  - revengfile: The name of a reverse engineering file to use when processing metadata information. See the discussion later in this section.

- <jpaconfiguration>: Mapping relationships are generated from JPA 2 and Hibernate annotations in conjunction with an EJB 3–compliant persistence.xml file.

  - persistenceunit: The JPA configuration will look for persistence units from persistence.xml on the classpath, or you can manually specify one.

The <configuration> element also allows you to specify a standard Ant <fileset> of *.hbm.xml mapping files. If you use this in conjunction with a *.cfg.xml configuration file, you must not permit any mapping resources to be duplicated, as this will result in duplicate import mapping exceptions.

Your choice of configuration element will be driven by the data sources that you have available to you. For example, if you have created your XML mapping files, you will want to use the standard configuration element, but if you have only a normalized database, you will want to generate the mapping information from this using the JDBC configuration (although you may well choose to create a reverse engineering file to control this).

Once you have correctly configured an annotation object, however, you can generate any of the other resources that you might need using one or more exporter elements. These are listed in Table B-2.

Table B-2. *The Available Exporter Elements*

Element	Description
<hbm2ddl>	Generates tables from the metamodel
<hbm2cfgxml>	Generates a *.cfg.xml configuration file from the metamodel
<hbm2java>	Generates entity POJOs from the metamodel
<hbm2hbmxml>	Generates Hibernate *.hbm.xml mapping files from the metamodel
<hbm2doc>	Generates HTML documentation for the database schema from the metamodel
<hbmtemplate>	Generates arbitrary user-defined output from the metamodel
<query>	Runs arbitrary HQL queries against the database using the mapping information in the metamodel

You may notice that the exporters available as Ant tasks correspond fairly closely to the exporters available in the Hibernate Code Generation tool—largely because they rely upon the same underlying implementations.

The two most commonly used tasks are <hbm2ddl>, which can generate a database schema directly from the mapping files or annotations, and <hbm2hbmxml>, which, conversely, can generate mapping files directly from the database.

The <hbm2ddl> element generates DDL scripts from the metamodel. These can be written to a file— or, if the configuration object is provided with database connection details, they can be run directly against the database. Table B-3 shows the attributes that can be supplied.

Table B-3. The Attributes Available to the `<hbm2ddl>` Element

Property	Default	Description
create	true	If set to **true**, causes the generated DDL to include commands to create database objects. This allows to distinct tasks to be created: one to drop all relevant database objects (using the **drop** attribute) and the other to create them.
delimiter	;	Specifies the delimiter to be used to separate DDL statements.
drop	false	If set to **true**, causes the generated DDL to include commands to drop preexisting database objects before it tries to create them. This may cause warning messages, depending upon the preexisting state of the database; and it of course has the potential to destroy existing data.
export	true	If set to **true**, causes the DDL to be run directly against the database (this has the potential to delete data—do not use carelessly).
format	false	If set to **true**, causes the generated DDL to be formatted using whitespace in a more readable fashion. We recommend using this option if you will be writing the DDL to a file.
haltonerror	false	If set to **true**, causes the script to halt if an error is encountered while generating the DDL (typically, this is used while exporting directly to the database to increase the visibility of any problems encountered while setting up the schema).
outputfilename		Specifies the name of the file name that the generated DDL should be stored in. If left unset, the generated DDL will not be stored.
update	false	Indicates that the tool should attempt to generate the appropriate statements to bring the existing schema inline with the model. We don't recommend using this option.

The task shown in Listing B-3, which completes the simple example that we've been building up in this section, creates a schema generation script from the annotation-based mappings referenced in the project's `hibernate.cfg.xml` file.

Listing B-3. A Complete Hibernate Mapping Target

```
<target name="exportDDL" depends="compile">
   <htools destdir="${sql}">
      <annotationconfiguration
         configurationfile="${src}/hibernate.cfg.xml"/>
      <hbm2ddl
         create="true"
         drop="true"
```

```
            format="true"
            export="true"
            outputfilename="${ant.project.name}.dll"/>
    </htools>
</target>
```

The `<hbm2cfgxml>` element generates a Hibernate XML configuration file from the metamodel information. Table B-4 shows the attributes that can be supplied.

Table B-4. *The Attributes Available to the* `<hbm2cfgxml>` *Element*

Property	Default	Description
destdir		If set, overrides, for this exporter only, the destination directory specified on the tools task.
ejb3	false	By default, causes entities to be mapped using `<mapping resource="..."/>` entries in the configuration file. If set to `true`, the entities will be mapped using the `<mapping class="..."/>` approach to pick up JPA/Hibernate annotations in the mapped classes. This setting does *not* cause a `persistence.xml` file to be generated!

Typically, the `<hbm2cfgxml>` element is used when the configuration task has been configured from a properties file—for example, when using `<jdbcconfiguration>`, you would typically start with a normalized database schema and a properties file containing the connection details, and use this exporter to create a `hibernate.cfg.xml` file containing both the connection details and the details of the mapped entities.

The `<hbm2java>` element generates the Java source code for POJOs for each of the entities held in the metamodel. Table B-5 shows the attributes that can be supplied.

Table B-5. *The Attributes Available to the* `<hbm2java>` *Element*

Property	Default	Description
ejb3	false	If set to `true`, causes the POJOs to be generated with EJB 3 annotations
jdk5	false	If set to `true`, causes the POJOs to be generated with Java 5 constructs (generics, enumerations, and so on.)

This exporter can be used to permit the mapping file–based creation of suitable classes or to create classes from the database schema when `<jdbcconfiguration>` is used.

The `<hbm2hbmxml>` element generates the XML mapping files from the information contained in the metamodel. There are no attributes for configuring this element.

This exporter is particularly terse because it only writes out the mapping information stored in the metamodel. This is all handled by the appropriate configuration element. The `<hbm2hbmxml>` exporter just needs to know which path to write the XML files into. And that is specified at the Hibernate tool level.

The `<hbm2doc>` element generates HTML documentation of the schema and entities in a style similar to the familiar javadoc output.

■ **Note** Nothing in any of the exporters intrinsically stops you from generating "silly" combinations of output—but this has its advantages; for example, it is possible to use an `<annotationsconfiguration>` configuration element with the `<hbm2java>` exporter to generate POJOs. While that might seem pointless, given that you have to start with POJOs to use an annotations-based configuration in the first place, it actually provides the useful ability to generate Java 1.4–compatible source code from annotated Java 5 class files!

In principle, the `<query>` element allows you to specify an arbitrary HQL query that will be run against the database using the configuration's mapping information. Table B-6 shows the attribute that can be supplied.

Table B-6. The Properties Available to the `<query>` Exporter Element

Property	Default	Description
destfile		If set, specifies the file into which the output of the queries will be written. If left unset, the query is carried out, but the output is not saved.

The HQL query itself is included as the body of the `<query>` element:

```
<query destdir="output" destfile="sql.log">
   select n.owner from Notepad n
</query>
```

If you want to include multiple HQL queries in the task, you can include multiple nested `<hql>` elements thus:

```
<query destdir="output" destfile="sql.log">
   <hql>select n.owner from Notepad n</hql>
   <hql>select n.owner from Note n</hql>
</query>
```

Reverse Engineering

As we discussed in the previous section, the `<jdbcconfiguration>` task can be used to create a configuration metamodel directly from a database schema. However, a database schema is not necessarily an exact match for the entity mappings that we want to create. It may contain tables and columns that we would prefer to omit from our entities. It may also lack some of the information that we want to express. For example, database types such as **VARCHAR** do not map exactly to Java types such as **char[]** and **java.lang.String**, and the tables will have names that do not conform to the Java naming conventions.

Used as is, the `<jdbcconfiguration>` task will select sensible defaults for the type names, and will assign the reverse-engineered tables suitable Java names derived from the table names. It also provides an attribute to allow you to directly specify a suitable package name. Even so, we would really like more control over the specifics of the reverse engineering process. Note that while it also provides a naming strategy attribute, this has no effect during the reverse engineering process, as naming strategy classes can only be used to determine schema names from mapping information, not vice versa.

Hibernate provides two ways in which this process can be controlled—you can specify one of two attributes on the `<jdbcconfiguration>` task to override the default behavior.

The `reversestrategy` attribute allows you to specify the fully qualified class name of a custom implementation of the `org.hibernate.cfg.reveng.ReverseEngineeringStrategy` interface. This interface defines methods that can be used to select the following:

- Class names from table details

- Property names from column details

- One-to-many associations from foreign key relationships

- Many-to-one associations from foreign key relationships

- Inverse relationships from foreign key relationships

- Lazy loading details from foreign key relationships

- Collection attribute names from foreign key relationships

- Entity names from foreign key relationships

- Tables and columns to include and exclude

- Primary key columns from table details

- The column to use for optimistic locking strategies

- Composite ID details from table details

It also allows you to provide information about how schemas should be *generated* from the resulting metamodel. This information is as follows:

- Additional foreign key relationships

- The table naming strategy to be used

The disadvantage of this approach to managing the reverse engineering process is that it is not particularly flexible, and it requires a lot of coding. Reverse engineering is often carried out only once to establish the mappings, with the schema thereafter being driven *from* the mappings, rather than being used to create them. The Hibernate tools therefore provide a second mechanism for controlling the reverse engineering process by specifying an XML configuration file using the `revengfile` attribute of the `<jdbcconfiguration>` task. This provides nearly the same degree of control, but is much simpler to create—especially if you intend to manipulate only minor details of the process.

The output of the reverse engineering tool described in the "The Reverse Engineering and Code Generation Tools" section is actually a reverse engineering XML file following this format. A very simple example reverse engineering file is shown in the following code:

```
<?xml version="1.0" encoding="UTF-8"?>
<!DOCTYPE hibernate-reverse-engineering
PUBLIC "-//Hibernate/Hibernate Reverse Engineering DTD 3.0//EN"
"http://hibernate.sourceforge.net/hibernate-reverse-engineering-3.0.dtd"
>

<hibernate-reverse-engineering>
    <table-filter match-schema="PUBLIC" match-name="NOTE"/>
    <table-filter match-schema="PUBLIC" match-name="NOTEPAD"/>
    <table-filter match-schema="PUBLIC" match-name="NOTEPAD_NOTE"/>
</hibernate-reverse-engineering>
```

The reverse engineering file in the preceding code limits the tables to be used when generating the mapping information from the schema to the three explicitly named tables (NOTE, NOTEPAD, and NOTEPAD_NOTE) in the database's public schema.

A reverse engineering file always consists of a single top-level `<hibernate-reverse-engineering>` element containing various additional elements. These daughter elements are given in order in Table B-7:

Table B-7. The Elements Used in Configuring the Reverse Engineering File

Element	Cardinality	Description
`<schema-selection>`	Zero or more	Allows the reverse engineering process to be limited by catalog, schema, and table name
`<type-mapping>`	Zero or one	Allows you to override the default mapping between database types and Java types
`<table-filter>`	Zero or more	Allows you to include or exclude tables by catalog name, schema name, and table name, and allows them to be grouped into a particular package
`<table>`	Zero or more	Allows you to override the default mappings of tables into entities

Rather than trying to exhaustively specify the syntax of a reverse engineering file, which is anyway available through the DTD at http://hibernate.sourceforge.net/hibernate-reverse-engineering-3.0.dtd, we think it is easier to follow the basic requirements of the file format with some examples of valid `<schema-selection>`, `<type-mapping>`, `<table-filter>`, and `<table>` elements.

Our first example specifies the following rule: tables should only be used for reverse engineering if they are in the public schema and their names begin with NOTE:

```
<schema-selection match-schema="PUBLIC" match-table="NOTE*"/>
```

Our next example enforces a rule that database INTEGER types for which the column is specified as NOT NULL must be represented using Hibernate's int type. It also enforces a rule that database VARCHAR types that have a specified length of 250 should be treated as Hibernate string types:

```
<type-mapping>
   <sql-type jdbc-type="INTEGER" hibernate-type="int" not-null="true"/>
   <sql-type jdbc-type="VARCHAR" hibernate-type="string" length="250"/>
</type-mapping>
```

These type mappings apply throughout the reverse engineering process—you cannot specify them on a per-table basis using the `<type-mapping>` element, but you can using the `<table>` element.

The `<table-filter>` element allows you to include and exclude groups of tables from the mapping process on the basis of pattern matches on their names. Where the `<schema-selection>` element allows you to specify a set of tables matching a single pattern to be reverse engineered, the `<table-filter>` element operates within this and allows multiple patterns to be applied to include and exclude tables. Here's an example:

```
<table-filter match-name="NOTEPAD_ARCHIVE*" exclude="true"/>
```

Although the previous `<schema-selection>` element included all tables within the current schema that matched the pattern `NOTE*`, this table filter excludes any tables that match the pattern `NOTEPAD_ARCHIVE*` from reverse engineering. Table filters are applied in order, so using this technique, you can build up a filter that only includes a specific set of tables.

The `<table>` task permits almost total control over the mapping details of the entity. You can select a specific table by catalog, schema, and name. You can specify the class name that it should take, how the primary key column(s) relate to that class's properties, the primary key generator that it should use, the column types and properties that they are associated with, and the details of the associations formed by foreign key relationships. Our simple example places the generated entity into an appropriate class, with a nonstandard primary key property name and a nonstandard type mapping for one of the columns (`note`). It also excludes one of the columns (`audit`) from the entity model:

```
<table schema="PUBLIC"
       name="NOTEPAD"
       class="com.hibernatebook.tools.Notepad">
   <primary-key>
      <column name="id"
              jdbc-type="INTEGER"
              property="notepadPk"
              type="int"/>
   </primary-key>
   <column name="note" jdbc-type="VARCHAR" type="char" property="note"/>
   <column name="audit" exclude="true"/>
</table>
```

If it looks like you will have to manage the reverse engineering process to this level of detail, it may in fact be more appropriate to create some or all of the mapping files manually, which gives you total control over the specification of those entities. Complex specification of mapping information in the reverse engineering file is really only appropriate if it is for exceptional classes when the general cases are common; or if you expect to need to regenerate the model from the schema very frequently in response to changes in the schema details.

Templates

With the exception of `<hbmtemplate>` and `<query>`, all the Ant exporter tasks take the metamodel information from the configuration, pass it to a set of FreeMarker templates, and write the output to files. For more information on the FreeMarker template scripting language, see the FreeMarker site at `http://freemarker.sourceforge.net`.

If the existing exporters do not meet your needs, you can specify your own additional code generation tasks using the `<hbmtemplate>` task. Table B-8 shows the attributes that can be supplied to this task.

Table B-8. The Properties Available to the `<hbmtemplate>` Exporter Element

Property	Default	Description
exporterclass		Specifies a class to use to generate output. It will be invoked once only, and the configuration object, output directory, template path and prefix, and any configuration properties will be passed into it.
filepattern		When using templates, represents the FreeMarker macro that should be used to determine the file name for the entity being processed.
template		Specifies the template to use to generate output. It will be invoked for each of the entities in the configuration metamodel.

Again, you have two options when carrying out this process. You can set the `exporterclass` attribute to the name of the class to be used to carry out the export process. This class must implement the `org.hibernate.tool.hbm2x.Exporter` interface. This is passed a reference to the current configuration object and any other attributes that were set on the `<hbmtemplate>` task.

Alternatively, you can specify the name of a FreeMarker template to be used in processing the configuration object and the name of a prefix:

```
<hbmtemplate
    destdir="generated_txt"
    templateprefix="foo"
    template="template/MyTemplate.ftl"
    filepattern="{package-name}/{class-name}.txt">
```

Note that `filepattern` contains FreeMarker macros that will be expanded at run time to determine the appropriate file names for the tool's output. The task will search for this file on the classpath, and then as a file resource.

If the configuration object does not contain some of the information that you need in order to produce the desired output, you can also specify additional arbitrary details using a standard Ant property or property set. Here's an example:

```
<hbmtemplate …>
    <property key="bar" value="BAR!"/>
</hbmtemplate>
```

In addition to any properties you add to the template task yourself, you will have access to the scripting variables listed in Table B-9.

Table B-9. *The Standard Scripting Variables Available to a Template Task*

Variable	Description
artifacts	An instance of `org.hibernate.tool.hbm2x.ArtifactCollector` that can be populated with values to reflect the actions taken during output generation
c2h	An instance of the `org.hibernate.tool.hbm2x.Cfg2HbmTool` class providing helper methods for converting configuration object values into Hibernate mapping files
c2j	An instance of the `org.hibernate.tool.hbm2x.Cfg2JavaTool` class providing helper methods for converting configuration object values into Java class files
cfg	A reference to the configuration object
outputdir	The path specified as the `<hbmtemplate>` element's `destdir` attribute
template_path	A list of the paths to directories containing FreeMarker templates

The standard Hibernate Tools exporter tasks are implemented in much the same way. Although we haven't shown this when discussing their attributes earlier, all the exporter tasks support the `templatepath` and `templateprefix` attributes, allowing you to override their default behavior by instructing them to use a different set of FreeMarker macros than those included in the `hibernate-tools.jar` file. All attributes also support the use of property sets to pass in information that is required by your custom macros but isn't available from the configuration object.

A very simple FreeMarker script is shown in the following code. This is not very useful in itself, as the first four variables simply display their hashcode representations from the default `toString()` implementation, but it provides you with a syntactically valid starting point for exploration of the code generation tools:

```
Configuration object: ${cfg}
Artifacts object: ${artifacts}
Cfg2Hbm Helper: ${c2h}
Cfg2Java Helper: ${c2j}
Output Directory: ${outputdir}
Template path: ${template_path[0]}
```

Configuring the Classpath

There are two distinct classpaths to consider when setting up the Hibernate Tools Ant tasks: the classpath of the task *definition*, and the classpath to be used by the *tasks*. The task definition needs to have in its classpath the Hibernate Tools JAR file, the Hibernate libraries, and the JDBC driver that will be used to access the database. A typical configuration of this classpath is as follows:

```
<path id="classpath.base">
    <pathelement location="${hibernate.path}"/>
    <fileset dir="${hibernate.lib}" includes="**/*.jar"/>

</path>
<path id="classpath.tools">
    <path refid="classpath.base"/>
    <pathelement location="${hibernate.tools.path}"/>
    <pathelement location="${jdbc.driver.path}"/>
</path>
```

The task definition (as shown earlier in this section) would use the classpath with the ID classpath.tools.

The tasks themselves will need access to two additional sets of resources: the configuration file(s) and the compiled classes.

```
<path id="classpath.apps">
    <path refid="classpath.base"/>
    <pathelement path="${src}"/>
    <pathelement path="${bin}"/>
    <pathelement location="${jdbc.driver.path}"/>
</path>
```

The configuration files will include the hibernate.cfg.xml and/or hibernate.properties files, along with any log4j configuration files, cache configuration files, and applicable XML mapping files.

If you are using annotations in any of your tasks, you will need to ensure that the task is assigned a dependency upon the compiled POJOs—annotations cannot be read at run time from Java source files, only from compiled classes.

Summary

In this appendix, we have discussed the installation and use of Hibernate Tools, including the Eclipse plug-in and the Ant tasks. Together, these remove most of the need to manually create boilerplate configuration code.

In Appendix C, we discuss how Hibernate can be used as the data access layer within the Spring Framework.

■ ■ ■

Hibernate and Spring

The Spring Application Framework offers developers an environment that ties together numerous APIs into a coherent whole. Spring applies the philosophy of "dependency injection" by providing appropriate configurable wrapper classes for all sorts of popular Java libraries.

The standard Spring API is immense, and its standardized approach to dependency management means that any existing API can in principle become a "Spring" API. If you want a good introduction to using Spring, then we recommend the excellent *Pro Spring 2.5*, by Jan Machacek, Jessica Ditt, Aleksa Vukotic, and Anirvan Chakraborty (Apress, 2008). We also recommend Dave Minter's *Beginning Spring 2* (Apress, 2007). For an overview, visit the Spring web site at `http://springsource.org`.

In view of its scope, we cannot and do not make any attempt to teach you even the basics of the Spring Framework in this appendix—instead, we assume that you are already familiar with Spring in general, and offer a focused introduction to the Hibernate-related components.

Throughout this appendix, we refer to a simple sample application that represents a "newsstand" of papers consisting of sets of articles. At the end of this appendix, we include the complete Spring bean configuration file for the example application; and as with all the examples in this book, the entire application itself can be downloaded from the Apress web site (www.apress.com).

For this chapter, we are using Spring Framework 3.0 with Hibernate 3.5.

Configuring Hibernate from a Spring Application

A conventional Hibernate application needs access to its database and the entity mapping information. The point of access to a fully configured Hibernate environment is the session factory, from which `Session` objects are obtained. Spring provides a bean to represent the session factory, but provides a few additional options in order to configure its resources.

In our example application, we take the line of least resistance and use a Hibernate configuration file (`hibernate.cfg.xml`) to represent both the mapping information and the database configuration. For easy reference when setting up a Spring application, we show a sample Hibernate configuration file in Listing C-1.

Listing C-1. Familiar Territory: A Standard Hibernate Configuration File Used in Spring

```
<?xml version='1.0' encoding='utf-8'?>
<!DOCTYPE hibernate-configuration PUBLIC
    "-//Hibernate/Hibernate Configuration DTD//EN"
    "http://hibernate.sourceforge.net/hibernate-configuration-3.0.dtd">
```

```
<hibernate-configuration>
    <session-factory>
        <property name="connection.driver_class">
            org.hsqldb.jdbcDriver
        </property>
        <property name="connection.url">
            jdbc:hsqldb:file:/spring/db/springdb;SHUTDOWN=true
        </property>
        <property name="connection.username">sa</property>
        <property name="connection.password"></property>
        <property name="hibernate.connection.pool_size">0</property>
        <property name="show_sql">true</property>
        <property name="dialect">org.hibernate.dialect.HSQLDialect</property>

        <mapping class="com.hibernatebook.spring.Paper"/>
        <mapping class="com.hibernatebook.spring.Article"/>
    </session-factory>
</hibernate-configuration>
```

Configuring Spring

The next step is to configure Spring to set up a Hibernate session factory. Spring represents the configured session factory as an `org.springframework.orm.hibernate3.LocalSessionFactoryBean`. Our example application uses annotations to manage the mappings, so we specify that the Hibernate `AnnotationConfiguration` type should be used in our bean instead of the default `Configuration`.

We also specify the location and name of the configuration file relative to the classpath as indicated by the `classpath:` prefix (see Listing C-2).

Listing C-2. Configuring a Session Factory Bean in Spring

```
<bean id="sessionFactory"
    class="org.springframework.orm.hibernate3.LocalSessionFactoryBean">
    <property name="configurationClass"
        value="org.hibernate.cfg.AnnotationConfiguration" />
    <property name="configLocation"
        value="classpath:hibernate.cfg.xml" />
</bean>
```

As noted, our simple web application derives its database connection details from the Hibernate configuration file. However, a larger web application typically needs to provide database resources to other applications, in which case a Hibernate-specific configuration file is not the appropriate location for its details to be stored. Moreover, a well-behaved web application will draw its database configuration from a JNDI-provided `DataSource` object so that connection details can be uniformly managed at deployment time.

Spring allows data sources to be managed centrally as beans, and if a `JndiObjectFactoryBean` bean is used, it can in turn draw its details from JNDI. The `LocalSessionFactoryBean` therefore provides a `dataSource` property into which the appropriate Spring `DataSource` bean can be injected.

Typically, to manage a data source from within the Spring configuration, but without deferring the details to a JNDI resource, you would use the `DriverManagerDataSource` bean (see Listing C-3).

Listing C-3. Configuring a Typical `BasicDataSource` *Bean*

```
<bean id="sampleDataSource"
    class="org.springframework.jdbc.datasource.DriverManagerDataSource"
    destroy-method="close">
    <property name="driverClassName">
        <value>org.hsqldb.jdbcDriver</value>
    </property>
    <property name="url">
        <value>
            jdbc:hsqldb:file:/spring/db/springdb;SHUTDOWN=true
        </value>
    </property>
    <property name="username" value="sa"/>
    <property name="password" value=""/>
</bean>
```

Alternatively, if the data source resources are to be drawn from an existing JNDI-accessible data source, then the Spring `JndiObjectFactoryBean` should be used to represent the data source (see Listing C-4).

Listing C-4. Configuring a Typical `JndiObjectFactoryBean`

```
<bean id="sampleDataSource"
    class="org.springframework.jndi.JndiObjectFactoryBean">
    <property name="jndiName" value="java:comp/env/jdbc/spring"/>
</bean>
```

It is not just the connection details that can be migrated from the Hibernate configuration file into the Spring configuration. The property attributes and the mappings (class names or mapping file names) can also be assigned during the configuration of a `LocalSessionFactory` bean (see Listing C-5).

Listing C-5. Configuring Hibernate Purely from Spring

```
<bean id="sampleSessionFactory"
    class="org.springframework.orm.hibernate3.LocalSessionFactoryBean">
    <property name="dataSource" ref="sampleDataSource"/>
    <property name="mappingResources">
        <list>
            <value>com/hibernatebook/spring/Paper.hbm.xml</value>
            <value>com/hibernatebook/spring/Article.hbm.xml</value>
        </list>
    </property>
    <property name="hibernateProperties">
        <props>
        <prop key="hibernate.connection.pool_size">0</prop>
        <prop key="hibernate.show_sql">true</prop>
        <prop key="hibernate.dialect">org.hibernate.dialect.HSQLDialect</prop>
        </props>
    </property>
</bean>
```

Note that in Listing C-5, purely in order to demonstrate the use of mapping files in a `LocalSessionFactoryBean` configuration, we omit the specification of a Hibernate - `AnnotationConfiguration` for the `configurationClass` property, causing it to default to the normal (mapping file–based) Hibernate `Configuration` object.

Typically, the mappings themselves are specified in the conventional Hibernate manner through XML mapping files or Java annotations. It would be entirely possible to arrange to configure these externally, but no default Spring classes are provided to achieve this, and it is difficult to see any obvious benefit that would accrue from such an approach.

Using Hibernate in Your Spring Beans

With your session factory configured as a Spring bean, you can now go on to create DAOs that take advantage of Hibernate's functionality. Previous versions of Spring and Hibernate required the use of the `HibernateDaoSupport` class and/or `HibernateTemplate` class to form the basis of your DAOs; however, recent versions of Spring and Hibernate have eliminated the need for these classes. Hibernate now supports a `getCurrentSession()` method on the `SessionFactory` that returns a `Session` object that is associated with the current transaction.

Ideally, you should define an interface to specify the methods that your DAO will contain. Our sample application requires a single DAO with a few simple methods (see Listing C-6).

Listing C-6. Declaring the Interface for Our DAO

```
package com.hibernatebook.spring.dao;

import java.util.List;
import com.hibernatebook.spring.Article;
import com.hibernatebook.spring.Paper;

public interface PaperDao {
    public List<Paper> getAll();
    public void createPaper(final Paper paper);
    public Paper getPaper(final Integer paperId);
    public Paper createArticle(final Integer paperId,final Article article);
}
```

With the interface clearly specified, your DAO class should then have a getter and setter for the `SessionFactory` class. Inside your DAO, get the current session and use it directly (without any Spring classes), as shown in Listing C-7.

Listing C-7. Implementing getAll() Inside a Spring/Hibernate 3 DAO

```
@SuppressWarnings("unchecked")
public List<Paper> getAll() {
    Session session = this.sessionFactory.getCurrentSession();
    List<Paper> papers = (List<Paper>)session.createQuery("from Paper").list();

    return papers;
}
```

Regardless of how you use it, configuring your Spring/Hibernate 3 DAO is extremely simple. The basic requirement is that you provide its `sessionFactory` property with a session factory bean from which to obtain Hibernate `Session` objects (see Listing C-8).

Listing C-8. Configuring a Spring/Hibernate 3 DAO

```
<bean id="sampleDao"
   class="com.hibernatebook.spring.dao.PaperDaoImpl">
   <property name="sessionFactory" ref="sessionFactory"/>
</bean>
```

In practice, however, this is usually made somewhat more complex by the need to declare the transactional behavior that applies to the DAO's methods.

Declarative Transaction Management

The `getAll()` method as implemented in Listing C-7 omits any explicit transaction management. However, you do have access to the Hibernate objects, so you can manage transactions yourself. If you are using Spring, you will most likely want to use Spring's transaction management capabilities with Hibernate, rather than Hibernate's transaction API.

One of the advantages of the Spring framework is that it abstracts away transaction management to a common base, no matter what type of programmatic transaction is used. As a developer, you can either work with Spring transactions manually through code written to the Spring Framework API, or you can declare transactional settings on the beans in the Spring configuration files. However, while managing transactions manually is possible, it is not recommended—the use of Spring's `OpenSessionInViewInterceptor` or `OpenSessionInViewFilter` (both of which we will discuss later in this Appendix) can prevent your programmatic transaction management code from behaving as you might expect, as can various other indirectly applied beans.

Because of these risks, you should favor the use of declarative transaction management. With this approach, the beans' methods are marked as being the boundaries of transactions, and the appropriate transaction isolation level and propagation behavior can be specified.

To support transactional behavior, a transaction manager bean must first be applied to the session factory. Typically, this would be a `HibernateTransactionManager` in a self-contained application, or a `JtaTransactionManager` in an environment in which the container is managing transactions. Our application uses the Hibernate transaction manager. We show the `HibernateTransactionManager` bean declaration from the Spring configuration file in Listing C-9.

Listing C-9. Declaring the HibernateTransactionManager Bean

```
<bean id="transactionManager"
   class="org.springframework.orm.hibernate3.HibernateTransactionManager">
   <property name="sessionFactory" ref="sessionFactory"/>
</bean>
```

The transaction manager must be notified of the session factory in use so that it can manage the transactions of the database connection configured in the session factory. If you want to be able to use nested transactions so that multiple calls to transactional methods can be made from a method that is itself enclosed in a transaction, you must set the `nestedTransactionAllowed` property on the

HibernateTransactionManager bean. Note that Hibernate does not support the use of savepoints within nested transactions because it is unable to rollback the session cache's state.

The transaction boundaries are applied to a bean by wrapping it in a proxy class that then honors the original bean's API as declared in its interface(s). Typically, the basis of the proxy is therefore declared as an abstract bean so that it can be applied to multiple DAO beans as required. For illustrative purposes, our example application also uses this approach (see Listing C-10).

Listing C-10. Declaring the Default Transactionality for Our DAO Beans

```
<bean id="daoTxTemplate" abstract="true"
class="org.springframework.transaction.interceptor.TransactionProxyFactoryBean">
    <property name="transactionManager" ref="transactionManager"/>
    <property name="transactionAttributes">
        <props>
            <prop key="create*">
                PROPAGATION_REQUIRED,ISOLATION_READ_COMMITTED
            </prop>
            <prop key="get*">
                PROPAGATION_REQUIRED,ISOLATION_READ_COMMITTED
            </prop>
        </props>
    </property>
</bean>
```

With the transaction manager's template prepared, the declaration of any DAO objects must be wrapped in a bean declaration derived from this template.

Our wrapped bean is shown in Listing C-11. The lines highlighted in bold are the wrapped bean's declaration—since it is only used as a property for the enclosing proxy, it does not need to be assigned an id—instead, the id of the paperDao proxy is used when a DAO reference is required. The proxy will honor the PaperDao interface declared earlier in Listing C-8.

Listing C-11. Wrapping the DAO Implementation Bean with Appropriate Transactionality

```
<bean id="paperDao" parent="daoTxTemplate">
    <property name="target">
        <bean class="com.hibernatebook.spring.dao.PaperDaoImpl">
            <property name="sessionFactory" ref="sessionFactory"/>
        </bean>
    </property>
</bean>
```

Managing the Session

A familiar problem encountered when using Hibernate is the LazyInitializationException. This occurs when you try to access the lazily loaded attributes of a detached entity—typically when the session that loaded it has been closed. This causes problems in Spring when you want to use information obtained from a DAO in a controller in the view to which it forwards the request.

Entities that have been retrieved from the DAO will therefore become detached from their session. If they are then passed to a view—typically a JSP—your client code will produce a LazyInitializationException when it tries to access any lazy properties of the entity that were not accessed prior to completion of the original DAO method (or forced to load in some other way).

Clearly, marking all the properties of your entities as being eagerly loaded is not practical—and typically, it is not possible to determine in advance exactly which properties of your entity should be actively loaded.

Instead, Spring provides a mechanism to implement the OpenSessionInView pattern of behavior. This ensures that the Session object is retained until processing of the view is complete. Only then is it closed—it must be closed at some point to ensure that your web applications don't leak a Session for every user request!

The effect is that with either an OpenSessionInViewInterceptor in your Spring configuration file or an OpenSessionInViewFilter configured in your web.xml file, you can access lazily loaded attributes of entities acquired from your DAOs without any risk of the dreaded LazyInitializationException. Note that only one of the two options is required—they differ only in their internal details, not the outcome of applying them.

Generally, we use the OpenSessionInViewInterceptor, as it is configured like any other Spring bean. Our example application makes use of this to ensure that the lazily loaded articles attribute of the Paper entity can be accessed from the JSP view implementations (see Listing C-12).

Listing C-12. Declaring the OpenSessionInViewInterceptor for Use in the Spring View

```
<bean name="openSessionInViewInterceptor"
class="org.springframework.orm.hibernate3.support.OpenSessionInViewInterceptor">
    <property name="sessionFactory" ref="sessionFactory"/>
    <property name="singleSession" value="true"/>
</bean>
```

The interceptor needs to control the behavior of the session factory, so we must provide it with a reference to the appropriate bean. We can also dictate whether a single Session object will be used for the entire duration of the user request. Setting this to true is the most efficient approach, and therefore the default; however, it has potential side effects, particularly if declarative transactions are not in use. When set to false, individual sessions will be acquired for each DAO operation.

The Sample Configuration File

Listing C-13 shows the full Spring configuration file of our example application as a handy reference to what's required in creating a Hibernate-based Spring application.

Listing C-13. The Complete Spring Configuration File

```
<?xml version="1.0" encoding="UTF-8"?>
<!DOCTYPE beans PUBLIC "-//SPRING//DTD BEAN//EN"
    "http://www.springframework.org/dtd/spring-beans.dtd">
```

```xml
<beans>
    <!-- Hibernate configurations -->

    <bean id="sessionFactory"
class="org.springframework.orm.hibernate3.LocalSessionFactoryBean">
        <property name="configurationClass"
            value="org.hibernate.cfg.AnnotationConfiguration" />
        <property name="configLocation"
            value="classpath:hibernate.cfg.xml" />
    </bean>

    <bean name="openSessionInViewInterceptor"
class="org.springframework.orm.hibernate3.support.OpenSessionInViewInterceptor">
        <property name="sessionFactory" ref="sessionFactory"/>
    </bean>

    <bean id="transactionManager"
class="org.springframework.orm.hibernate3.HibernateTransactionManager">
        <property name="sessionFactory" ref="sessionFactory"/>
    </bean>

    <bean id="daoTxTemplate"
        abstract="true"
class="org.springframework.transaction.interceptor.TransactionProxyFactoryBean">
        <property name="transactionManager" ref="transactionManager"/>
        <property name="transactionAttributes">
            <props>
                <prop key="create*">
                    PROPAGATION_REQUIRED,ISOLATION_READ_COMMITTED
                </prop>
                <prop key="get*">
                    PROPAGATION_REQUIRED,ISOLATION_READ_COMMITTED
                </prop>
            </props>
        </property>
    </bean>

    <!-- DAO configurations (note use of template) -->

    <bean id="paperDao" parent="daoTxTemplate">
        <property name="target">
            <bean class="com.hibernatebook.spring.dao.PaperDaoImpl">
                <property name="sessionFactory" ref="sessionFactory" />
            </bean>
        </property>
    </bean>

    <!-- Basic Spring MVC configurations -->
```

```xml
    <bean id="viewResolver"
class="org.springframework.web.servlet.view.UrlBasedViewResolver">
        <property name="prefix" value="/WEB-INF/jsp/" />
        <property name="suffix" value=".jsp" />
        <property name="viewClass"
            value="org.springframework.web.servlet.view.JstlView"/>
    </bean>

    <bean id="urlMapping"
class="org.springframework.web.servlet.handler.SimpleUrlHandlerMapping">
        <property name="interceptors">
            <list>
                <ref bean="openSessionInViewInterceptor" />
            </list>
        </property>

        <property name="mappings">
            <props>
                <prop key="/viewPapers.do">viewPapersController</prop>
                <prop key="/createPaper.do">createPaperController</prop>
                <prop key="/viewArticles.do">viewArticlesController</prop>
                <prop key="/createArticle.do">createArticleController</prop>
            </props>
        </property>
    </bean>

    <!-- Message resources -->

    <bean id="messageSource"
class="org.springframework.context.support.ResourceBundleMessageSource">
        <property name="basename" value="message"/>
    </bean>

    <!-- Validators -->

    <bean id="createPaperValidator"
class="com.hibernatebook.spring.validator.CreatePaperValidator"/>

    <bean id="createArticleValidator"
class="com.hibernatebook.spring.validator.CreateArticleValidator"/>

    <!-- Controller configurations -->

    <bean id="viewPapersController"
        class="com.hibernatebook.spring.controller.ViewPapersController">
        <property name="paperDao" ref="paperDao" />
    </bean>
```

```xml
    <bean id="createPaperController"
class="com.hibernatebook.spring.controller.CreatePaperController">
      <property name="commandClass"
        value="com.hibernatebook.spring.form.CreatePaper"/>
      <property name="commandName" value="paperForm"/>
      <property name="formView" value="createPaper"/>
      <property name="successView" value="viewPapers"/>
      <property name="validator" ref="createPaperValidator"/>
      <property name="paperDao" ref="paperDao"/>
    </bean>

    <bean id="viewArticlesController"
class="com.hibernatebook.spring.controller.ViewArticlesController">
      <property name="paperDao" ref="paperDao"/>
    </bean>

    <bean id="createArticleController"
class="com.hibernatebook.spring.controller.CreateArticleController">
      <property name="commandClass"
value="com.hibernatebook.spring.form.CreateArticle"/>
      <property name="commandName" value="articleForm"/>
      <property name="formView" value="createArticle"/>
      <property name="successView" value="viewArticles"/>
      <property name="bindOnNewForm" value="true"/>
      <property name="validator" ref="createArticleValidator"/>
      <property name="paperDao" ref="paperDao"/>
    </bean>
</beans>
```

Summary

The Spring Framework offers excellent support for Hibernate as a persistence mechanism. It offers excellent support for creating Hibernate-based DAOs and various convenient features to smooth over the problems that you would otherwise encounter in building web applications based around Hibernate.

APPENDIX D

■ ■ ■

Upgrading from Hibernate 2

Hibernate 3 represents a major change from the ways of doing things in Hibernate 2. On the whole, it is a better product, and we applaud the Hibernate developers for their efforts. One particular group of users will be made nervous by all the changes: the existing users of Hibernate 2.

Well, there is good news, and there is . . . no bad news! Hibernate 3 has gone the extra mile to allow earlier users to get along. In this appendix, we will discuss the differences between the two versions and explain how a Hibernate 2 user can take advantage of them without conducting a major code rewrite.

Hibernate 3 does make changes: the package names have changed, the DTDs have changed, the required libraries are different, and some of the method names and signatures have been altered. Even so, we don't think that these differences will cause you much grief when upgrading to the new version.

Once you have read this appendix, we also recommend that you consult the Hibernate 3 Migration Guide in the Documentation section of the Hibernate web site (`http://hibernate.org`). The Hibernate team maintains and updates this section to reflect users' experiences, so you can find hints and tips gathered from developers at the cutting edge of just this sort of upgrade.

Package and DTD Changes

The package names for Hibernate 2 have changed with Hibernate 3. Hibernate 2 used a base package of `net.sf.hibernate`, while Hibernate 3 uses a base package of `org.hibernate`.

This is, in itself, a completely trivial difference—you might imagine that it is purely the result of a migration from Hibernate's hosting from SourceForge (`http://sf.net` or `http://sourceforge.net`) to their own web site (`http://hibernate.org`); but, in fact, there is another reason for the change.

Because of the package name change, it is possible for an application to use Hibernate 2 and Hibernate 3 simultaneously, allowing legacy Hibernate 2 code to run unmodified within the same application as more recent Hibernate 3–based components. If the same package name had been used, then it would be nearly impossible to achieve this.

This is not a coincidence—in addition to the package name, there are now two versions of the DTDs for the XML configuration files. Unchanged Hibernate 2 code should use the usual mapping DTD reference of

`http://hibernate.sourceforge.net/hibernate-mapping-2.0.dtd`

And for your new Hibernate 3 code, you will use

`http://hibernate.sourceforge.net/hibernate-mapping-3.0.dtd`

Similarly, for the Hibernate configuration file, your version 2 code will use

`http://hibernate.sourceforge.net/hibernate-configuration-2.0.dtd`

And your version 3 code will use

`http://hibernate.sourceforge.net/hibernate-configuration-3.0.dtd`

■ **Caution** If you do not update your mapping configuration from the Hibernate 2 form to the Hibernate 3 form, the time it takes to create a configuration and session factory will increase from around 20 seconds to a matter of minutes.

Obviously, it will not be possible for you to have two configuration files with the same (default) name of `hibernate.cfg.xml`, but either version of Hibernate permits you to construct a `Configuration` object and then specify an explicit location for the configuration file using the `configure()` methods (as shown in Listing D-1). If you are using both versions of Hibernate simultaneously, you must make sure that POJOs are not passed from one version's `Session` object to another's. If you need to persist your old POJOs using the new version, you must update the older code to use Hibernate 3. For an explanation of how this sort of upgrade is supported by Hibernate 3, see the description of the "classic" API in the following section, "New Features and Support for Old Ones."

Listing D-1. Using an Explicitly Named Configuration File in Hibernate 3

```
File configFile = new File("hibernate3.cfg.xml");
Configuration v3Config = new Configuration();
v3Config.configure(configFile);
SessionFactory sessionFactory =
   v3Config.buildSessionFactory();

Session session = sessionFactory.openSession();
// ...
```

You should be aware that in your Hibernate 3 logic, some of the defaults for entries in the mapping file have changed. If you have logic that relies upon implicit settings, you should review your converted mapping files against the version 3 DTD to check that they will behave as expected. The most significant change is that all mappings now default to lazy loading.

New Features and Support for Old Ones

If you are a Hibernate 2 developer and you have browsed through the earlier chapters, you will have realized that Hibernate 3 offers a lot of new features. You will have also realized that some of the Hibernate 2 features that you rely on may no longer be supported in version 3. For the most part, though, this is not the case.

Changes and Deprecated Features

If you do not plan to take advantage of the Hibernate 3 features in any of your existing code, you can, as discussed, simply run the two versions side by side without concern. If you are prepared to make some changes to your existing code, then it is better to take the opportunity to update your existing code to use Hibernate 3 directly. In order to make this second choice a little easier, Hibernate 3 provides a number of "deprecated" APIs that permit fewer changes than a full-blown conversion.

This reduces the immediate impact of the change, and allows you to conduct the rest of the conversion at your leisure, while still allowing you to remove the legacy Hibernate 2 libraries from your application.

■ **Tip** Hibernate exceptions are now thrown as unchecked exceptions. This will not impact existing code, but you may want to revisit APIs that explicitly declare HibernateExceptions. This change is intended to increase the clarity of API signatures by removing the need for the explicit throws clause in code, which uses Hibernate but does not catch its exceptions. There are ongoing debates over the relative merits of the two approaches, but certainly the change *from* checked *to* unchecked does not introduce any incompatibilities (whereas the reverse would).

Some changes to HQL have occurred between versions 2 and 3. If you have a substantial body of existing HQL syntax, you can elect to retain the old syntax. The selection is made with the `hibernate.query.factoryclass` configuration attribute, which selects the class to load for translating HQL into database queries. The options are listed in Table D-1.

Table D-1. The HQL Processing Classes

Query Factory Class	HQL Version
`org.hibernate.hql.ast.ASTQueryTranslatorFactory`	3 (default)
`org.hibernate.hql.classic.ClassicQueryTranslatorFactory`	2

It is not possible to switch between the two query translators within a `SessionFactory` instance. Because HQL queries are not parsed until run time[1], you will need to run extensive tests to ensure that your modified queries are correct if you decide to convert to the Hibernate 3 syntax.

The object retrieved from the session factory in Hibernate 3 implements both the pure Hibernate 3 `org.hibernate.Session` interface and a Hibernate 2–friendly `org.hibernate.classic.Session` interface. By using a classic `Session` reference instead of the usual one, you will have access to the methods that have now been deprecated. Despite their deprecated status, all of these methods are fully implemented at the present time. Most of them are backward-compatible with their Hibernate 2 counterparts—but the `delete(String)` method has changed slightly in that deletions are no longer cascaded to associated entities.

A fully converted Hibernate 3 application will not need to invoke any of these methods, so you should use a reference to the standard interface unless you're absolutely compelled by existing logic.

Other deprecated features reside in the classic package and its subpackages. Notable examples are listed in Table D-2.

Table D-2. *Feature Replacements in Hibernate 3*

Feature	Location in Hibernate 3	Use in Preference
Life cycle	`org.hibernate.classic`	Interceptor or event
Validatable	`org.hibernate.classic`	Interceptor or event

Some of the changes to Hibernate 3 have not justified the creation of a replacement class. A few methods will have been removed, replaced, or renamed. In these few cases, if you do not want to run Hibernate 2 and 3 side by side, you will be forced to update your code. When compilation produces errors, consult the javadoc API at `http://hibernate.org` to see whether the API has changed, and to determine how to alter your code to work in the new environment. In practice, there are few changes in the core API between versions 2 and 3, and the changes that do exist have well-signposted successors in the new API documents.

Additions

The `Event` class is new to Hibernate 3. If you are familiar with the `Interceptor` class (which is retained), you will have some idea of what to expect. This topic is discussed in Appendix A.

The Criteria and Filter APIs have been extended considerably. These are discussed in detail in Chapter 11.

The flexibility of the mappings has been improved. For example, the `join` element permits a single class to be represented by multiple tables. Support for stored procedures allows better integration with legacy databases. The mapping file format is discussed in Chapter 8, and support for stored procedures and other new features is discussed in Appendix A.

Changes to Tools and Libraries

As you may expect, the libraries upon which Hibernate is based have changed in version 3. Some have been added and others have been brought up to date. Rather than enumerate these here, we refer you to the `lib/README.txt` file in your Hibernate 3 distribution, which explains in detail whether or not individual libraries are required, and what purpose each serves.

Hibernate 2 provided a number of aids to the generation of POJOs, mapping files, and database schemas. Hibernate 3 has started a process of migrating to external support for these processes. Where these tools are retained, they can be found in the `org.hibernate.tool` package and its subpackages. For example, previously a facility provided by the `CodeGenerator` class to generate DDL from your mappings existed in Hibernate 2. This is still provided in Hibernate 3, but the fully qualified name of the `SchemaExport` class is now `org.hibernate.tool.hbm2ddl.SchemaExport`—but even though the tool still exists, the generation of mapping files from POJOs in Hibernate 3 would usually be conducted by an Eclipse plug-in, or the Hibernate Tools Ant tasks. See Appendix B for an extensive discussion of the use of the Eclipse plug-ins and Ant tasks.

Changes with Java 5

The release of Java 5 introduced some pretty substantial changes to the language. It also introduced some incompatibilities with the previous class file format.

The only significant addition to Hibernate 3 that relies directly upon a Java 5–specific feature is the annotations support. Otherwise, a 1.4 JVM will work fine. The use of annotation-based mapping in Hibernate 3 is discussed in depth in Chapter 6.

Summary

In this appendix, we examined some of the changes that have been introduced with Hibernate 3, and showed how code written for Hibernate 2 can be run in parallel with Hibernate 3, or be readily adapted to run directly under Hibernate 3.

Index

■F

■Q

You Need the Companion eBook

Your purchase of this book entitles you to buy the companion PDF-version eBook for only $10. Take the weightless companion with you anywhere.

We believe this Apress title will prove so indispensable that you'll want to carry it with you everywhere, which is why we are offering the companion eBook (in PDF format) for $10 to customers who purchase this book now. Convenient and fully searchable, the PDF version of any content-rich, page-heavy Apress book makes a valuable addition to your programming library. You can easily find and copy code—or perform examples by quickly toggling between instructions and the application. Even simultaneously tackling a donut, diet soda, and complex code becomes simplified with hands-free eBooks!

Once you purchase your book, getting the $10 companion eBook is simple:

❶ Visit **www.apress.com/promo/tendollars/**.

❷ Complete a basic registration form to receive a randomly generated question about this title.

❸ Answer the question correctly in 60 seconds, and you will receive a promotional code to redeem for the $10.00 eBook.

eBookshop

233 Spring Street, New York, NY 10013

Offer valid through 11/10.